Steven Dietz:
Four Plays for Family Audiences

Book Thirty-Seven
Louann Atkins Temple Women & Culture Series

STEVEN DIETZ:
Four Plays for Family Audiences

Edited by
Coleman A. Jennings

Including comments by
Linda Hartzell *and* Susan Mickey

Foreword by
Kim Peter Kovac

University of Texas Press, Austin

The Louann Atkins Temple Women & Culture Series is supported by
Allison, Doug, Taylor, and Andy Bacon; Margaret, Lawrence, Will, John,
and Annie Temple; Larry Temple; the Temple-Inland Foundation; and
the National Endowment for the Humanities.

Requests for permission to reproduce material from this work should be sent to:
Permissions
University of Texas Press
P.O. Box 7819
Austin, TX 78713-7819
http://utpress.utexas.edu/index.php/rp-form
⊗ The paper used in this book meets the minimum requirements
of ANSI/NISO Z39.48-1992 (R1997) (Permanence of Paper).

Library of Congress Cataloging-in-Publication Data

Dietz, Steven.
[Plays. Selections]
Steven Dietz : four plays for family audiences / edited by Coleman A. Jennings ;
including comments by Linda Hartzell and Susan Mickey ;
foreword by Kim Peter Kovac. — First edition.
pages cm. —
(Louann Atkins Temple women & culture series ; Book 37)
ISBN 978-0-292-77255-7 (cl. : alk. paper)
ISBN 978-0-292-77256-4 (pbk. : alk. paper)
1. American drama—20th century.
I. Jennings, Coleman A., 1933– editor.   II. Title.
PS3554.I385A6 2015
812'.54—dc23
2014024547

Contents

Foreword

Memory, Family, and the Boundaries of Reality: Steven Dietz's Writing for Young Audiences

Burned into my theatrical memory is a complex twenty-six-year-old image of a sassy teenage girl, a bicycle with two bowling pins with pinwheels on top in its basket, and a graveyard. It was a 1988 production of *More Fun Than Bowling* at the Round House Theatre in Bethesda, Maryland—my first encounter with a Steven Dietz play. While *Bowling* is not for young audiences, it has so many elements that resonate with the plays in this anthology—a smart and somewhat odd-duck young character, memory as an important part of the landscape, life and death, family, the long view.

It's all too easy to define plays for young audiences in simple terms: This is a play about bullying, or about a young man making tough choices, or about a girl who wants to be a scientist. Often this serves as easy shorthand for the children's "gatekeepers," the parents and teachers who buy the tickets. If they think a play's story or theme is familiar and safe enough, they will send their children. However useful we might think these simplistic definitions are, they do many disservices—to the play (if it's a good one), and to the young people in the audience who are capable of understanding and appreciating a lot more than we often give them credit for. Because of this, when asked what a play I'm producing is "about," more often than not I answer, "It's about sixty minutes," or "It's about seventy-five minutes."

You won't find here any attempt to categorize Dietz's marvelous plays— *The Remember, Still Life with Iris, Honus & Me*, and *Jackie & Me*. That said, there *are* some recurring threads in all the plays. They are well crafted, smart, and filled with believable dialogue. (The Dutch playwright Ad de Bont once said, "If your play is for ten-year-olds, write for twelve-year-olds"; Steven himself said, "Play in the bracket above you.") Their protagonists are strong, resourceful, and slightly eccentric, and come from families that are closely bonded in spite of difficult circumstances. The plays contain a straightforward, unapologetically blue-collar sensibility that's aligned with an often-loopy humor. In their worlds magic is important, and the boundaries of reality are fluid. The stories themselves are filled with light moments and elegant transitions.

Welcome to Steven Dietz's charming, direct, humane, witty, and wise worlds for young audiences. I guarantee there will be moments that you'll never forget.

Kim Peter Kovac, producing director of Theater for Young Audiences
at the John F. Kennedy Center for the Performing Arts, Washington, D.C.

Acknowledgments

Steven Dietz,
playwright

Allison Gregory,
playwright, co-author of *Go, Dog. Go!*

Dramatic Publishing
(for permission to reprint *The Rememberer,
Still Life with Iris, Honus & Me, Jackie & Me*)

Gayle Sergel,
vice president of Dramatic Publishing

Kim Peter Kovac,
producing director of the Kennedy Center Theater
for Young Audiences at the John F. Kennedy Center
for the Performing Arts, Washington, D.C.

Corey Atkins,
associate producer at Cleveland Play House

J. Richard Smith,
department coordinator/adjunct faculty at
Cornish College of the Arts, Seattle, Washington

Susan Mickey,
senior associate chair and head of Design & Technology
in the Department of Theatre & Dance at the
University of Texas at Austin

Linda Hartzell,
artistic director of Seattle Children's Theatre

Chris Bennion,
photographer based in Seattle, Washington

Acknowledgments

Jacqueline Russell,
artistic director of Chicago Children's Theatre

Derrick Sanders,
director of *Jackie & Me* at Chicago Children's Theatre

Lawrence "Bret" Brookshire,
professor of photography
at Austin Community College

The Houston Endowment, Inc.,
for support from the Jesse H. Jones Regents
Professorship in Fine Arts, Department of Theatre & Dance,
the University of Texas at Austin

The Actors

A Conversation with Susan Mickey
Go, Dog. Go!
Red Dog: Reed Sigmund
Yellow Dog: Dean Holt
Hattie, French Poodle: Janet Hanson
Big Dog: Luverne Seifert
Photographs for *Go, Dog. Go!* courtesy of
Children's Theatre Company, Minneapolis

The Rememberer
Stefan Enriquez, Richard H. Restoule, Jane Lind

Still Life with Iris
Julyana Soelistyo, Leslie Law, Sue Guthrie, William Salyers,
John Abramson, Steffan Soule, David Scully

Honus & Me
Charles Leggett, Troy Fischnaller, David Drummond

Photographs for *The Rememberer*, *Still Life with Iris*, and *Honus & Me*
courtesy of Chris Bennion, photographer based in Seattle, Washington

Jackie & Me
Ron Rains, Tyler Ross
Photograph courtesy of Michael Brosilow, photographer

Plays by Steven Dietz

1. *Brothers and Sisters* (1981)
2. *Railroad Tales* (1983)
3. *Random Acts* (1983)
4. *Wanderlust* (1984)
5. *More Fun Than Bowling* (1986)
6. *Painting it Red* (1986; music by Gary Rue and Leslie Ball)
7. *Burning Desire* (1987; short play)
8. *Foolin' Around with Infinity* (1987)
9. *Ten November* (1987; music by Eric Bain Peltoniemi)
10. *God's Country* (1988)
11. *Happenstance* (1989; music by Eric Bain Peltoniemi)
12. *After You* (1990; short play)
13. *Halcyon Days* (1991)
14. *To the Nines* (1991; short play)
15. *Trust* (1992)
16. *Lonely Planet* (1993)
17. *Handing Down the Names* (1994)
18. *The Rememberer* (1994; from the unpublished memoirs of Joyce Simmons Cheeka)
19. *Silence* (1995; from Shusaku Endo's novel of the same name)
20. *The Nina Variations* (1996; variations on the final scene of Chekhov's *The Seagull*)
21. *Dracula* (1996; from Bram Stoker)
22. *Private Eyes* (1996)
23. *Still Life with Iris* (1997)
24. *Rocket Man* (1998)
25. *Force of Nature* (1999; after *Elective Affinities* by Goethe)
26. *Fiction* (2002)
27. *Left to Right* (2002; short play)
28. *Go, Dog. Go!* (2003; co-written with Allison Gregory, from P. D. Eastman's book of the same name)
29. *Over the Moon* (2003; from P. G. Wodehouse's *The Small Bachelor*)

30. *Inventing Van Gogh* (2004)
31. *Paragon Springs* (2004; from *An Enemy of the People* by Henrik Ibsen)
32. *Last of the Boys* (2004)
33. *The Spot* (2004; short play)
34. *Honus & Me* (2005; from Dan Gutman's book of the same name)
35. *September Call-Up* (2006; short play)
36. *Sherlock Holmes: The Final Adventure* (2006; from William Gillette and Arthur Conan Doyle)
37. *Yankee Tavern* (2007)
38. *Shooting Star* (2008)
39. *Becky's New Car* (2008)
40. *Jackie & Me* (2010; from Dan Gutman's book of the same name)
41. *360* (Round Dance) (2011; from Arthur Schnitzler's *Reigen,* or *La Ronde*)
42. *Mad Beat Hip & Gone* (2013)
43. *Rancho Mirage* (2013)

Steven Dietz:
Four Plays for Family Audiences

Steven Dietz

Introduction

Twenty-Six Letters and Thousands of Days: How Steven Dietz Is Crafting a New Generation of Plays, Playwrights, and Audiences through Curiosity, Collaboration, and Community

Corey Atkins

EDITOR'S NOTE: *Even though the four plays in this collection are regularly performed around the country in professional and amateur theatres for young audiences, Steven Dietz is primarily known for his writing for adult audiences. In my preparation for this anthology, I read and saw many of the adult plays of this master playwright who, with more than forty plays to his name, is one of America's most-produced playwrights. During the research process I kept returning to the same question: What is the connection between Dietz's work for adults and his work for young audiences? That question is addressed in the following interview essay by Corey Atkins, associate producer at the Cleveland Play House, as he explores the life, work, and philosophy of Steven Dietz, playwright, director, educator, and parent.*

In a much-discussed 2012 blog post on the popular theatre field website Howl-Round, Steven Dietz asked readers to envision with him "the perfect audience for [a] new play." He described this audience as eager, engaged, open, demanding, vocal, and committed, writing, "There's a name for this ideal audience. They are called kids." Dietz continued:

> Kids get outraged by stories that are stupid. Plays that have crappy endings. They get outraged about characters that do really obvious and dumb things, speeches that are boring, and stagecraft that looks fakey or dopey. Kids get outraged about being talked to like "kids." Kids get outraged at the theatre's bright, earnest, pleasant, upbeat and relentless inability to astonish them.

It might surprise some that a man who may be best known for plays about the AIDS crisis, white supremacists, and Sherlock Holmes believes that children are the perfect audience. Consider, however, that Dietz has made a life for himself in the perhaps less-than-practical field of the theatre but is a self-avowed "shameless pragmatist"; he prefers the title "working playwright" to the loftier-sounding "professional playwright," and he favors elbow grease and routine to waiting for the muses' call. Given these seeming paradoxes, perhaps it makes perfect sense that the response of a young audience—a group simultaneously demanding yet generous, munificent yet frank—would be his trusted yardstick of a play's success.

Dietz has been described by his fellow playwrights, educators, and students in similarly dichotomous terms: he's both "tough" and "positive," and someone who can "sit alone in a room and wrestle with the universe before being on time to take his kids to the Spaghetti Warehouse." He's "neither too humble nor too arrogant," and, by his own wife's account, he's both "a freak" and "beautifully put-together as a human being." Dietz himself has argued that playwriting demands both madness and patience, and that poetry is imperative while inspiration is not.

It's been said that contradiction is at the core of most of the theatre's truly memorable characters. So Dietz may be right in tune with the openhearted outrage of young audiences who demand only what is simultaneously honest, urgent, beautiful, and surprising. Is there any period more caught between confusion and conviction, hope and despair, bravery and terror, than youth? After all, Dietz has said, youth is itself a paradox, a time when "we both live our lives and make up our lives."

> And your past is a tide which crashes inside
> and you speak aloud the story of your life.
>
> Annabel Lee, *Still Life with Iris*

Steven Dietz was born and raised in Denver, Colorado. He had no exposure to theatre as a child, and read few books—"not because my upbringing was bereft in some sort of way," he says, "but my interests were just to be outside horsing around, riding my bike and playing baseball." Dietz says his path to playwriting comes down to a lifelong "obsessive curiosity": "I liked writing—bad poetry, song lyrics, stuff like that. But primarily I was fascinated with people and situations." He didn't see any theatre until his senior year of high school, but then it literally changed his life:

> My first theatre experience was not even a play. It was a musical revue of songs that I saw at Loretta Heights College in Denver, Colorado. I maybe had been in a couple of plays in high school, but I still had never sat and watched one. It was a dark space, and there was a shaft of light from up right to down left, a beautiful shaft of light—I'd never seen anything like

that before—and a woman in a sort of simple, off-white tunic started up right and crossed down left in that shaft of light. She was singing Neil Young's "After the Gold Rush." She sang that song, and it lasted from when she started up right to when she got down left, and then the lights went out. And I thought, "I want to do this forever!" I hadn't even heard anyone say any lines, there was no story. This was just a performer, in space.

Dietz attended the University of Northern Colorado, in Greeley, where he earned a B.A. in theatre arts. The day after graduation he got into his car and started driving, guided by the sense that he'd like to be a director. He visited several cities—Louisville, Washington, D.C., New York City—before deciding to stay with friends in the Twin Cities for a while. No sooner had Dietz pulled into Minneapolis, in the middle of a March snowstorm, than his car broke down. He walked into what he thought was a church to use a phone; in fact, he had stumbled into The Playwrights' Center (PWC), then in its infancy but now one of the major American organizations devoted to new plays and their writers. "This huge man came up to me when I was on the phone and handed me some literature," Dietz recalls. "It was [PWC founding director] Tom Dunn. He said, 'We work on new plays here, we have actors and directors, these are our writers.'" It was like a sign from the theatre gods. After his car was repaired, Dietz says, "I drove back to Denver, got my stuff, and moved up [to Minneapolis]." He spent the next ten years there—his "honeymoon phase with this business."

Dietz was hired as a resident director at PWC, to direct new play readings and workshops with writers in the early stages of their careers, like Lee Blessing, August Wilson, John Olive, and Kevin Kling. He found himself directing a new play every week. "It was like theatre boot camp. I was watching these writers just do their work. [. . .] And I assumed that's what a playwright did: got in, rolled up his or her sleeves, and made the words better. Made the story better. It wasn't until later that I realized, no, a lot of playwrights don't do that. A lot of playwrights are arm-folders. They walk into the room, and they fold their arms, and they don't want to collaborate." While Dietz was bringing writers' plays to life, he found himself getting the urge to work on a play of his own.

Dietz's first script was a play for young audiences called *Brothers and Sisters*. It was produced by the Children's Theatre Company in Minneapolis, which also toured it around the country during their 1981–1982 season. Though it would be several years before one of his plays got such national exposure again, the work Dietz created in the intervening time set the precedent for his remarkable output: He wrote four plays during the next five years. In 1986 his play *More Fun Than Bowling* was produced at several regional theatres, and while he continued to direct, becoming artistic director of Midwest PlayLabs, a PWC umbrella organization, his work as a playwright began to garner national attention, too.

But Dietz says it wasn't until 1987 and his ninth play — *Ten November*, about the 1975 wreck of the Edmund Fitzgerald on Lake Superior — that he began to realize his purpose as a playwright. "It taught me my place in the world," he says. "My job — that I'm fortunate to do — is to tell these stories and give them back to the people they belong to." Shortly thereafter, he was able to further explore that purpose when Jeff Steitzer, artistic director of A Contemporary Theatre (ACT) in Seattle, Washington, contacted him. He offered Dietz a commission to adapt the true story of a Northwestern white supremacist group and the related killing of Alan Berg, a Jewish talk-radio host from Denver whom Dietz had listened to while growing up. The resulting work, the docudrama *God's Country*, was Dietz's breakout hit and remains one of his most-produced and best-known plays. Three years later, in 1991, Dietz moved to Seattle, where he quickly found a new artistic home. Under Steitzer's leadership, ACT premiered or produced a play from Dietz's growing canon nearly every season, including *Halcyon Days, Trust, Lonely Planet, Handing Down the Names*, and *The Nina Variations*. Dietz also found ideas within the local theatre community. Two prominent Seattle actors, Michael Winters and Laurence Ballard, inspired his meditative two-man play *Lonely Planet*. In Dietz's words, the play is about "a couple of guys, both with their eccentricities, neither of whom initially come off as stereotyped gay characters. The play attempts to have [the unnamed epidemic of HIV/AIDS] sneak up on the audience in the same way that this disease sneaks up on us." *Lonely Planet* premiered in 1993 at Northlight Theatre, a regional theatre in the Chicago suburb of Evanston, and was the first of Dietz's plays to receive a major national award, the PEN Center USA West Award in drama.

While working on *Lonely Planet*, Dietz was approached by Linda Hartzell, artistic director of Seattle Children's Theatre (SCT), about dramatizing the unpublished memoirs of Joyce Simmons Cheeka, a "Rememberer" for the Squaxin Indian tribe. Dietz agreed, returning full circle to where he began as a playwright: theatre for young audiences. The resulting play, *The Rememberer*, premiered in 1994. During that time Dietz also found the next stage of his personal life. In 1990 he met the actress and playwright Allison Gregory, whom he directed in a play at the Denver Center Theatre Company. They were married in 1996, and three years later their daughter Ruby was born.

Seattle had been Steven Dietz's home base for almost ten years when, in 2006, the University of Texas at Austin offered him "a situation I felt I couldn't turn down." The university's Theatre & Dance and Radio-Television-Film departments had created a prestigious joint professorship that would allow Dietz to teach and continue to work professionally around the country. Dietz and his family—including son Abraham, recently adopted from Ethiopia—left their home in Seattle's Queen Anne neighborhood and moved to the Lone Star State.

As Dietz nears a decade of service at the university, he continues his prodigious output as both writer and director, in addition to teaching. His more than forty plays have been seen at more than one hundred regional theatres in the United States, as well as in off-Broadway theatres. International productions have been seen in England, Japan, Germany, France, Australia, New Zealand, Sweden, Austria, Russia, Italy, Slovenia, Argentina, Brazil, Peru, Greece, Singapore, Thailand, and South Africa. His work has been translated into ten languages. Dietz's numerous awards include the Kennedy Center Fund for New American Plays Award, for both *Fiction* and *Still Life with Iris*; the PEN USA West Award in Drama for *Lonely Planet*; the 2007 Edgar Award for Drama for his widely produced *Sherlock Holmes: The Final Adventure*; and the Yomuiri Shimbun Award (the Japanese equivalent of a Tony Award) for his adaptation of Shusaku Endo's novel *Silence*. He has received new play commissions from the Guthrie Theater, Steppenwolf Theatre, Actor's Theatre of Louisville, McCarter Theatre (Princeton), ACT, Arizona Theatre Company, Milwaukee Repertory Theater, and the Denver Center Theatre Company, among others.

Despite Dietz's prodigious output and success, interviewers throughout the years have pointed out that his work has rarely been seen in New York City. His only production by a major New York City company was the 2004 Roundabout Theatre Company production of *Fiction*. "I've made a living on my plays for twenty-some years. But I don't have a 'hit' play," Dietz says. Instead he has a reputation for integrity, consistency, variety, and longevity, not to mention hundreds upon hundreds of productions at theatres of all sizes around the world, from major regional theatres to universities to community theatres. Few "hit" writers can claim the success of these individual accomplishments; together they make Dietz a truly unique specimen in the theatre ecosystem.

Twenty years ago, when *Lonely Planet* established Dietz's national reputation, the *New York Times* said, "Dietz is [. . .] able to set up and work out his conceits with intelligent precision." *New York Newsday* reported, "Dietz owns all the tools of a crackerjack writer." These reviews point to a feature of Dietz's work that many, including Dietz, cite as the foundation of his career: crafts-

manship. Dietz is a wordsmith who employs the tools of language and structure with precision to tell his stories. The author's note at the end of the acting
edition of *Lonely Planet* conveys Dietz's artistic philosophy and reveals the
motivation behind his writing:

> My parents taught me that an act of kindness is its own reward. That
> took a while to sink in. Over time, I have begun to appreciate the depth
> of their wisdom. I thought of this recently while doing research for a new
> play I'm writing about Joyce Cheeka, a Squaxin Indian girl growing up
> in the Northwest in the '20s. One phrase from the teaching of her elders
> keeps coming up again and again: *Be useful.*

Are you curious or lost? [. . .] It's better
to be curious than lost, don't you think?

Iris, *Still Life with Iris*

The answer to why Steven Dietz writes may indeed be, in part, to be useful.
But unpacking that statement presents other questions: Why write the stories
he does? Why write for young audiences? Why, in a world of possibilities,
write for the theatre at all? A close look at the author's writing and the inter-
views he's given shows that the answers lie in four words: curiosity, collaboration, community, and craft.

One of the many theatre essays Dietz has published over the years, a 1988
piece titled "Developed to Death (or How to Hamstring a Playwright)," partly
addresses the question of why he writes for young audiences. Taking to task
those organizations, individuals, and processes that would seek to define a
"good play" in neat, often TV-related terms—at a time when "digital" was a
clock without hands and before "e" and "i" were prefixes—he said:

> The fact is that the Tube 'n' Screen does miniaturizations [. . .] while the
> theatre does magnifications. Because of its immediacy theatre prioritizes
> the world, while Tube 'n' Screen, under the guise of offering limitless
> opportunities, actually homogenizes it. When it deals in action, the
> theatre creates a desire to grapple with the world.

That desire to grapple, synonymous with Dietz's confessed "obsessive curiosity," is as much the impetus for his work as the audience response. "I would
say that when I'm starting a new play I'm moving toward the very questions
that I encounter in thinking about the world. I don't think of writing as a retreat. I might close the door to my studio but I'm not trying to close the door
to the world," he says. Just as a play might stay with a viewer for a lifetime, for

Dietz "certain fundamental things don't change: my fascination with the magic of a proximate, onetime, live event, my belief in the power of language and metaphor, my love of the collaborative theatre-making process."

Throughout the course of his career, Dietz's curiosity has led him to interrogate not just his own world and work but the American theatre at large. He's been vocal about the perils of isolation and hierarchy in an ostensibly collaborative field and art form: playwright over here, designers and actors over there, and director on top and in charge of it all. In Minneapolis he observed that, in the playwright-dramaturg relationship, "for the sake of fairness, passion was being lost. For the sake of logic, which has never been the theatre's strong suit, amazing voices were being rendered quiet or normal or mediocre." In his essay "On Directing: A Modest Proposal," published in *American Theatre* in 2007, he said:

> [A] new century requires a new approach. To be clear: What must be achieved is not the abolition of the director's role, but its continued evolution. As with any ongoing experiment, the director's role must be regularly interrogated—with the goal of having it grow and change at the pace of the art form.

Dietz argues that the word "director" could be replaced with any theatre artist's role:

> Let us seek to eliminate the hyphenization of artists ("playwright-director," "actor-director," "choreographer-director") and instead actively foster the integration of these disciplines. Let us recognize that the essence of the director's craft must be inculcated in not only our directors, but in each generative artist—be they writer, performer or designer.

This theatrical raison d'être, collaboration, is something Dietz has seamlessly integrated into his teaching. As part of his three-hour playwriting class, Dietz created "The Last Hour," opening the final portion of the class as a sort of incubator of collaboration for all first-year MFA students studying acting, design, or filmmaking. For Dietz, says Suzan Zeder, a former University of Texas teaching colleague and fellow playwright, "collaboration is not something that just happens in production but something that happens in the generation of work from all the artists that are involved. Steven has been at the forefront of it."

Why Dietz sees theatre—and particularly theatre for young audiences—as so essential might ultimately be summed up elegantly and pragmatically in a sort of theatrical theorem: curiosity + collaboration = community. Under this would lie his ever-active axiom that "theatrical art is fundamentally 'transitory' — it builds upon its past, engages with its present, ponders its future." This is true whether we're conscious of it or not, and so, Dietz says, it's vital that theatre artists ask:

> What part of your city, and the kids in your city, is in your work? Are the concerns of the kids in your city replicated and evidenced in your theatre? It's opening the doors to what a city is dealing with and what those kids are dealing with and making a connection. People do want to see themselves on stage. And as happy as I am when our *Go, Dog. Go!* adaptation goes around the country, and I'm as proud of that as I am of anything I've ever created in my life, I would hope that hand in hand with that, when the play is in "X" city, that the theatre in that city is also looking at what's specific to the kids in that city. What are the kids in that city going through?

But Dietz also knows that community = children + their parents. In his HowlRound article Dietz states that all too often "we don't write for kids. We write for their gatekeepers." He goes on to ask his adult readers to be as frank with themselves as young audiences are when considering a play:

> [L]et's please admit this: we don't dumb things down for our kids — we dumb things down for us. To mollify our own fears. We don't make upbeat endings or "easy morals" for our kids — we make them for us. To avoid what might be the harder discussion. We don't censor (and please let's drop the euphemisms and use the word) plays for our kids — we censor them for ourselves. And why? Because we get "outraged" — or, more commonly, we live in fear that someone else will get "outraged." [. . .] Gatekeepers tend to get outraged about words, bodies, "issues" and "themes" — especially those that bespeak a less-than-sunlit world. Kids get outraged, too — but in my experience their outrage is not about nouns, verbs, butts, boobs, dark thoughts or moral complexity.

By truly engaging with the youth of our communities, Dietz says,

> We go to the source of the art form. [. . .] The thin part of our audiences' thinking is a very thin pop culture layer. But if I talk to the thick part of my audiences, the deep part of my audiences, they're going to want something about loss, they're going to want something about joy, they're going to want something about passion, they're going to want a journey or an adventure. If we keep talking to that thick part of our audiences, which is in kids, I believe we will make the plays that they need. And we will get the theatre that we deserve.

Nothing gets finished until you make a start.

Mom, *Honus & Me*

How exactly do we create the theatre that we, our children, and our communities deserve? Dietz takes guidance from a former employee of the Colorado and Southern railroad—his father. "Work is a celebrated thing in my family and my upbringing," Dietz says. As a working playwright, he asserts, "This is my job—this is what I do. So whether I'm inspired or not, I get up and go to my desk and plug away." He approaches the writing task with the same matter-of-fact diligence that a round-the-clock conductor (like his father) might show when guiding a train through the snow-packed Rockies. "I either don't believe or don't trust that great ideas for plays will just arrive in my head," he says. "The sobering thing when you write is that your imagination doesn't get your play written. Your craft does. I have a healthy skepticism of my imagination, which forces me to practice my craft."

The suffix in playwright, "wright," means "worker" or "maker," and emphasizing craft has been Dietz's modus operandi almost from the start. "I have always admired his plays because I think they're some of the most solidly crafted plays [I know]," says Suzan Zeder. "There's nothing trendy about Steven's work. It's there for the long term. It's like going into a really beautiful furniture store and seeing hand-done craftsmanship in the way his plays are put together [and] that is a very refreshing ethos." Zeder is quick to point out that Dietz's "craft over inspiration" approach doesn't devalue his art, rather, "It's getting the art in the right category: it's a thing we make with our hands, and we do it together."

The unique dichotomy of Dietz becomes apparent again when discussing the most fundamental of a playwright's tools: language. Pragmatic and practical as Dietz may be, he insists that "the theatre's first language is poetry, not prose, and to think otherwise is to sever our ties with greatness." Language, he says, "connects the primitive and contemporary in us." Dietz admits this has been the source of many arguments between his inner writer and director. Yet many of his peers and collaborators have pointed out that Dietz's experience as a director has a strong positive impact on his writing. David Ira Goldstein, artistic director of Arizona Theatre Company and one of Dietz's collaborators, says, "What makes him a particular joy to be with is, since he's a director and was an actor, he understands the theatrical process—the journey actors, directors, and designers need to take from reading the script to opening night."

While Dietz's adult plays are rooted in a specific approach to craft, he understands that writing for young audiences requires a special approach. Anyone who's ever tried to do anything with or for children—eat a meal, choose clothes for school, go shopping without experiencing a mysterious emotional meltdown—knows that rules for children are different than for adults. Theatre is no exception. "Writing plays for children is harder than for adults," says Dietz. But he can relate to both of his audiences. Even as he works his way toward his fortieth play, he still considers himself a student of his craft. "I still find myself having to relearn again and again, one play after the next," he says. Each new play is a lesson in the basics: story, structure, sentences, and rewriting. Dietz knows that his perfect audience of young people will surely make it known whether or not he's succeeded.

Like any good student, Dietz takes a lot of notes. He keeps a notebook filled with thoughts and ideas—snippets of conversations, interesting sights that capture his imagination and haunt him, questions that nag at him—to draw ideas from, a failsafe against inspiration's inevitable absence. And, like so many students and young people, he's simultaneously troubled by and drawn to things that make him nervous, situations he doesn't understand. "I've built very few successful plays on my certainties," he says, "I've built my plays on my doubts. Or my wonder, or my worry. As optimistic in some fundamental way as *Honus & Me* or *Jackie & Me* are, there's a worry in those kids. There's a worry in those adults. And certainly that holds true for *Iris* and *The Rememberer*. Somehow that worry, which I guess is just another way to say 'leaning into the questions' instead of propagating the answers, keeps me connected."

If writing plays for young audiences is harder than for adults, is it harder to write young characters too? Just as Dietz's HowlRound article argues that the youngest, least experienced audiences are actually the ideal, it also makes the point that even the oldest person isn't a stranger to the perspectives of youth. This is true, writes Dietz, because

> our youth is the very oldest part of us. We have carried it longer, had the chance to know it more fully than any self we have concocted in the interim. When we write for "children," we are writing for our most fundamental selves. And thus a "children's play" is not a play about "children" any more than an "adult play" is about "adults." These are plays about our Youth. These are not plays that move faster or play brighter or end better, these are plays that dig deeper, that reach back farther. These are plays that do not settle for the facile adult surface of a man, but instead burrow to his core, his past, his youth. A "children's" play can surely be about five young girls having a grand adventure, but it can also be about five women in their eighties who gather to rekindle the girls that still reside inside them. All of our ages conspire within us and continue to underscore our days. We are all the young.

In crafting worlds and stories for the young, Dietz has had to access a buried part of himself. "I have learned that young audiences demand a profound and ruthless interrogation of my own Youth: What became of the child in me? What did I know back then in my heart and gut and bones before the world began to teach me everything else?" Watching his own children grow (both are teenagers now) has deeply affected his thoughts on those questions, and one can find his children's youth in his writing, too:

> I guess I can trace a great deal of my life in these plays. If you throw out all of my quote-unquote adult plays, and look at the plays in this anthology, that's a roadmap of me as a person and a parent. *Jackie & Me* was written when our African son came to America. What were we talking about when suddenly we had an African American son in a family that loves baseball? Well, it shows up in the play. *The Rememberer* and *Iris* were written before we had kids, but I wonder whether *Honus*, *Jackie*, and maybe the plays that are still coming—I really wonder what these plays would be if we hadn't become parents.

> The time will come, little one, when you will take my place. You will hold our history and our stories in your mind. And you will pass them on. [. . .] It's a great responsibility little one. But, you've been chosen. And we are never chosen for something we don't have the power to do.
>
> Mud Bay Sam, *The Rememberer*

Dietz's desire to "write towards someone else's experience" speaks to the sense of duty he finds in playwriting. And just as his diligent commitment to craft, full-hearted collaboration, and connection to community were passed to him by parents and mentors, he endeavors to pass them on to the next generation of theatre artists and audiences. For those making theatre, Dietz has distilled his pragmatic approach down to three points:

1. Seek expertise: If you are the best writer, director, or actor in your group, then you are in the wrong group. Play in the bracket above you.
2. Invite scrutiny: Don't just wait for feedback/criticism—seek it out, welcome it, and use it to sharpen yourself against it. Working in theatre is not for the faint of heart.
3. Diligence and patience: Do today's work, do the next day's work. Keep showing up—whether the muse (or whatever) shows up or not. Take the long view.

After nearly a decade at UT, Dietz continues to instill in his students the same respect for the nuts and bolts that he himself holds. He says,

> I'm trying to fill up a toolbox for them, and my job is to give them more tools than they need. They're going to write that first rock and roll song with those three chords that they know, but eventually they're going to need a diminished seventh, and their craft is going to have to grow with their ideas. As I tell them, my job is to make myself unnecessary. I want to be there for my students, but ultimately I want them to say, "This is mine now, and I don't need that Dietz to tell me where to put the short word in the sentence."

Dietz is also intent on modeling for his students the career they're pursuing. Even with a well-stocked toolbox, "you can't be a playwright until you learn how to rewrite at rehearsals and work with actors." He says,

> I feel like when my position was created here, it was created to put a professional playwright, including the good, bad, and ugly of what goes on in one's career, on the faculty. My students are on deadline for something that they have to write for me, and I'm on deadline for a play for the Guthrie Theater, and we have the same twenty-six letters, and we're struggling with them every day. On the days when you don't have any ideas, you still have to write that play. And when the actors are staring at you, and it's Tuesday, and they're waiting for you to fix that scene, it's a deadline-driven art form.

When he works at theatres across the country he often takes a student along to observe. On these trips, Dietz says, "It's watching me cut, watching me change, really demystifying the process."

Dietz acknowledges, though, that the profession his students are pursuing is not what it was when he was starting out. He knows that no matter how well stocked their toolbox, his students' careers will require a healthy measure of McGyver-like improvisation and ingenuity. "I can give clues and hints, I can give examples and strategies," he says, "but theatre is like any other discipline: it is wholly inner-driven, self-dependent. You have to *work* at it. You are beholden to its ongoing demands, and you must meet them daily, head-on."

In addition to the demands of writing are the demands created by new generations of audiences and a rapidly shifting cultural landscape. Particularly in relation to theatre for young audiences, Dietz worries about shrinking budgets and declining arts exposure in public schools, about socioeconomic and cultural barriers to attending the theatre, about the ways social and digital media are impacting live theatre, and about the diminishing role of regional theatres in the national new play and TYA landscape. He wonders how theatre professionals can debunk the myth of theatre being an art form apart: "How do we engage a rapidly moving world in a traditionally reflective art? How do we put change into context?"

Does Dietz think we can answer these questions before our theatres go the way of the handwritten letter, the landline telephone, MySpace? "If the regional theatre has been dying this many years, it is dying very inefficiently," Dietz says. He admits that it's probably not as alive as we want it to be, "but this is no time to throw up our hands. We have plenty to move forward with. I'm hopeful, probably just because I'm stubborn, and I've seen plays land. I got to write the Jackie Robinson play, and I got to watch that play with a group of African American children in Chicago. They didn't need to be told how to behave in the theatre. They didn't need to be told about Stanislavsky and Brecht. They needed a story that they could relate to and some terrific actors and a terrific production."

"I believe in the regional theatre, and I've had such great fortune in it," Dietz says, but he would like to see the field hew more closely to "the essence of the Tyrone Guthrie days, the Zelda Fichandler days." For example, though he still sees a role for that old warhorse, the student matinee, in exposing young people to the theatre, he also pushes back at the notion that such formal "benchmark" arts experiences are a panacea. "As soon as [theatre] gets rarified I think it's in danger," he says. Yet in many communities across the country, the formerly vaunted regional theatres don't hold the same position within their region that they once did. Whereas baby boomers perhaps saw these institutions as essential temples of the arts, today's youth are more likely to perceive them as ivory towers with "keep out" signs on the doors. Asked why so many younger people today have such a different relationship to the arts than past generations, Dietz says,

> One of the prime possessions that families used to buy was a piano. Now it's maybe a flat-screen TV, or for a while it was an automobile. They would buy the piano so that the family could gather around and someone could pound on it and they could sing. And music—the experience of music, the creation of music—became less rarefied because it was brought into the home. I absolutely fear the rarefication of the theatre experience, that it's not built into the fabric of our children's cultural experience because of expense, because of time, and more importantly, because it's not in the fabric of the parents' lives.

Part of the problem, Dietz says, is that "the model is still 'build it in the center of the town and hope that people will come,' rather than identify the need and go out to the people, which is what we tend to do through touring, but the theatres who do that best are the ones that reach out with subject matter: 'We're going to do a play for *these* people, for *these* kids.' I believe that is the way we become necessary."

Dietz does see hope, though, in the example of his own upbringing:

> I find in my own history the fact that I was the kid not exposed to theatre, but there was theatre in my heart. I fell into it as a profession. When we talk about "the untapped audience," I *was* that audience. I just needed exposure.

> You know what Satchel Paige said about that, don't you? "How old would you be if you didn't know how old you were?"
>
> Miss Young, *Honus & Me*

More than three decades into his professional career, Dietz says, "I think I am more candid now about how my plays are made, and at the same time less certain of their ultimate effect." "This is a curious and maddeningly illusive medium, which is probably what I secretly love about it. We learn and we fail and we work and we push on. Mr. Dylan of course said it best: 'I was so much older then, I'm younger than that now.'"

Though each new generation, person, place, and time will have different cultural needs, Dietz believes that theatre is essential when our storytellers act on the knowledge that "job one is to be aware of your time. You write to your heart and hope that in doing so you write to your time."

Dietz would also have us remember that the theatre's primary function is as a place in which we "see others do and say things we cannot do or say. [. . .] Through these events, we experience emotions ourselves. We are given the theatre's most profound gifts: participation and reflection." The characters in the plays in this anthology comprise a range of ages, races and ethnicities, cultures and socioeconomic classes, experiences and day-to-day realities. They stand up to those who would strip them of their culture, they investigate how hardship can make a hero, they learn to listen to the sound of their intuition even when external forces would silence them. They are prime examples of the ways in which theatre can be a window to possibility for new, younger, and more diverse audiences.

Among the many characters and worlds contained in this anthology, one line from *Still Life with Iris*'s eponymous character could stand as a clarion call from Steven Dietz to future artists and audiences alike, and it serves as both warning and mandate: "You've given me everything but the thing I want the most: *the story of who I am*."

There is a harsh reality to be extrapolated from Iris's lament: We could provide free theatre to every child in the country, every day for a year, and still fail to be "useful" if the stories are not connected to the community, not born of an unquenchable curiosity about our world as it is or could be, not forged in the collaborative fire of multiple perspectives and experiences. But the opposite is also true: One child's experience can change the world, as in Dietz's case. And he's seen this possibility in the many and varied students he's taught, in the audiences of his plays, and in the future of his most precious young audience: his children.

> What they're going to need is not necessarily a working knowledge of theatre names and dates that I can quiz them on. But the world will require from my children a story: Tell me why you want this job, why you want to marry me, why you want to move to this city. And the kinds of narratives these questions will generate—alive, personal, proximate—are the heart of our art form. We're teaching to the most central aspects of what our children need to learn when we expose them to theatre. I don't think of it as "They should know about Shakespeare." Of course they should know about Shakespeare, but I think about it way more viscerally than that. People are affected by what goes on in rooms; theatre is events that happen in rooms, imaginative events, real events. [. . .] That notion of spontaneous, proximate contact is the heart of communication; it's the heart of the culture—and I think we do a disservice to our kids, and perhaps to our art, when we try to find a villain to help explain why theatre is not in the fabric of our kids' lives. It's easy to make money the villain, to make time the villain, to make schools the villain, to make the NEA the villain. But one of the main questions is—for those of us who are parents, for those of us who make theatre—have we really made it central?

With both his writing and his teaching Dietz continues his part in crafting a future where audiences of all ages can experience meaningful stories on stages in their own communities. He says his students "are an amazing group" who he hopes "will surpass my generation in what they bring to the theatre." If the toolbox with which he supplies each student were a physical object—complete with the necessary implements for crafting the theatre's next stage—it's easy to imagine one last pragmatic yet poetic lesson from Dietz engraved (by hand, of course) on the box's side:

You have twenty-six letters and thousands of days.

Time to get to work.

Works Cited

Atkins, Corey. Interview with Steven Dietz, 7 November 2012.

———. "Play Time: Renowned playwright and director Steven Dietz brings his energy and experience to University of Texas faculty." University of Texas at Austin College of Fine Arts newsletter, summer 2006.

Berson, Misha. "'Rememberer' Poses Many Questions." *Seattle Times*, 21 March 1994.

Dietz, Steven. "An Audience Manifesto." *American Theatre*, January 1993.

———. "Author's Note." *Lonely Planet*. Dramatists Play Service, 1994.

———. "How to Hamstring a Playwright." *Los Angeles Times*, 28 February 1988: K45.

———. "Playwright's Notes." From the performance program for *Mad Beat Hip & Gone*, 2013: 50.

———. "Stage Wanted: A Return to a Theater of Eloquence." *Los Angeles Times*, 20 March 1988: 45.

———. "Theater of the Young, For the Young." HowlRound, 23 May 2012. http://www .howlround.com

Drake, Sylvia. "Steven Dietz: A Playwright Sink or Swim." *Los Angeles Times*, 11 June 1989.

Dramatists Guild of America, Inc. "Ten Questions." *Dramatist*, 2009: 6.

Faires, Robert. "Working Playwright." *Austin Chronicle*, 7 November 2008.

Faubion, Rob. *Five Questions with Steven Dietz*, March 2009. http://www .austinonstage.com/interviews/stevendietz

Jones, Kenneth. "PLAYBILL ON-LINE'S BRIEF ENCOUNTER with Steven Dietz," 22 July 2004. *Playbill On-line*. http://www.playbill.com/celebritybuzz/article /print/87507.html

Jones, Rosemary. *Steven Dietz: resisting a brand-name image*, 28 August 2010. 1 April 2013. http://www.examiner.com/article/steven-dietz-resisting-a-brand-name-image

Longenbaugh, John. "Brick-Solid." *Seattle Weekly*, 15 October 2008.

Meadows, Olin. *Steven Dietz speaks about his inspirations in an exclusive interview*, 15 April 2013, 1 June 2013. http://austinentertainmentweekly.com/2013/04/15 /steven-deitz-speaks-about-his-inspirations-in-an-exclusive-interview/

Merriam-Webster Dictionary. *Merriam-Webster Dictionary*, 4 June 2013. http://www .merriam-webster.com/dictionary/wright

Sales, Laurie. "Interview with Steven Dietz and Emily Mann." From McCarter Theatre's *Last of the Boys* resource guide, August 2004.

Sandys, Nick. *Remy Bumpo Theatre Company, Interview with Steven Dietz*, August 2007. http://www.remybumppo.org/interview-with-steven-dietz-pages-216.php

Truzzi, Gianni. "Honus and Me brings the prolific playwright Steven Dietz full circle in Seattle." *Seattle Post-Intelligencer*, 30 March 2006.

Tu, Janet I-Chin. "Busy, Busy, Busy: Playwright Steven Dietz Juggles Many Projects." *Seattle Times*, 1 February 1998.

———. "Magic Tricks Add Charm to 'Iris.'" *Seattle Times*, 23 September 1997.

———. "Playing With Magic — 'Still Life With Iris' Is a Fanciful Story With Bagfuls of Tricks at Seattle Children's Theatre." *Seattle Times*, 8 September 1997.

University of Texas Department of Theatre and Dance. *Faculty Spotlight*, 1 April 2013.
    http://www.utexas.edu/finearts/tad/people/dietz-steven
Valenzi, Peter Bonilla and Shane. *Talking With ... Steven Dietz, Playwright of 'Last
    of the Boys'*, 2007, 1 April 2013. www.interacttheatre.org/staging/talkingwith
    stevendietz.htm

.

Dramatic Impact

A Conversation with Linda Hartzell

J. Richard Smith

EDITOR'S NOTE: *Another significant consideration that playwrights and artistic directors encounter when working together to develop new plays for any audience is addressed in the following interview. Theatre designer and director J. Richard Smith spoke with Linda Hartzell, artistic director of Seattle Children's Theatre, about her years of working with Steven Dietz. The plays in this collection have all been produced at Seattle Children's Theatre—*The Rememberer *in 1994,* Still Life with Iris *in 1997,* Honus & Me *in 2006, and* Jackie & Me *in 2011.* Jackie & Me *premiered at Chicago Children's Theatre in 2011.*

Few individuals have had the impact that Linda Hartzell has had in the field of drama and theatre for youth and communities. For nearly thirty years, operating under her leadership as artistic director, Seattle Children's Theatre (SCT) has been one of the major professional theatre companies for children and families in the United States. In this time, Hartzell has cultivated and nurtured not only young audiences and their families, but also the artists who create the work that will feed their imaginations and souls for generations to come.

Our profession has existed for more than a century, continually evolving as a barometer of an ever-changing world. Even as the cultural climate swings like a pendulum, censoring and at the same time engendering our art form, SCT continues to be an essential measure of our progress. Not only is it an instrumental part of the cultural climate in the Pacific Northwest, but it also plays a large role in a global community that continues to expand and enrich the canon of dramatic literature for young audiences. Given the depth and breadth of Hartzell's experience, I wanted to explore her relationship with Steven Dietz and the scripts in this anthology, as well as how her arc of leadership figures into the genesis of the profession as a whole.

J. Richard Smith

JRS: How did you come to be artistic director of Seattle Children's Theatre?

LH: One day, in November 1984, the artistic director left for lunch and never came back. He turned in his resignation to the newspaper and quit without telling the staff or board. So there was no artistic director, and the baby of the woman who was directing the main stage shows had just died of SIDS. The theatre was in an absolute crisis! Yet the defining thing about theatre is that you've got to open the show.

One of the six women on the board knew me, since I had taught her children at Lakeside School,[1] and she had seen shows I had directed. By that point, I had become an independent director and I had four productions that had been big hits. She came to me in the middle of a rehearsal and said, "We just need an interim person. You know how to direct and I've watched you teach." I had been a member of the original company of actors for the theatre, but I had no administrative skills. I didn't know anything. But as her friend and the theatre's, I just wanted to get them through that fall and winter. So I helped stage that first production and stepped in to direct the play that was going to open right after that. They decided they had to do a national search, and dear Kathleen Collins,[2] I've heard many times, is someone who gave me a good review. They did a national search, but ultimately I got the position. I think, honest to god, that if I had gone through a professional search the way people have to do these days, I would have never gotten the job. I had no experience as an artistic director!

JRS: One aspect of your leadership is your commitment to new work. All of Steven's plays that you've produced have been premieres. What is the process and goal for commissions and new adaptations?

LH: Richard Edwards before me is the one who said, "Let's do *The Count of Monte Christo.* Let's commission new works." Fortunately or unfortunately, we have become a Book-It[3] theatre. In the old days, it was a means of getting away from just doing *Aesop's Fables* or *Hansel & Gretel*, because there is so much great literature for young audiences. Today, with very limited marketing dollars and the need for capacity audiences in order to make payroll, we need some name recognition. So I'll read a book and like it. I talk to people. It sort of starts there.

Also, I'm such a history and politics buff, and I try to tie in relevant discussions we're having as a society right now, like Suzan Zeder's *The Edge of Peace*,[4] about war veterans coming home and feeling displaced or not connecting. That's the part of the job I like—and worry about—the most.

JRS: Why do you worry about it?

LH: You're introducing people to theatre, and many people want familiar titles more than ever. It would be very easy to just do a whole season of *Give a Mouse a Cookie*. But we're not going to do that. It would be very easy for me to say I'm sick and tired of having a playwright sitting next to me, developing the new play. It's ten times more work! [*laughs*] As many people as there are who know SCT, there are also those who don't know who we are. And I'm constantly surprised that there are many adults who have heard of us but haven't been here.

Currently, about 180,000 people a year see our work; it used to be 286,000. However, I don't think you'd find a child who grew up in Seattle who hasn't been here, which is pretty extraordinary. We've gone into three generations. But the bigger dilemma is that many people don't think theatre is interesting. They don't think it's engaging.

JRS: Because of technology and films, and everything else that theatre competes with?

LH: Right. "Theatre is boring . . ." I'll use my family as an example. One portion of our family will spend $146 per ticket to see *The Lion King* but won't subscribe to our theatre for their children. To them, theatre means spectacle. That's why all of us are having trouble getting ticket buyers—because they want spectacle rather than a bare stage with just four actors. In producing plays for the last three generations, we first saw children who couldn't listen as long as our grandparents, who sat around and focused on a radio. But the thing that is scaring me a little now is I'm seeing some sociopathic behavior—because of video games, where the image changes every second. For the human psyche, that second of seeing the action or event is just the first step. We need an extra beat or two to connect to how we feel about that action. He's injured: (beat) *That's bad*. He's dead: (beat) *I'm sad*. It's scaring me that it doesn't matter that somebody is hurt, that they die, that there's no sense of empathy.

More than ever it's really important to present the basic kind of storytelling, Storytelling 101. You introduce children to character. If they care about that person, if they connect, they will buy into the character's story and have some emotional response. Basically children are fair-minded, but there are so many kids today who watch so much TV and are ignored by the adults in their lives that fairness goes away in the child. It doesn't take long. Don't forget: two-year-olds either bite or they come home and they've been bitten; there's a little animal in there! You have to, on a regular basis, nurture that fairness.

I like the challenge of the work that we have to do. I love this field. I've had chances to work in adult theatre but I like our young audiences much better. But it's been frightening at times. I put my car and house up for collateral to make payroll when I first came here. I cleaned the bathrooms. There have been times as scary as that as recently as a few years ago. We have this crazy imbalance of paying the most we can for the best artist, for the highest level of work, while keeping the tickets affordable. We continue to give away $1.2 million dollars of free or discounted tickets to needy children every year, and we are now providing arts education for the public schools. So we fill a huge niche in this community, but boy, it's hard to do that. Yet I hope we can continue.

JRS: With the changes you've seen in your career, is there anything that's remained consistent?

LH: First of all, somehow the marketing people can tell you that this theatre has sold five million tickets. We have entertained five million people. It is incredible! I mentioned our three generations; we are now seeing people who were coming when I was first in the company, in 1977, and they are now having their own little ones attend. Where I have been consistent is to always insist, "I know we have to cut cost, but you know what? The children deserve this [high quality work]." If we are going to change the perception in America that art is not important, that theatre is just an elitist thing, our work is just starting. Since the 1980s, the arts have been eliminated in many public schools. They haven't been recognized as essential elements of the curriculum.

JRS: And yet the national standards for arts education remain.

LH: They do!

JRS: English playwright David Wood, who wrote the theatrical adaptation of *The Big Friendly Giant* and other adaptations of Roald Dahl stories, has said, "I believe that children are born with an innate sense of justice. This has nothing to do with morality, or knowing the difference between right and wrong. It is to do with fairness. [. . .] It is very rare to find a child who backs the baddie. The vast majority of children instinctively want justice to prevail."[5]

LH: The ideas of education and politics are inextricably linked. They shape or inform what we do, and are also sort of a cautionary tale. Really good children's theatre provides an opportunity for audiences to think critically about the world. I believe that is why we do what we do, in many instances.

One thing that is different between adults and children is that children are not cynical. My husband was a Waldorf teacher, and in the Waldorf education system there is a saying that summarizes what we do in the arts: "We educate children to use their head, their heart and their hands."[6] They are developing the whole person, and I know good theatre for young audiences does that too, because we're doing more than teaching them how to appreciate theatre. We're storytellers and we're telling parables, which is the most ancient form of teaching. We are engaging the children, entertaining them, and introducing them to good people and bad people, interesting and new ideas. We're not presenting didactic, condescending, "teachy-preachy" programs or plays. We are offering good storytelling, good drama.

JRS: As we've been talking about the connections between adults and the child audience, I'm reminded of an essay Steven wrote on the theatre blog HowlRound. He said:

> In case running an American professional theatre in 2012 was not hard enough, [theatre managers] must program their seasons for a Double Audience. These leaders always seek to astonish and inspire their young audiences—but make no mistake: they must cater to the parents. And the schools. And the funders and the marketers and the Board. They must constantly assuage the well-intentioned gatekeepers . . .[7]

How do you see the future for theatre in terms of this "double audience," and what I see as a sociopolitical conservatism that has galvanized the country?

LH: Well, we've been dealing with that for over twenty-five years. We saw its influence in the arts probably before the rest of Middle America, in the 1980s—Mapplethorpe[8] and the movement he was part of was pretty extreme for Middle America.

But let me give you one anecdote. We had a major earthquake in Seattle in 2001, and we had both theatres filled with children. We were taking care of kids for four hours when parents couldn't get here. [There were] these two little boys, I think they were turning eight, in second grade or maybe third—one boy said to me, "You know why we have earthquakes?" And I said, "No, why?" And he said, "The Devil. The Devil turns over, that's why we have earthquakes." Then his little friend went like this [slides one hand over the other] and said, "You see, what happens is two tectonic plates shifted and . . ." [laughs]. So we have, and always have had, all kinds of people walking through this door. We have every aspect of American society, every Muslim, Jewish, Christian kid sitting in the same seats. And that is a wonderful thing. We have to love all of our children. And for them we strive to present a season of beloved stories that are G-rated, not out of concern for violence and sexual content, but G so as not to offend anyone in this group or that group. All you can do is try.

JRS: The quality of the writing on your stage is in part a credit to SCT and the other children's theatres in the country that have helped nurture relationships with really fine playwrights like Steven, who cross boundaries between genres.

LH: Yes! Others we have commissioned to create new works are Y York, Suzan Zeder, John Olive, Cheryl West, and Robert Schenkkan.

JRS: What makes Steven a great author for young audiences? What drew you to him in the first place?

LH: It's obvious that Steven loves his own two children so much that he sees the world a little differently because of them. But he had the love and respect of children before he was married. I hired him because, first, he's a generous person and artist. He's also a skilled craftsperson who writes great dialogue, who is theatrically innovative and knows how to solve playwriting and production challenges.

JRS: Do you have an example of his craftsmanship?

LH: With *The Rememberer*, his first production with us, dramaturgically he took what was a bit of an epic story and did a great job of keeping us connected to the lead characters. He kept it from being one of those coat-rack shows where there is a new event on every page. He always kept the plot moving along and the story of the main character the most important thing.

He also gave a sense of the Squaxin and Salish cultures through dance and song and storytelling without truncating their story. He took many, many different things and made them one world.

With *Go, Dog. Go!*, which he co-wrote and directed, he and Allison [Gregory] made the decision not to add any more words to the book. In figuring out how to move the story along in a nonverbal way, he'd switch hats, problem solving as a director and then putting it on the page as a playwright. For example, Steven approached the circus scene first as director, then as playwright. He took the end of the bedspread, lifted it up until it became the canopy of the tent, and pulled out a miniature Ferris wheel for the action to continue. So in the script he was able to give specific staging ideas for a small puppet world. He's really good at seeing and solving things in a nonliteral way, and communicating that in text and stage directions. He's so savvy. Steven sees the physicality of what is needed in the theatre, and sometimes playwrights don't get that.

Children are not interested in plays where people sit and talk and talk—they want to see the story played out, in action. Steven's children's plays are perfect examples of the fundamental concept of "show me, don't tell me."

JRS: Of the four plays in this collection, *The Rememberer* seems the most challenging because of the subject matter. What was the hardest part about staging the premier production?

LH: Did Steven ever tell you how *The Rememberer* came about?

JRS: No.

LH: Agnes Haaga[9] had a friend who knew Joyce Cheeka, the protagonist of *The Rememberer*. As Joyce Cheeka was getting older, she asked her friend to help her write down her stories. Later, Agnes Haaga came to me with a cardboard box this large [*gestures*] with yellowed typing paper, that beautiful old-fashioned typing paper, with Joyce Cheeka's stories. Everything she was supposed to have known as designated Rememberer of her tribe. With that box of memories, I went to Steven and said, "I think there is a play in here." If one is designated from age ten to be their tribe's Rememberer, as Joyce Cheeka was, and then is suddenly forced to forget, you have conflict, the crux of good drama.

We put together a proposal and received a $250,000 Lila Wallace Grant. This was in the days when large amounts of money were available from philanthropic foundations in support of the arts. We were fortunate to be one of the seven companies that got a Wallace grant—money we'd never had before, and haven't had since—which gave us the time to do our research. Steven and I were privileged to spend time with members of the Squaxin tribe of the Salish Nation, who shared their ideas concerning design, directing, acting, staging. Their expertise was an amazing thing.

JRS: Can you talk more specifically about the ways that the grant money influenced the creation of the play?

LH: We had money to bring in artists and craftsmen, rather than have our prop shop do everything. I was able to pay Squaxin and Macaw artists to create the cedar-bark capes, carve the masks, put authentic work on stage. We were able to train Native Americans as actors. The choreography was taught by Native Americans who were relatives of Joyce Cheeka. We had the time to fully do the research and development part. We always do that, starting a year or two ahead of time, especially if we're dealing with another ethnic group, a different culture, a different time or place. But with *The Rememberer* we had an exceptional amount of time to really do the research, to meet these people. And we had the money to pay them for their time and expertise. Rather than just tell us the stories, they actually helped us create them onstage.

The hardest part of staging the play, which is often difficult, was finding the actors. But fortunately we had the money to solve that. The grant gave us the money to do two things: go outside of Seattle to cast the play, and provide the types of Equity contracts that we can hardly ever afford. And more importantly, when I identified people who were eager, who wanted to act but had never been trained, I was able to put them in acting lessons for a year. We'd never been able to do that before.

JRS: Of the plays collected in this anthology, I think *Still Life with Iris* is the only work without preexisting source material. Am I correct?

LH: Well . . . no, that's not true. *Still Life with Iris* was inspired by the stage illusions of Steffan Soule and Cooper Edens, who brought me ideas for eight illusions that they wanted to use in a production. God bless Steven, he wrote around these illusions. Since other producers might not be able to afford the illusions, Steven published a version of *Still Life* without them, and the play still stands well on its own.

JRS: How did collaborating with designers affect the creation of *Still Life with Iris*?

LH: Working with Steffan was the starting point for *Still Life*. We paid him as a consultant for the illusions. He worked with the set designer and the costume designer—so that all would match and compliment the illusions.

JRS: Let's talk about the two baseball plays, *Honus & Me* and *Jackie & Me*. Each was adapted from a book by Dan Gutman. What is it that drew you to these stories? Were the adaptations initiated by you or by Steven?

LH: *Honus & Me* was initiated by Seattle Children's Theatre. I read the book, I liked the book. As the mother of a son who was passionate about baseball and baseball cards and what they meant, these stories are relevant and important to me. Also, I loved that the book involves time travel. As a kid I read all of Jules Verne's science fiction novels.

JRS: How did you obtain the rights for the adaptation?

LH: I called Dan Gutman for the rights, and fortunately he was interested. In the old days, you could just call the author. I called Judy Blume at home, Maurice Sendak, Shel Silverstein. They all took my calls many times. Now you can't find their numbers, or they've sold rights to so many publishing companies they don't even know what they own anymore.

Steven loves baseball—it's God to him!—and along the way he and Dan got to be friends, then wanted to work on another play together. So after the success of *Honus & Me*, Steven, with Chicago Children's Theatre and Seattle Children's Theatre, proposed the idea of dramatizing *Jackie & Me*. With Dan's approval and support, Steven began adapting this story that so boldly illustrates the bigotry of the time. With racism an ongoing challenge for society, it was and still is imperative that people be shown what Jackie Robinson went through as the first African American to break the "color line" in Major League Baseball in 1947. And what a hero he was—an everyday hero as well as a baseball hero.

JRS: Did the play spur the kinds of conversations you'd hoped it would?

LH: Initially we were concerned about the scene between Brooklyn Dodgers general manager Branch Rickey and Jackie. It is exactly what happened that day. During an interview Branch Rickey called Robinson "nigger," to see his reaction. Then he said, "You're going to be tested, as a person, on the field." We made certain that the story and the content were shared with teachers and administrators before they agreed to bring children to the production. Then we sent letters to all the schools with a discussion about the word "nigger," and sent teachers that particular scene from the play. The outreach sparked a discussion about that term, its history, what it signifies, and the whole issue of racism.

JRS: Was there any objection to the use of that word and the other racist remarks? What responses did you get to the production?

LH: We had some who said, "We don't want our child to hear that," so they didn't attend, and we might have had one school group who chose not to come. But we had done a good job showing teachers and leaders in the community how we could create productive conversations about racism.

Also, I think it's helpful that *Jackie & Me* is a story seen through the eyes of a young person. So we aren't just looking at Jackie Robinson's and Branch Rickey's stories. We're seeing a kid's experience. So for a child today, who doesn't know that this happened, the play becomes a history lesson. And the children loved it. There were no restless spots during the performances. There were gasps when the word "nigger" was used. To get that reaction from an audience of young people is great. *Jackie & Me* is a timely and immediate story, and yet exotic—in the sense that it's another time, another place.

JRS: What are some of the particulars of working with Steven?

LH: Steven is not one of those playwrights who wears me out when he's sitting next to me in rehearsals. He's easy and he knows how to rewrite. Do you know how many playwrights do not know how to rewrite? You give them notes and the next draft comes back and they've dropped all the stuff that was working. They often don't know how to rework one thing and still leave all of what was working.

With Steven every character has different idiomatic phrases; they use different rhythms. Look how varied *Jackie & Me* and *Still Life with Iris* are in style and tone. Also, he's flexible, which is the reason I want someone like him on a project as sensitive as *Jackie & Me*. He's so mature, and he's so generous of spirit. It was the same with *The Rememberer*. He loved learning about the history he so respected, what he was getting from the people. It really was a marriage of ideas.

His plays for young audiences and his plays for adults are equally rich and textured. He never condescends to his young audience. In fact, I think *Go, Dog. Go!* is unique in that it is very much a European style of theatre for young audiences. You don't have to put actors in fake, fully realized animal costumes and have a fully painted set. That's what I learned from watching European plays, and it's really affected how we are doing our work. I was not producing anything for children under age seven until I started seeing productions overseas.

For *Go, Dog. Go!* I hired Allison and Steven, not just because they are successful playwrights, but because Steven is a really excellent director and Allison's an outstanding choreographer. It was those skills, those kinesthetic, nonverbal talents, that I knew were going to be successful. And as you know, there are only a few words, many repeated, in the P. D. Eastman book. Allison and Steven did not add one extra word.

JRS: You and your SCT staff have had a major part in the creation of the plays in this anthology. What do you hope the effect, or legacy, of Steven's plays will be?

LH: I hope that all plays being written for young audiences are being written the way Steven Dietz writes. That should be the norm, not the exception, that level of dramaturgy. Every character has a different voice, the plots are always interesting, and the stories are important. His historical plays aren't boring, didactic history lessons without dramatic tension. In all of his stories I want to turn the pages quickly when I get the first draft to find out what's going to happen. And it's such a joy to work with Steven. His plays are just fun to act in, they're fun to direct, and they're fun to watch.

As we concluded our conversation, I was reminded of a line spoken by Jackie Robinson at the end of *Jackie & Me*: "A life is not important except in the impact it has on other lives." It was one of those glorious few summer days here in the Pacific Northwest, when everyone is outdoors enjoying the sunshine. Outside Linda's office, on the Seattle Center campus at the foot of the Space Needle, I could hear the excited voices of countless children. They were all participants in the theatre's summer programming: dozens upon dozens of young, eager spirits just beginning a summer of discovery, about themselves and about others. That was what Linda and I had been discussing—what the work by Steven, Linda, and this exceptional organization are all about: young people who we hope will take away something from the theatre and, in turn, learn and grow and continue the process.

I was reminded too of something Steven Dietz said that perfectly sums up the hopes shared by Linda and Steven, and, I hope, by all who read this anthology:

To make plays for young audiences asks a playwright to wrestle with essences—a challenge often just impossible enough to summon our very best work. It has the feel of trying to grab at fireflies in an endless field at night. But if we catch one—if our craft proves worthy of our story and we connect with the oldest and deepest parts of ourselves—I can promise you this: the perfect audience awaits."[10]

Notes

1. Lakeside School is a private school for grades five through twelve in Seattle, Washington.

2. Kathleen Collins cofounded Seattle Children's Theatre in 1975 while pursuing her MFA in theatre at the University of Washington. She has since served as artistic director of the Honolulu Theatre for Youth and the Fulton Opera House in Lancaster, Pennsylvania. She has recently directed for Seattle Children's Theatre, New Century Theatre, American Contemporary Theatre (San Francisco), and Seattle Rep. As an educator, she has taught at the University of Hawaii, at Lesley University (Cambridge, MA), and at her alma mater. She is currently a professor of theatre at Cornish College of the Arts.

3. This is a reference to the style of theatre practiced by Book-It Repertory, a small, professional theatre in Seattle that is known for its narrative style of theatre.

4. The last play in Zeder's *Ware Trilogy*.

5. David Wood and Janet Grant, *Theatre for Children: A Guide to Writing, Adapting, Directing and Acting* (London: Faber & Faber, 1997). 21.

6. Waldorf education, also known as Steiner education, was founded in 1919 by Rudolf Steiner.

7. Steven Dietz, "Theatre of the Young, For the Young." HowlRound, 23 May 2012.

8. Robert Mapplethorpe (1946–1989) was a well-known photographer who reached the height of his fame during the 1990s. An open homosexual, Mapplethorpe was a central figure in a large national debate over sexuality, censorship, and public funding for the arts when his solo exhibition, *The Perfect Moment* (1989), set in motion a huge controversy culminating in the United States Supreme Court case *National Endowment for the Arts v. Finley*, which led to the abolishment of funding for individual artists by the NEA.

9. Agnes Haaga (1916–2006) was an internationally recognized pioneer in children's drama. She studied with Winifred Ward, and moved to Seattle in 1947 to join the University of Washington School of Drama.

10. Dietz, "Theatre of the Young, For the Young."

On Stage with *Go, Dog. Go!*

A Conversation with Susan Mickey

Coleman A. Jennings

EDITOR'S NOTE: *In 2003 the book* Go, Dog. Go! *by P. D. Eastman was drama-tized by Allison Gregory and Steven Dietz with music by Michael Koerner. Re-grettably, the reprint rights of the play were denied for this anthology. I decided that the essence of the dramatization could be imagined through a discussion with Susan Mickey, costume designer of the 2003 production of* Go, Dog. Go! *at the Children's Theatre Company in Minneapolis.*

The original plan was for our conversations to be limited to discussing Mickey's designs for Go, Dog. Go! *But Mickey also described some of the chal-lenges of designing costumes for other plays that include animals, such as* Char-lotte's Web, Ferdinand the Bull, *and* Lilly's Purple Plastic Purse. *Mickey's ex-periences and insight are significant for those within the theatre profession and for this book.*

Dressed in Mickey's costumes, actors are able to successfully portray ani-mals while talking and expressing emotion. In Go, Dog. Go! *actors allude to the "dogginess" of their characters rather than appear in full makeup and whole-body dog suits.*

The play includes an assembly of dogs: red, blue, green, and yellow; big dogs, little dogs, dogs who prefer cars, and dogs that favor skis. The story line is very simple: two dogs meet and one asks if the other likes her hat. "I do not like that hat" is the latter dog's constant response until the end, when the answer is posi-tive. The single-syllable words in rhythmic repetition, with humor and action, replace a conventional plot. The playwrights use only the minimal text from the book. The scenes are linked by the addition of Latecomer, or MC Dog. The lack of a forceful conflict does not hinder the effectiveness of the script—the play is basically a fanciful romp with songs, dances, and physical comedy. The musi-cians onstage, who play musical themes for selected characters, emphasize the connection between words and action.

Ears, paws, and tails are a challenge you face time and time again when design-ing costumes for young audiences. Many of the children's plays I've designed have animal characters. *Charlotte's Web* has the pig, the spider, the rat, geese, and everything else. In *Lilly's Purple Plastic Purse*, everyone's a mouse.

Red Dog and Yellow Dog in a car

In *Go, Dog. Go!* everyone is a dog. You constantly have to solve the problem of how an actor can portray an animal while telling the story, talking, and expressing emotion. The audience needs to see the actor's face, eyes, eyebrows, and mouth in order to know where to focus their attention. For more physically active characters, who must stand upright rather than crawl, the designer must decide how to portray the animals with the least amount of decoration to allow for mobility.

Although simple, straightforward, visual animal details are essential, the key to a successful portrayal most often lies in the movements and voice of the actor. You can give an actor very, very little: a little mark on their nose, a simple ear alteration. You don't have to do a lot. If the actor is fully embodying a pig, he will be a pig. But first, the director, designer, and actors must answer the question of how the transformation will occur. After the concept is decided, there are the practical and technical considerations. Perhaps a designer must make the tail springy, so that it can move on its own and survive being rolled over when the actor does summersaults. Animal ears should not impair the actor's hearing. Since the locations of the eyes and ears of an animal are very different from those of human beings, special attention must be paid to making sure their angles on the costume are correct.

Children don't process new experiences in a filtered, intellectual way, as adults do. Their reactions are often emotional and visceral. In order to connect with a character, they need to see the face. Small details lend credibility.

For example, it's easy to make a pig look like a dog by accident, and vise versa. Children will tell you if the pig looks like a dog. They are completely honest; they go with their gut instinct, and they are very vocal about it.

The successful designing and execution of costumes in theatre for young audiences is not in any way different from the philosophy of doing good theatre for adult audiences. Designers and their designs should not be pedantic or condescending. Costumes are condescending when they are overly simple and in big, broad, crayon strokes of color. The fact that children are capable of responding to incredibly subtle designs should be honored.

One of the ideas that I always stress to young designers is that details are really important in telling the story. The trim that you choose, the length of the sleeve—the minute considerations that go into making the costume are the crux of the matter. Details, whether in the acting, directing, or design, are what make the production believable, honest, and ultimately enjoyable.

Visual direction is also significant. It is indicated by the choices that I make as a designer to tell a young audience where to look onstage at any given time. Because children's reactions are often emotional, designers in conjunction with one another must make certain that the audience is focusing on the specific actions that help them better understand the story from beginning to end. Working together is one reason why we do what we do. If we did not want to be collaborators, we would be artists who work alone, like poets or painters.

Artistic collaboration was essential in creating the 2003 production of *Go, Dog. Go!* at the Children's Theatre Company in Minneapolis. In the musical dramatization by Steven Dietz and Allison Gregory, as in the 1961 book written and illustrated by P. D. Eastman, all of the characters are dogs. In the book there are many red, blue, green, and yellow dogs, whereas in the play there is only one dog in each of those colors, as well as Hattie, the French poodle, and MC Dog, the master of ceremonies.

Designers, director, actors, and theatre staff collaborated to create a production about dogs that behave like human beings. In the opening scene of the dramatization, one human character appears, a man known as Latecomer. He quickly transforms into MC Dog in full view of the audience, thus firmly setting the action in the world of dogs. Dogs wearing hats, riding unicycles and scooters, skiing, roller-skating, and driving cars are on their way to a dog party held on top of a tree. In both the book and play the humorous encounter between two dogs is told in only seventy-five words.

When the director and I initially discussed the script, his first image was that of visual clowning. European clowning is not what we think of as Barnum & Bailey Circus clowns but rather old-fashioned storytelling in a physical way, much like the overt action of characters of Italian *commedia dell'arte*. This approach became the heart of each adventure. Scenes are basically miniature plays: dogs playing baseball, dogs going to work, dog in a tree, dogs in a boat, dog under moon, and on and on.

During the continuing collaboration I met with each actor individually, some of the best I have ever worked with. I took pictures of them, talked with them, and watched them move. Then, back in my studio, I sat for days studying an encyclopedic book of dogs: pictures, descriptions of every dog imaginable. I sought to match each actor's physical movements and characteristics with a specific breed. Designing with the European model of clowning in mind, I created each clown dog specific to its breed. There was nothing general about the dogs: each had a personality and temperament according to its breed. The actors came to understand their costumes as an extension of their characters, of their "doggie-ness." The addition of clown noses, attached to the actors' faces with elastic string, enhanced the overall design concept.

Red Dog

During the fabric shopping that followed soon after the renderings, we selected terry cloth and fake fur with different textures. The material had to be flexible and stretchable, as the active dogs moved all over the set, climbing, jumping, and rolling. Each dog had his own basic fabric color. The shopping was great fun.

Red Dog in a tree

Yellow Dog

Yellow Dog, a Labrador Retriever

Working with the excellent costume craftsmen, I designed noses that were crafted out of clay: a tiny one, a snout, a pug nose, a pointed one. Creating tails that had to stay alive performance after performance took more research and development than the noses. With wires and harnesses worn around their waists, the actors, with very little movement, were able to wag their tails when they sat. It was charming and believable. A last-minute addition to the cast for the dog party in the final scene were nine to twelve high school students from the theatre arts training program, as black-and-white Dalmatians. They added to the joyfulness of the celebration.

Hattie

As in the book, each of the poodle's hats is very different. Unique in shape and texture, they were designed to highlight Hattie's moods as she seeks Big Dog's approval. Although he's in love with Hattie, he can't express his feelings.

Hattie, a French Poodle

He's frustrated every time she comes out asking him, "Do you like my hat?" He can't tell her that he loves her, because he doesn't know how to say it. Instead he says, "I do not. Goodbye!" Hattie then runs off, heartbroken. Big Dog's panting sounds emphasize his frustration at not understanding what he has done wrong or what he should have said, until Hattie arrives wearing her last hat. As Hattie rises slowly from beneath the stage, we see that her hat is made up of many different hats stacked one on top of another, like a huge birthday cake. First it was one little hat, then a second, somewhat larger hat, and finally Hattie is seen wearing the stack of hats, as in the book. After a long pause, Hattie asks Big Dog: "And now . . . do you like my hat?" The Big Dog's "I do" is followed by a jazzy, explosive dog party.

Throughout the performance, music by two dog musicians on stage, costumed as hobo clowns in old, traditional morning suits, cleverly highlights the play's ingenious staging of the various events.

The designs for scenes with cars are remarkable. The actors, as dogs, wear

Big Dog's "I do."

Hattie wearing a stack of hats, as in the book.

period driving caps and lightweight cars. They can set the cars down, get out, open the hoods, and make adjustments as smoke flows out.

The Ferris wheel design was also brilliant. During the bed scene, before turning out the lights, MC Dog reminds the dogs that it's "not time for playtime but for sleep." After MC Dog leaves, the other dogs, instead of sleeping, begin playing the game "going around." As a huge Ferris wheel rises from the back of the bed and lights up, the dogs go tumbling. In the midst of the romp the dogs, realizing that MC Dog is returning, jump in bed, freeze, and begin snoring.

We must not forget that the most important collaborators in a performance are the audience members. Since children are more vocal and participatory than adult audiences, they become our evaluators, sharing their assessments vocally and through their behavior. Another of the beauties of doing theatre for younger audiences is that when they see a fascinating animal or unusual character in a comic or dramatic situation, they often "become" it, reliving moments of the theatre experience as they leave the performance.

The Plays

The Rememberer

Steven Dietz

Premiere production, Seattle Children's Theatre, 1994

Production credits from the premiere of *The Rememberer* and details concerning performance rights are included in the acting edition of the play as published by Dramatic Publishing.

Your ancestors are looking through your eyes
when you are carving.

Al Charles, canoe carver,
Lower Elwha Reservation, 1993

Playwright's Note

Joyce Simmons was born in Mud Bay, near Olympia, Washington, on January 31, 1901. She was the third of seven children of Julian Sam Simmons and John D. Simmons, both members of the Squaxin Indian tribe.

The people of the Squaxin tribe, lacking a written language, passed knowledge from one generation to the next through the stories and recollections of a chosen member of the tribe—the "Rememberer." Early in life, Joyce was chosen to succeed her grandfather as the Rememberer for her people. In 1964, Joyce Simmons Cheeka began to tell her stories to educator and child drama advocate Werdna Phillips Finley. Over the next five years, Ms. Finley taped hundreds of hours of Joyce's memories of growing up as a Squaxin Indian girl in the Lower Puget Sound. These reminiscences were edited down to a 270-page manuscript titled *As My Sun Now Sets*. In chapter four of the manuscript, Joyce is forcibly taken from her home and placed in the Tulalip Training School, a government-run boarding school under the jurisdiction of the Bureau of Indian Affairs. That is where this play begins.

I have always told theatres—especially those outside the Pacific Northwest—to feel free to substitute a Native American language from within their own community for the Squaxin dialect called for in the script. I don't want to discourage any theatre from tracking down the actual Squaxin, but it is very difficult, even when in full consultation with the tribe, as we were when we premiered the show. Cecil Cheeka, Joyce Simmons Cheeka's son, agrees with this approach. He believes that because the events of this play happened nationally to many other tribes, it is appropriate to use the native language of one's choice. Mr. Cheeka has offered to assist production groups with information and can be reached at (360) 352-7227. Other possible resources for aid include the Daybreak Star Cultural Center in Seattle and the Squaxin Museum in Shelton, Washington.

On the music: same note. Find the Squaxin, if possible, but feel free to use other native melodies that suit the needs of the production.

Steven Dietz

Cast of Characters

(5m., 4w., 8 children, dancers, musicians, pairing of characters indicates suggested actor doubling)

JOYCE: a 12-year-old Squaxin Indian girl

ADULT JOYCE: Joyce as a 40-year-old woman

EMILY SAM: Joyce's grandmother
SQUAXIN WOMAN: a distant relative of Joyce's family
AUNT SOPHIE: a deceased relative of Joyce's
PITCH WOMAN: a mythical old woman

MUD BAY SAM: Emily Sam's husband, the tribal Rememberer

HENRY: Joyce's cousin, in his 20s
DARIN LONGFEATHER: a student, age 17

LONGHOUSE: Henry's father
TWIN RIVER: Kwakiutl Indian, employed by the B.I.A.
CHIEF SEATTLE: a Duwamish chieftain

MULLIN: the county sheriff
MR. CONRAD: a teacher at the Tulalip Training School

SUPERINTENDENT: head of the U.S. Indian schools, in her 40s
MISS BRENNAN: a teacher at the school

NURSE WARNER: a nurse at the school, in her 30s

DR. BUCHANAN: head of the Tulalip Training School

OTIS: a student, age 6

GIRL ONE: student, age 15
GIRL TWO: student, age 12

BOY ONE: student, age 13
BOY TWO: student, age 12

YOUNG GIRL: student, age 8

YOUNG BOY: student, age 8

Time and Place

1911 and the present. The Squaxin Indian reservation in southern Puget Sound, Washington, and the Tulalip Training School, near Marysville, Washington.

Setting

A dark, open playing space, which will be transformed into a variety of locales. This transformation will be done primarily through lighting, as well as through the use of a few set pieces, as noted. The ability to move quickly from scene to scene, without blackouts, should be the defining principle of the design.

Upstage, a cyclorama envelops the stage. When lit from the front, the cyclorama features a huge image of Mount Rainier. When actors are lit from behind it, the cyclorama becomes filled with their huge shadows.

The musicians are in plain view to the side of the stage. All costumes, masks, and props are true to both the era of the play and to the specific tribe or tribes from which they come.

ACT I

(Silence. The stage is bare, except for a large SCREEN, which is hanging fully to the floor at center. The DRUMMERS/SINGERS enter and take their positions to the side of the stage. A crash of DRUMS — sudden darkness. Another crash of DRUMS — a shaft of light on JOYCE CHEEKA ["ADULT JOYCE" in this text], 40 years old, dressed in a simple skirt, blouse, and sweater. Around her neck hangs a small, woven pouch. A FLUTE plays under the following.)

ADULT JOYCE. My name is Joyce Simmons Cheeka. I am from the Squaxin tribe, in the southern reaches of Puget Sound. This area has been known as Washington State for over a hundred years. This continent has been home to the United States of America for over two hundred years. My family has lived and worked here for seven hundred and fifty years. *(She smiles.)* There is a lot to remember. *(Crash of DRUMS. On the screen a FILM begins: the famous Edward S. Curtis footage of the arrival of the long canoes from "In the Land of the War Canoes," circa 1914.)* Think about your parents and grandparents and great-grandparents. Think about how they lived, many years ago, when they were young, like you. You may know about them because of movies you've seen. Now, imagine you have no movies. *(She claps her hands. The FILM goes to black.)* You may know about them because of photographs you've seen. *(CRASH OF DRUMS. ON THE SCREEN A SERIES OF PHOTOGRAPHS ARE PROJECTED: THE FACES OF SALISH WOMEN AND TWO CHILDREN, TAKEN BY CURTIS, CIRCA 1915.)* Your parents may have shown you pictures and said, "That is your great-uncle, that is your great-great-grand-mother." You looked at them and tried to imagine their lives. Now, imagine you have no photographs. *(She claps her hands. The PHOTOGRAPHS go to black.)* So instead, you read about them. *(Crash of DRUMS. On the screen a series of*

SLIDES are projected: pictures of numerous books about the Indian people, past and present.) And as you read, you thought about the past. You thought about what you would have done if you had lived long ago. Now, imagine your language has never been written down. That means you have no books. (*She claps her hands. The SLIDES go to black.*) Without movies, without pictures, without books—how will your history be remembered? How will you learn the story of your family, your tribe, your people? (*Crash of DRUMS as the screen flies away, revealing a CANOE, suspended roughly three feet above the ground on a pivoting pedestal. Deep blue sidelights flood the stage floor, providing a vast expanse of WATER around the canoe. We hear the sound of WAVES lapping against the canoe. A man paddles the canoe toward us. This is MUD BAY SAM. DRUMMING continues, under, as does the FLUTE. Upstage, looming over the scene, is MOUNT RAINIER. ADULT JOYCE remains in a shaft of light, watching.*) Among my family, and among my people, the past was brought to you in the form of stories. And the stories were brought to you by a chosen member of your tribe. That person was known as the Rememberer.

[*Note: All dialect typed in italics will be spoken in the Lushootseed language—the language of JOYCE's people—or some other Native American dialect.*]

MUD BAY SAM. Wake up, Joyce. Wake up, *little one.* (*A young JOYCE CHEEKA ["JOYCE" in this text], age 12, sits up in the canoe.*) The mountain is out. It's telling us to get home before the storm.

JOYCE. How do you know it will storm?

MUD BAY SAM. The clouds are sitting on the west side of the mountain. That means rain.

JOYCE. But Grandfather, how do you know?

MUD BAY SAM. I know because my father knew, and his father, and his. The mountain always tells us when a storm is coming.

(*LIGHTNING and THUNDER as JOYCE ducks down again and MUD BAY SAM paddles through the water.*)

ADULT JOYCE. His name was Mud Bay Sam. He knew about the mountain. He knew the story of the Great Flood. It seemed like he knew about everything. In our tribe, he was known as the Rememberer.

MUD BAY SAM. Don't be frightened, little one. We'll be home soon.

JOYCE (*peeking back up*). I'm not frightened.

(*LIGHTNING and THUNDER as JOYCE screams and ducks down again, quickly. MUD BAY SAM smiles.*)

MUD BAY SAM. Not even a little?

JOYCE. No.

MUD BAY SAM. The sparrow is frightened of the crow, the crow is frightened of the hawk. Sometimes the Great Spirit gives us fear to protect us.

JOYCE. I'm not frightened of anything.

MUD BAY SAM. I knew a little girl just like you. She said she wasn't afraid of the night.

JOYCE. I'm not either.

MUD BAY SAM. So she disobeyed her father and went walking. But one night, this little girl met up with the Pitch Woman.

JOYCE. Who's that?

ADULT JOYCE. And that's when he told me.

(*LIGHTNING and THUNDER as the PITCH WOMAN, covered in black rags, runs around the floating canoe and enacts/dances the following as it is described. BURSTS OF DRUMMING accompany her movements.*)

MUD BAY SAM. The Pitch Woman lives far away.

ADULT JOYCE. She is very big and covered in pitch, black as night.

MUD BAY SAM. At twilight time, the Pitch Woman throws her basket over her back—

ADULT JOYCE. Takes a handful of pitch—

MUD BAY SAM. And goes forth into the night, looking for—

ADULT JOYCE. Looking for—

JOYCE. Looking for what?

MUD BAY SAM. Disobedient children.

(*THUNDER. JOYCE screams, frightened. MUD BAY SAM smiles. The PITCH WOMAN unveils a small wooden figure that will represent the "child."*)

JOYCE. What happens if she finds one?

MUD BAY SAM. The Pitch Woman sneaks up behind the child—

ADULT JOYCE. Quiet as can be—

MUD BAY SAM. And then GRABS HER—

ADULT JOYCE. Before she can make a sound—

MUD BAY SAM. And puts a gob of pitch over each of her eyes—

ADULT JOYCE. Tosses the little girl in her basket—

MUD BAY SAM. And disappears into the night.

(*The PITCH WOMAN, having tossed the "girl" into a basket on her back, disappears into the darkness. The DRUMMING fades away.*)

JOYCE. What happens to the little girl?

MUD BAY SAM. She belongs to the black night now. She will never be seen again.

(*THUNDER. JOYCE grabs hold of MUD BAY SAM and hangs onto him as he paddles.*)

ADULT JOYCE. I was taught to remember the story of the Pitch Woman.

MUD BAY SAM. You're a brave girl, Joyce. And bravery is a great teacher. But we must learn from our fears as well. (*He touches her face tenderly.*) Come on, *little one.* It's time to go home.

ADULT JOYCE. It was an honor to ride in Mud Bay Sam's canoe. He loved that canoe more than anything in the world. He had carved it himself from a twenty-foot cedar tree. He was fond of saying—

MUD BAY SAM. When I go to the next world, I will carve a new canoe and paddle it across time.

(*The canoe turns, pivoting on its pedestal, and paddles away, facing upstage. Light on the canoe fades.*)

ADULT JOYCE. The year was 1911. I was living with my grandparents in Mud Bay. My father knew they'd teach me the ways of our people. (*The YARD IN MUD BAY. EMILY SAM enters and kneels near a campfire. She is making "ashes" bread. ADULT JOYCE moves toward her, watching. MOUNT RAINIER remains prominent upstage.*) In the fall, we'd travel to pick berries. In the spring, the salmon would run. And Emily Sam, my grandmother, would teach me how to make "ashes" bread.

(*JOYCE enters, holding a DOLL carved of cedar. She kneels down next to EMILY SAM.*)

EMILY SAM. Dig a hole near the campfire, Joyce, and line it with hot coals. Wait till the coals have burned down to nothing but embers— (*She reaches out her hands. JOYCE sets down her DOLL and hands EMILY SAM an unbaked loaf of bread that was sitting next to them.*) Then put the bread inside. Make sure it's covered with lots of flour, or— (*She makes a bad face and pretends to spit. JOYCE laughs. EMILY SAM smiles.*) Then . . . fill the hole with hot ashes.

(*They cover the bread with ashes during the following.*)

ADULT JOYCE. The bread baked in the ground just like in a real oven. There was no difference . . . (*smiles*) except I remember the "ashes" bread tasted better.

EMILY SAM. Learn to accomplish one thing, Joyce. Even if it's a small thing. A loaf of bread, a whistle made of alder, a small, carved stone. Accomplishing even *one small thing* will build strength into your character. And you will have that accomplishment with you for life. (*The bread is covered. JOYCE is holding her DOLL.*) We'll need a lot of bread for the potlatch. *Do you want to bake some on your own?* (*JOYCE understands what she's said but slowly shakes her head no, not knowing if she knows how.*) *Why don't you try? Just one loaf.* Just one little loaf. (*JOYCE stares at her. EMILY SAM smiles.*) If it's bad, we'll feed it to the ducks. (*JOYCE smiles. Then she nods. She hands EMILY SAM her DOLL.*) That's my girl. I'll meet you inside.

(*JOYCE runs off excitedly. EMILY SAM looks at the DOLL as ADULT JOYCE stands near her.*)

ADULT JOYCE. And so I baked my first loaf of "ashes" bread—and lucky for the ducks, at least it floated. (*She smiles. SINGING and DRUMMING begin.*) The day of feasting and celebrating arrived . . . the "potlatch" had begun.

(*A flurry of activity: The KIDS run on from all directions, playing a game of hide-and-seek with JOYCE. LONGHOUSE and OTHER ADULT GUESTS are playing the "bone game," in which two teams try to amass twenty-one sticks by guessing whether a "bone" held by the other team is marked or unmarked. EMILY SAM is preparing food. HENRY, JOYCE's cousin, stands at a conspicuous distance from the others. He reads from a book. He watches the festivities. Unlike the others, HENRY wears a suit with a white shirt and tie. Shiny black shoes. A carved and painted HOUSE POST is featured prominently, rising high into the air. MUD BAY SAM joins the OTHERS at the "bone game." JOYCE is "tagged" by BOY TWO.*)

BOY TWO. *C'mon, Joyce. You've got to sing while we hide!*

JOYCE. *What are we playing?*

GIRL ONE. Hoo-hoo-hoo.

BOY TWO. I tagged you!

YOUNG BOY. *You've got to sing!*

GIRL TWO (*points across the stage at HENRY*). *Joyce, go tag Henry!*

(*JOYCE looks across the stage at HENRY. He is reading a book. She approaches him as the others run off. She "tags" him.*)

JOYCE. *You're it.*

HENRY. What?

JOYCE (*in English now*). You're it. You've got to sing while we hide.

HENRY. Do you remember me?

JOYCE. You're Henry, my cousin.

HENRY. You were just a baby last time I saw you.

JOYCE. Who made you wear that?

HENRY. It's my new suit. What do you think?

JOYCE. I think you look stupid.

HENRY. I've been away at school, Joyce. I've —

JOYCE. Do they make you wear shoes, too?

(*Before HENRY can respond —*)

KIDS (*calling from their hiding places*). You're it! C'mon, Henry! *Sing, Henry!* Hoo-hoo-hoo! Hoo-hoo-hoo! (*etc.*)

HENRY. Joyce, I don't —

JOYCE. C'mon. Sing "Hoo-hoo-hoo!" while we go hide. Then come find us.

HENRY. Have you ever read a book, Joyce?

(*JOYCE grabs the book from HENRY and tosses it to one of the KIDS, who runs off with it.*)

JOYCE. Close your eyes and sing.

KIDS (*as before*). Henry, c'mon! *Come find us, Henry!* Hoo-hoo-hoo! Hoo-hoo-hoo! *Close your eyes!*

(*Kids continue singing. HENRY looks at Joyce. He looks at the others. Then he covers his eyes and begins to sing as JOYCE runs off and joins the OTHER KIDS, hiding.*)

HENRY. Hoo-hoo-hoo. Ha lay-ay-ay. Hoo-hoo-hoo. Ha lay-ay-ay . . .

BOY TWO. Louder, Henry!

(*MUD BAY SAM walks up very close to HENRY and inspects his clothes as HENRY keeps singing, louder now, his eyes still covered with his hands.*)

HENRY. Hoo-hoo-hoo. Ha lay-ay-ay. Hoo-hoo-hoo. Ha lay-ay-ay . . .

(*When HENRY uncovers his eyes, MUD BAY SAM is standing right in front of him, startling him.*)

MUD BAY SAM. The boy who went away to school! How are you, Henry?

HENRY. I'm fine, Sam. You frightened me.

MUD BAY SAM. And you frightened me, Henry. *Look at yourself.* You've joined the Sears & Roebuck tribe. How can you fish in those clothes?

HENRY. I'm not a fisherman, Sam. I'm going to be a teacher.

MUD BAY SAM. We have guests coming, Henry. Today I need you to be a fisherman.

JOYCE and OTHERS (*offstage*). Henry! Come find us! (*etc.*)

(*LONGHOUSE, Henry's father, joins them, carrying a fishing net and spear.*)

MUD BAY SAM. Come help your father.

LONGHOUSE. *Do as he says, son.* We're catching fish for the potlatch.

MUD BAY SAM. I saw a school of porpoises out on the water. They are our cousins. They'll give us some fresh fish if we ask them.

HENRY. Oh, not the story about our "cousins" again. I thought I'd heard the last of that.

JOYCE and OTHERS (*offstage*). *Henry, come find us!* Henry! (*etc.*)

LONGHOUSE (*firmly*). They are our cousins. After the Great Flood, many of our ancestors came back to this world as porpoises. They are our cousins.

HENRY. Why do you talk so crazy?

MUD BAY SAM. They will help us find food for the potlatch.

HENRY. It's superstition, nothing else.

LONGHOUSE. Henry, you must respect the teachings of—

HENRY. *No one believes that old nonsense anymore.*

(*Silence. LONGHOUSE turns away. JOYCE rushes on.*)

JOYCE. Henry, you have to come find us!

(*HENRY looks at her, then looks at his father.*)

HENRY. Joyce, I want you to have something. (*HENRY takes a pouch—the one we saw ADULT JOYCE wearing earlier—from around his neck. He puts it around JOYCE's neck.*) This pouch was my father's. (*JOYCE admires the small pouch.*) He believes it holds a spirit that will protect me. I want you to have it now.

(*LONGHOUSE stares at HENRY, hard.*)

JOYCE. Will this protect me from the Pitch Woman?

HENRY (*to MUD BAY SAM*). Are you still scaring kids with stories of the Pitch Woman?

JOYCE. She finds little children and she—

HENRY. Joyce. There is no Pitch Woman. It's a foolish old myth.

MUD BAY SAM. Henry, don't *ever* do that to your old people. (*pause*) You've been away, you've learned things from your white teachers. It's all right to learn those things, but you must also honor your elders. They know things that you don't.

HENRY. *I* know those porpoises are not going to bring us gifts!

(*Silence. LONGHOUSE stands very close to HENRY, speaks firmly.*)

LONGHOUSE. *You left here, my son, and you return as a stranger.*

HENRY. What are you saying?!

LONGHOUSE. I'm speaking our language. Have you forgotten that, too?

HENRY. Father, I don't—

LONGHOUSE. You say you'll be a teacher—but what will you teach? You've turned your back on everything we've taught you.

HENRY. Father—

LONGHOUSE. You've given the *little one* the pouch I made for you.

HENRY. Those are your beliefs, Father. Not mine.

ADULT JOYCE. Henry and his father looked each other in the eye for a long time. I had never seen two men do that.

MUD BAY SAM. Henry is going out on the water, *little one.* Would you like to go with him?

HENRY. I'm not going out on—

LONGHOUSE. It's the only way that you'll learn, son.

MUD BAY SAM (*to JOYCE*). Take him out on the water and be very still.

JOYCE (*nods*). *I will.*

MUD BAY SAM. And Joyce.

JOYCE. Yes?

MUD BAY SAM. Remember what you are about to see.

(*MUD BAY SAM begins to chant. EMILY SAM, LONGHOUSE, and the OTHER GUESTS join in the chanting. JOYCE hands her doll to EMILY SAM. JOYCE grabs HENRY's hand, and they get in the canoe. Lights shift. The CANOE floats in the BLUE-LIT WATER, as before. As JOYCE paddles, the canoe pivots until it is facing the audience. Then she and HENRY sit in the canoe in silence, keeping very still. The DRUMS join in with the chanting.*)

MUD BAY SAM and OTHERS (*chanting, repeat as needed*). *Oh, our great cousins, we are traveling. We have traveled far. We are tired. We are camping here and have not much meat. Would you honor us by sharing with us the fruits of the sea?*

(*The FOUR COUSINS—four DANCERS wearing wooden hand-carved PORPOISE MASKS—move in a pattern around the canoe. They respond and react to both the chants from the shore and the canoe in their midst. CHANTING and DRUMMING continues. One by one, each COUSIN comes very near the canoe. HENRY and/or JOYCE touches each COUSIN's head, taking hold of a small fish that is attached there. Then, as each COUSIN moves away, a brightly colored string of fish and other sea animals—depicted in the style of the porpoise masks—unfurls from inside the COUSIN's costume. After each COUSIN's string of fish has been unfurled, they stand at the four corners of the stage, still attached to HENRY and JOYCE via the string. They then begin to circle the canoe, wrapping HENRY and JOYCE in the fish and sea animals, filling the canoe. Then, as a group, the COUSINS leave. HENRY and JOYCE*) *are smiling, amazed, their canoe and their arms filled with the fish and sea animals. The CHANTING and DRUMMING fade. Lights shift to the YARD. The canoe is now ashore. EVERYONE helps carry the fish and sea animals up to the house for cooking. JOYCE, HENRY, EMILY SAM, MUD BAY SAM, and LONGHOUSE remain behind. EMILY SAM hands JOYCE her doll.)*

JOYCE. What do you think of our cousins now, Henry?

HENRY (*his arms full of fish*). I think they're very kind—

JOYCE. It's enough to feed the whole potlatch.

HENRY. But there are other things to learn, Joyce. Things your grandfather can't teach you.

(A SQUAXIN WOMAN appears at the side of the stage.)

SQUAXIN WOMAN. Mud Bay Sam—

(MUD BAY SAM sees her and goes to her.)

MUD BAY SAM. *Hello, friend. How are you?*

SQUAXIN WOMAN. *I have something to ask you . . .*

(She continues to talk to him, softly.)

ADULT JOYCE. Often, people from all over the area would come to ask the Rememberer questions. To learn about their ancestors.

(MUD BAY SAM turns and calls to JOYCE.)

MUD BAY SAM. *Little one*, our friend wants to know the name of Klook-kwa-kay's father. (*Pause. He smiles a bit—a challenge.*) Do you remember?

(JOYCE looks at him. He nods. JOYCE looks around, then steps forward and begins talking—softly at first, then with increasing confidence.)

JOYCE. Deeaht was succeeded by his brother, Odiee. (*pause*) His descendants were Kat'hl-che-da, then Wa-wa-tsoo-pa, then Wat-lai-waih-kose, Klatch-tis-sub, How-e-sub, Ko-shah-sit . . . (*HENRY and LONGHOUSE look on amazed. MUD BAY SAM and EMILY SAM look on proudly. The OTHERS look on as well.*) And then Tai-is-sub . . . who was the father of Klook-kwa-kay.

(Very pleased, the WOMAN looks at JOYCE, takes her hand.)

SQUAXIN WOMAN. *Thank you. You are a fine young girl.*

JOYCE. Thank you. Now, go hide, Henry.

(The OLD WOMAN leaves. EMILY SAM exits with her.)

HENRY. Joyce, how did you know all that?

MUD BAY SAM. She listens to her elders.

LONGHOUSE. Go hide, now. She'll find you.

HENRY. Father, I—

LONGHOUSE. Go.

(HENRY looks at JOYCE, who smiles a bit. He looks back to his father, then runs off to hide. LONGHOUSE exits opposite. SEVERAL KIDS rush on, calling to JOYCE, then run off.)

KIDS. Sing hoo-hoo-hoo! Hurry, Joyce! Come find us! (*etc.*)

(JOYCE covers her eyes. The yard has emptied. Just as she is about to begin singing, MUD BAY SAM approaches her.)

MUD BAY SAM. Joyce, I have something for you.

(She uncovers her eyes and looks at him. He holds a small oyster shell in his hand.)

MUD BAY SAM. Put this shell in the pouch Henry gave you. Keep it with you. (*He hands her the shell.*) The oyster's shell protects him, just as the Great Spirit protects us. And remember that all things, even the smallest things, are worthy of protection.

JOYCE. *Thank you, Grandfather.* (*She puts the shell in her pouch.*)

MUD BAY SAM. The time will come, *little one*, when you will take my place. (*She looks up at him, curious.*) You will hold our history and our stories in your mind. And you will pass them on.

JOYCE. But how do I learn them?

MUD BAY SAM. You watch. You listen. And no matter what happens to you, or to your family, or to your people—you *remember.* (*puts his arm around her*) It's a great responsibility, *little one*. But you've been chosen. And we are never chosen for something that we don't have the power to do.

(MUD BAY SAM leaves. JOYCE watches him go. Then, slowly, she covers her eyes and begins to sing to herself.)

JOYCE. Hoo-hoo-hoo Ha lay-ay-ay Hoo-hoo-hoo Ha lay-ay-ay ... (*Behind her, we see the HUGE SHADOWS OF TWO MEN on the upstage wall.*) Hide yourself good, Henry, or I'll find you! (*returns to singing*) Hoo-hoo-hoo Ha lay-ay-ay Hoo-hoo-hoo Ha lay-ay-ay ... (*During the following, the MEN enter the stage quietly, approaching JOYCE from behind. She does not see or hear them. The MEN are MULLIN, a United States Marshall, and TWIN RIVER, a Klickitat Indian, employed by the Bureau of Indian Affairs.*) I'm almost there, Henry! Get ready! (*returns to singing*) Hoo-hoo-hoo Ha lay-ay-ay Hoo-hoo ...

[Note: TWIN RIVER speaks the Sahaptin language, not spoken or understood by JOYCE or her family. This language will be indicated by underlined italics.]

MULLIN. Joyce Cheeka, come with us.

TWIN RIVER. *Do as he says, little girl.*

(JOYCE turns and sees them. She is frozen in fear. Her doll drops to the ground.

DRUMMING and WAILING *begin to pierce the following scene at random intervals. The MEN approach her slowly.*)

MULLIN (*simultaneously*). Be a good girl now.

TWIN RIVER (*simultaneously*). <u>We have spoken with your father</u>.

JOYCE. GRANDFATHER!

MULLIN (*simultaneously*). Be a good girl now—

TWIN RIVER (*simultaneously*). <u>We have spoken with your father</u>—

MULLIN (*simultaneously*). It won't help to call—

TWIN RIVER (*simultaneously*). <u>Just do as we say to do</u>—

JOYCE. EMILY SAM!

(*The MEN grab her and carry her away. She kicks and screams.*)

MULLIN. You're coming with us.

JOYCE (*hideous scream*). NOOOOOOOOO!

(*The DRUMMING and WAILING crescendo. JOYCE is carried away by the MEN as lights shift abruptly to the upstage wall: A HUGE SHADOW of the PITCH WOMAN dances wildly. The DRUMMING, WAILING, and JOYCE's SCREAMING continue for a few moments—then suddenly stop. Lights snap out on the SHADOW as lights rise on ADULT JOYCE at center stage. She slowly picks up the abandoned DOLL and holds it. The sounds of WIND and HORSES' HOOVES are heard under the following.*)

ADULT JOYCE. The men put me in a wagon and drove away. (*The rear of a horse-drawn, uncovered WAGON is visible at one side of the stage. JOYCE is inside, tethered to the wagon with a rope. The wagon shakes JOYCE about as it travels. Two other Indian children—a YOUNG BOY and a YOUNG GIRL—are with her, also tethered to the wagon as it travels.*) We rode for several days, but they never told us where we were going. Sometimes we stopped and the men got out and grabbed more children. (*The wagon stops shaking. JOYCE looks into the distance.*) I remember I saw a little boy playing in his yard. I saw the men approaching him—

JOYCE. *RUN, LITTLE BOY!*

ADULT JOYCE. The little boy looked up when he heard me—

JOYCE. RUN BACK IN YOUR HOUSE!

ADULT JOYCE. The men reached out to grab him—

JOYCE. RUN BEFORE THEY CATCH YOU!

ADULT JOYCE. The men took the little boy from his yard. I heard him scream for his mother.

OTIS (*offstage*). *MOTHER!*

ADULT JOYCE. They brought the little boy to our wagon. (*MULLIN and TWIN RIVER bring OTIS, an Indian boy from a neighboring tribe, to the wagon and set him down next to Joyce in the back. OTIS is crying and very frightened.*) I had to hold onto him so he wouldn't fall out as we drove.

(*MULLIN and TWIN RIVER exit to the unseen front of the wagon. OTIS looks at JOYCE, the YOUNG BOY, and the YOUNG GIRL, saying nothing. The wagon shakes as they begin to travel again. Gradually, the image of MOUNT RAINIER fades away and is gone. JOYCE puts her arms around OTIS and holds him, protecting him. He holds onto her tightly. Long silence. Then . . .*)

OTIS (*quietly*). Were we bad?

JOYCE. No.

OTIS. Then why are they taking us away?

(*JOYCE stares at OTIS. She takes the shell out of the pouch around her neck. A FLUTE begins to play, melancholy and distant.*)

JOYCE. My grandfather gave me this shell. He said it would keep me safe. (*She hands him the shell and he looks at it.*) The oyster's shell protects him, just as the Great Spirit protects us. (*Long silence as the WAGON travels. OTIS gives her back the shell, then looks away sadly.*) What's your name? (*pause*) My name's Joyce. (*pause*) If I don't know your name, I can't be your friend.

OTIS (*pause, then quietly*). I'm Otis.

JOYCE (*smiles a bit*). Say you'll be my friend, Otis.

OTIS (*pause, then speaks tentatively*). I'll be your friend.

(*A CRASH OF DRUMS as lights shift to the SUPERINTENDENT of Indian Schools, a woman in her 40s holding a book and a Bible.*)

SUPERINTENDENT. In our efforts to humanize, Christianize, and educate the Indian, we should endeavor to divorce him from his primitive habits and customs. He should be induced to emulate the white man in all things conducive to his happiness and comfort.

(*During the following, we see JOYCE and the YOUNG GIRL sitting on small stools lit by a lone shaft of harsh sidelight. NURSE WARNER stands behind them. She is cutting off the girls' long, black hair with scissors. She tosses the cut-off clumps of hair onto the ground near their feet. RANDOM DRUMMING, under.*)

ADULT JOYCE. The government started with the children, stating they needed to be taken from their homes at an early age—before their parents could instill in them the principles of Indian life. With the girls, one of the first things they did was cut off our hair. We had been raised to be very careful with our hair, to let it grow and take care of it, because our hair has a connection to our life, and mistreatment of it could bring harm to us. And if someone in your family died, you would cut your hair as a way of mourning, and to show honor to the dead. But none of us said anything about that. We just sat there. And none of us cried until we were alone in our rooms.

(*NURSE WARNER leaves. The GIRLS sit on the stools, hair cut short, staring front, motionless. The DRUMMING fades away and is gone.*)

SUPERINTENDENT. Experience has shown that it is possible to do a great deal for the Indian, that it is possible to educate them and that it is possible to prepare them to take their places along with us as citizens in this great republic.

(*A TRUMPET plays "REVEILLE" loudly. Lights shift to the SCHOOLYARD. SEVERAL STUDENTS in uniforms enter and walk past JOYCE, OTIS, the YOUNG BOY, and the YOUNG GIRL laughing and pointing at the new arrivals.*)

ADULT JOYCE. And so we were given our uniforms. And shoes for our feet. And we were marched outside to meet the other students. They still hadn't told us where we were, or why we'd been brought there. What I remember most about that first day is the buildings. Brick and mortar, rising far into the sky. They were the biggest buildings I'd ever seen.

(*The HOUSE POST is quickly and efficiently "walked down" onto its side by TWO BOYS in school uniforms. The BOYS carry the HOUSE POST away revealing, in its place, a tall FLAGPOLE. TWO GIRLS in school uniforms hoist an AMERICAN FLAG up the flagpole as the MUSIC CONTINUES. "REVEILLE" CONCLUDES as DR. BUCHANAN enters and addresses the four new arrivals.*)

DR. BUCHANAN. Welcome to the Tulalip Training School. I'm Dr. Buchanan. (*Silence. JOYCE and the OTHERS just stare at him.*) Good. Well, let me show you around. The Tulalip school was, until recently, an abandoned Catholic mission. We have converted the buildings into — (*He points into the distance, showing them.*) A schoolhouse. A shop. A hospital. An office. A sawmill. A laundry. The headmaster's house (that's where I live). And two dormitories. One for boys. One for girls. You'll spend your mornings in the classroom, learning to read and write and do basic arithmetic. And you'll spend your afternoons on work detail. The boys will learn carpentry, farming, and general upkeep. The girls will learn weaving, sewing, cooking — and a few girls will be selected to learn nurse's training. We also will put together a marching band and a drill team. (*OTIS has walked up and is tugging on DR. BUCHANAN's coat.*) Young man, the first thing you'll have to learn is how to raise your hand. If you have something to say, you must raise your hand. (*OTIS looks up at him, blankly.*) Do you have something to say? (*OTIS looks at him for a moment, then walks back and stands in the line.)* Very well. Now, first of all— (*OTIS raises his hand.*) Yes, young man. What is your question?

OTIS (*simply*). Can I go home now?

(*DR. BUCHANAN stares at him. Silence. He walks over to OTIS.*)

DR. BUCHANAN. You know, I've asked myself that question a lot over the past few years. I'm away from home, too. What's your name, young man?

OTIS. I'm Otis.

DR. BUCHANAN. What tribe are you from, Otis? (*OTIS just stares at him. Then OTIS looks to JOYCE. She also stares at DR. BUCHANAN. Awkward silence.*) Well, what about the rest of you? Don't be shy. (*Silence. The STUDENTS all stare at him.*) I'd like to know who your people are, what tribes you're from. (*More silence. NURSE WARNER and MR. CONRAD enter and join the others.*) Well. This is Nurse Warner, our head nurse.

NURSE WARNER. Welcome.

DR. BUCHANAN. She'll show the girls to their rooms. And Mr. Conrad, our history teacher—(*MR. CONRAD nods*)—will show the boys to theirs. I'll see you all bright and early tomorrow morning. And remember, listen for the bells.

(*DR. BUCHANAN turns and leaves.*)

NURSE WARNER. Well, ladies, shall we go? (*JOYCE and the YOUNG GIRL look at her, then nod.*) Follow me. (*NURSE WARNER turns and starts off. JOYCE and the YOUNG GIRL follow. MR. CONRAD turns to OTIS and the YOUNG BOY.*)

MR. CONRAD. Off we go, gentlemen.

(*MR. CONRAD turns and starts off. The YOUNG BOY follows him. OTIS follows for two steps, then turns and runs after JOYCE.*)

OTIS. *Joyce, don't go*—

MR. CONRAD. Young man, get back here. (*OTIS grabs JOYCE before she leaves, holding onto her tightly.*) Get back here this instant.

(*OTIS just holds onto JOYCE, terrified.*)

JOYCE. Otis, it's all right.

NURSE WARNER (*to OTIS*). You'll see her soon. Don't worry.

MR. CONRAD. Young man, something you will learn is that orders are meant to be followed. Now, let go of her and stand up straight.

JOYCE. He wants to see his mom. He wants to—

MR. CONRAD. I'm not talking to you, girl. Follow Nurse Warner to your room. (*to OTIS*) *Let go of her and look at me.* (*OTIS slowly lets go of JOYCE and looks* up at MR. CONRAD.) Your mother is not here, son. From now, until you are a grown and civilized young man, this is your home. We are your family. And when we tell you to do something, you do it. Now. Are you ready to go? (OTIS looks at JOYCE. Then he nods sadly.) Good day, ladies.

(MR. CONRAD starts off. The YOUNG BOY follows him. OTIS, too, follows him. Unseen by MR. CONRAD, JOYCE follows OTIS for a few steps. As she does, she takes the small pouch from around her neck and places it around OTIS's neck. OTIS turns and starts to say something to her. She gestures "Ssshhh." She gestures "Now, go on." OTIS holds the pouch tightly and follows MR. CONRAD off. JOYCE turns back and looks at NURSE WARNER. NURSE WARNER turns and exits, followed by the YOUNG GIRL and JOYCE. A FLUTE plays.)

ADULT JOYCE. They took us to what was called "the Girls' home." Our rooms were on the second floor. At night, they made us take off our shoes and leave them in the basement. (This was done to soften our footsteps. They were very concerned with "quiet.") In the morning, we had to walk down barefoot to get our shoes. The basement was always the coldest place of all. In the winter, this made for a very cold walk. There were many of us in one room. But my bed was at the end of the room, near a window, away from the other girls.

(Lights rise on JOYCE's ROOM. A small tin box is on the bed. Also on the bed is the bundle of JOYCE's own Indian clothing. GIRL ONE and GIRL TWO enter, looking around.)

GIRL ONE. What's her name?

GIRL TWO. I think it's Joyce.

(GIRL ONE has found something underneath JOYCE's pillow.)

GIRL ONE. Look . . . (She pulls a large piece of JOYCE's HAIR out from under the pillow.) It's her hair. She kept it after they cut it off.

GIRL TWO. Let me see.

GIRL ONE. *She saved it.*

(A BELL RINGS loudly. The sound is made by a triangle struck with a piece of metal. The GIRLS quickly put the hair back under the pillow as JOYCE enters wearing a school uniform.)

JOYCE. What's that noise?

GIRL ONE (urgent, frightened). Hurry up!

JOYCE. Where are you going?

GIRL TWO. Grab your box and come!

(The YOUNG GIRL joins them.)

JOYCE. My what?

GIRL ONE. Hurry!

(*The BELL rings again. JOYCE looks around, grabs her tin box, and follows the OTHER GIRLS as light shifts to the WASHROOM, indicated by a long board that represents the counter and the sinks. The GIRLS enter, marching in a line, holding their identical tin boxes in front of them.*)

ADULT JOYCE (*during the above action*). Everything happened by bells. Every night, we'd be marched into the washroom just before bedtime. (*Sound of MILITARY DRUMMING. The GIRLS turn in unison and face their individual mirrors and sinks. In unison they set their tin boxes on the counter in front of them. Then they take their toothbrushes out of the box and hold them in their right hands, at the ready. NURSE WARNER enters holding a container of tooth powder. She stops, looking at the GIRLS. In unison, the GIRLS all extend their left hands in front of them, palms up. NURSE WARNER walks down the line of GIRLS, putting a small amount of tooth powder in the each girl's left palm. Then she stops, stands nearby, and observes. A BELL rings. The GIRLS all avidly brush their teeth in an identical pattern.*) The school was very strict about grooming. They thought we didn't know any better. This was funny to us, because our families were always very concerned with daily bathing and having good, clean teeth. (*In unison THE GIRLS all spit. A BELL rings. The GIRLS put their toothbrushes back inside their tin boxes and remove their hairbrushes. In unison they brush their hair.*) We had been taught by our parents to watch the animals, and to care for ourselves as well as they do. (*In unison the GIRLS put their hairbrushes in their tin boxes. Then they turn and face NURSE WARNER, smiling. NURSE WARNER walks down the line and quickly inspects each girl for cleanliness.*) Of course, the teachers didn't know any of this. Their job was to "clean us up," and we did our best to help them along. (*Another BELL rings. Still in unison, the GIRLS pick up their tin boxes, turn, and march past NURSE WARNER in a line, leaving the washroom. NURSE WARNER checks her hair in the mirror and quickly applies a dab of perfume to each of her wrists, then follows the GIRLS out as lights shift back to JOYCE's ROOM. JOYCE enters, sets her tin box on the chair. She goes to the window and looks out. Then she goes to her "own" clothes, picks them up, and holds them tightly. She carries them to the bed with her and sits. She rocks back and forth, holding her clothes in her arms. The MILITARY DRUMMING fades out as a FLUTE plays, melancholy and distant. During the following, NURSE WARNER enters. She takes JOYCE's clothes from her. She hands JOYCE a store-bought DOLL. She leaves. JOYCE looks at the DOLL, then lets it fall to the ground. She curls up on her bed and cries.*) I'd never been so far from home. We asked how long we'd be gone . . . and they said nothing. For all we knew, and for all our families knew, we were gone for good.

(LOUD DRUMMING as the room goes suddenly dark except for a shaft of moonlight streaming through the window and onto JOYCE's face. SINGING in Salish is heard, distantly at first. This SONG will come to be known as "JOYCE's SONG.")

Hoo lad chad sthloo la ha ha ob

Hoo lad chad sthloo la ha ha ob

Ha woo, ha woo, ha woo, ha woo . . .

(Upstage, against the back wall, the SHADOW OF A WOMAN dances. The WOMAN wears a long dress, a fringed shawl, moccasins, and a kerchief on her head. She carries and dances with a "khawa"—a shoulder-high staff, or walking stick.)

JOYCE *(looking around fearfully).* Who is it? Who's there? *(The SINGING and DRUMMING continue. The SHADOW OF A WOMAN continues to DANCE upstage.) Who are you? What do you want? (SINGING grows louder. DRUMMING continues. The WOMAN's DANCING continues, growing wilder.)* Nurse Warner! Nurse Warner, someone's here! *(JOYCE jumps into her bed and pulls the covers over her head, hiding herself. The SHADOW OF THE WOMAN grows larger and larger upstage as the SINGING and DRUMMING reach a crescendo. Suddenly the SHADOW VANISHES and the WOMAN HERSELF pops up directly behind JOYCE's bed. The SINGING and DRUMMING stop abruptly. Though JOYCE doesn't know it yet, this is her AUNT SOPHIE. AUNT SOPHIE stares down at the still-covered JOYCE. Hearing the silence, JOYCE gets curious. Slowly, she pulls the covers back from her head. When she uncovers her eyes, she is looking directly up into the face of AUNT SOPHIE. JOYCE screams and covers her head again. AUNT SOPHIE laughs. AUNT SOPHIE sings while she does her DANCE in JOYCE's room. After a moment, JOYCE is more curious than afraid. She uncovers her head slowly and listens to the SONG. She watches AUNT SOPHIE dance.) Who are you? (No response.)* What do you want? *(Again, no response.)* Are you the Pitch Woman? My grandfather told me about you. You take a handful of pitch and you— *(Suddenly AUNT SOPHIE stops singing, turns, and looks directly at JOYCE. AUNT SOPHIE walks slowly, threateningly, toward JOYCE. JOYCE, still in bed, cowers with fear. When she is very near JOYCE, AUNT SOPHIE slowly shakes her head "no." Silence. Then JOYCE speaks.)* You're *not* the Pitch Woman? *(AUNT SOPHIE shakes her head "no" again.)* You're not here to hurt me? *(AUNT SOPHIE again shakes her head "no.")* Then why *are* you here? Why don't any of the other kids see you? *(AUNT SOPHIE smiles. Then, quietly and beautifully, she sings one final, brief PHRASE of the SONG, looking directly at JOYCE. On the last note of the SONG, AUNT SOPHIE points to the upstage wall with her walking stick. JOYCE looks and sees the SHADOWS OF MUD BAY SAM, LONGHOUSE, and HENRY. DRUMMING is heard under. Facing upstage, JOYCE speaks, amazed.)* It's Mud Bay Sam. And Henry. *(JOYCE turns back to the room, saying—)* It's my family. *(AUNT SOPHIE is gone. JOYCE looks all around, under the bed, out the window.)* Hello? Hello!? Where'd you go? *(JOYCE sits down on her bed.)* Tell me who you are!

(A crash of DRUMS, then silence. JOYCE sits for a while, then lies back on her bed.)

ADULT JOYCE. I lay awake all night that first night, wondering what I'd seen. Wondering if it was only my imagination. *("REVEILLE" sounds, loudly followed by MILITARY DRUMMING. JOYCE sits up quickly. Then she rushes into the WASH-ROOM and joins the other GIRLS, once again, at the counter. NURSE WARNER joins them, as before. The GIRLS and NURSE WARNER repeat the entire teeth-and hair-brushing routine from before, except this time they do it at double the speed.)* And at five in the morning, we had to get all cleaned up again — even though we hadn't done anything except *sleep!* *(A BELL rings as lights shift to the SCHOOLYARD. Dawn. MR. CONRAD blows his WHISTLE and begins to lead all the BOYS and GIRLS in calisthenics. ADULT JOYCE speaks while watching the calisthenics.)* The school knew that, from living with our families, all of us were used to a great deal of exercise — hiking, swimming, hunting, fishing. But they were determined to direct our energies into what were called "useful channels."

(Another WHISTLE, a new exercise. As before, a shaft of light rises on the SUPERINTENDENT.)

SUPERINTENDENT. "The Indian is splendidly equipped for *manual labor.* However, in a literary or professional sense he is apt to be deficient." *(A WHISTLE, a new exercise)* "Therefore, rather than requiring an Indian boy to solve hypothetical equations or study the geography of countries he will never visit, we believe *industrial training* should have the foremost place in Indian education." *(A WHISTLE, a new exercise)* "Similarly, Indian girls should study and practice the 'domestic sciences' since culture can be obtained as readily from baking a pumpkin pie as through studying Greek mythology."

(A WHISTLE, a new exercise)

ADULT JOYCE. Be gentle in your judgments. These men and women were the social reformers of their day. And they had inherited, from the government that had displaced the Indian people, the task of "righting a great national wrong." *(A WHISTLE, a new exercise. Lights snap out on the SUPERINTENDENT.)* But even though they may have had the best of intentions, to this day I don't think Mr. Conrad knew the *slightest thing* about calisthenics.

(Led by MR. CONRAD, the BOYS and GIRLS are now engaged in a particularly weird, uncomfortable, seemingly pointless exercise. The STUDENTS, however, give it their best. DR. BUCHANAN enters and observes.)

DR. BUCHANAN. What do you call this one, Mr. Conrad?

MR. CONRAD (*from his very awkward position*). I call this one the "Hackensack High-Topper."

DR. BUCHANAN. Fascinating.

(*A BELL rings. MR. CONRAD stands.*)

MR. CONRAD. Up and at 'em, now. Flag drill at noon. Marching at three. Good day.

(*MR. CONRAD exits. The STUDENTS stop their exercise and stand in one line, facing DR. BUCHANAN.*)

DR. BUCHANAN. Good morning, troops. Those of you who are new here have discovered this morning that we like to spend as much time in the open air as possible. (*OTIS raises his hand.*) Yes, young man. What is it?

OTIS. My leg hurts.

DR. BUCHANAN. I'm not surprised. I'll talk to Mr. Conrad about his exercises. In the meantime, let's all have a seat. (*DR. BUCHANAN sits on the ground. The STUDENTS, surprised at first, follow his lead and sit in a line facing him.*) Now, Thanksgiving is just around the corner and I'm planning to— (*OTIS raises his hand again.*) Yes, Otis. What is it now?

OTIS. Duwamish.

(*silence*)

DR. BUCHANAN. I'm sorry, what?

OTIS. My tribe.

DR. BUCHANAN. Your—

GIRL TWO. Wynoochie.

(*DR. BUCHANAN looks at her. Then, one by one—and not "down the line"—the other STUDENTS state the names of their tribes.*)

YOUNG GIRL. Nisqually.

BOY ONE. Skagit.

GIRL ONE. Chehalis.

BOY TWO. Kikiallus.

YOUNG BOY. Makah.

JOYCE. Squaxin.

(*Silence. DR. BUCHANAN looks at them all for a long moment.*)

DR. BUCHANAN. I had no idea there were so many tribes represented here. No idea at all.

OTIS. What about you?

DR. BUCHANAN. Pardon?

OTIS. What's your tribe?

DR. BUCHANAN. (*pause*) Well . . . I guess I come from a tribe called Philadelphia.

ADULT JOYCE. I liked Dr. Buchanan. (*A BELL rings. During the following, the BOYS exit one direction, and the GIRLS exit the other. DR. BUCHANAN exits, also.*) But sometimes at Tulalip, the more they taught me, the more I missed my family, and the way things were done at home.

(*A CLASSROOM. MISS BRENNAN enters carrying a small quilt. The GIRLS each hold small blocks of fabric and a sewing needle.*)

MISS BRENNAN. Joyce, are you stitching? (*JOYCE moves to the classroom.*) This is called the log cabin quilt. Each square is sewn individually, then added to the rest. (*hands the quilt to the GIRLS*) There are many kinds of quilts you can make, and each kind tells a story.

(*ADULT JOYCE moves and stands behind EMILY SAM, who is sewing a quilt. JOYCE, also, is looking at EMILY SAM.*)

ADULT JOYCE. My mother and grandmother made blankets using designs inspired by stories of the raven, the eagle, the whale, and the salmon. Stories that went back to the days of the Great Flood, and before.

MISS BRENNAN. Joyce, did you hear me? (*JOYCE turns and watches MISS BRENNAN.*) Now, this quilt comes from the pioneer women, women who came west with their families. Who can tell me the story of those women's journey? (*GIRL ONE raises her hand.*) Lillian?

GIRL ONE. The gold rush in California in 1849, and in Colorado in 1859, brought hundreds of families to the West in covered wagons.

MISS BRENNAN. Good. Perhaps our next quilt can be a covered-wagon design.

JOYCE. I want to make a salmon quilt.

MISS BRENNAN. What's that?

JOYCE. I want to tell the story of my family, how they travel in the spring to catch salmon.

MISS BRENNAN. That's not what you're here to learn, Joyce.

JOYCE. I want to make a salmon quilt.

MISS BRENNAN. Someday you will. But first you must learn this log-cabin design and—

JOYCE. *I think your quilts are stupid.*

(*The GIRLS laugh for a moment, startled. Then, silence. MISS BRENNAN does not understand what JOYCE has said.*)

MISS BRENNAN. Joyce, you know you're to speak English, and English *only*, at this school. You know that, don't you?

JOYCE. Yes.

MISS BRENNAN. Now, what did you say? (*silence*) Joyce? (*JOYCE stares at MISS BRENNAN, who then turns to GIRL ONE.*) Lillian, tell me what Joyce just said.

GIRL ONE (*after an apologetic look to JOYCE*). She said your quilts are stupid.

MISS BRENNAN (*to JOYCE*). Is that true? (*JOYCE nods.*) You must learn to sew, Joyce. You—

JOYCE. I know how to sew. My grandmother taught me.

MISS BRENNAN. But you must learn to sew *this way*. This is the way quilts are made now. You'll be able to make them for your family, but you'll also be able to sell them, to make a living with them. Wouldn't you like that?

JOYCE (*holds up a corner of the quilt*). But this is your story, not mine. I want to remember my stories. Mud Bay Sam told me to remem—

MISS BRENNAN. But don't you want to learn new stories?

JOYCE. Yes, but I—

MISS BRENNAN. That's all I'm asking you to do. To learn new stories, in addition to your own. That's why you're here. So you'll have the skills to live as well as you can when you leave here.

JOYCE. But when I leave here, I'm going home.

MISS BRENNAN. Home to the reservation?

JOYCE. Home to my *home*. To my family, at Oyster Bay.

(*silence*)

ADULT JOYCE. And Miss Brennan just looked at me. I don't think she'd ever thought about what I'd just said—that maybe they were preparing me for a world I would never enter.

MISS BRENNAN. Girls, let's finish up. We'll continue tomorrow.

(*MISS BRENNAN takes the quilt and exits. The GIRLS exit opposite. JOYCE stands alone.*)

ADULT JOYCE. I remember wanting to stay in my room and not go to class.

(*As EMILY SAM leaves the stage, she stops and puts her arms around JOYCE.*)

EMILY SAM. Each day is a gift from the Great Spirit. To waste one of your days is inexcusable. You must account for yourself and your time on Earth. You must learn to be *useful*.

ADULT JOYCE. So . . . I started a quilt of my own.

(*JOYCE's ROOM. Night. A FLUTE plays. JOYCE and the OTHER GIRLS sit on the floor in the darkened room, their faces lit only by a few CANDLES in their midst. JOYCE is sewing the first few squares of her quilt. GIRL TWO has a small knife, and is carving a small toy out of cedar. GIRL ONE is painting a toy she has carved. The YOUNG GIRL is weaving a small bracelet.*)

GIRL ONE. *What kind of quilt will it be?*

JOYCE. A salmon quilt.

GIRL TWO. Where'd you get the cloth?

JOYCE. Where'd you get that knife?

GIRL TWO (*smiles*). *Secret.*

JOYCE (*smiles*). *Secret.* (*They shake hands.*)

GIRL ONE. I'm hungry.

GIRL TWO. Potatoes, stewed in fish oil.

GIRL ONE (*nods*). And berries for dessert.

JOYCE. And Emily Sam's "ashes" bread.

(*They make hungry moans and groans, playfully. Except for the YOUNG GIRL, who begins to cry quietly.*)

YOUNG GIRL. I want to go home.

(*The OTHER GIRLS look at her.*)

GIRL ONE. It's all right, Sarah.

(*GIRL ONE holds the YOUNG GIRL. Then GIRL ONE looks up at JOYCE.*)

GIRL TWO. Joyce . . . tell her a story.

(*JOYCE begins to tell a story. As the story progresses, the GIRLS lift a sheet off the bed and drape it up behind the candles. They then use the props in the scene [brush, knife, fabric, bracelet, piece of cedar, etc.] to "act out" a tiny shadow play in the candlelight.*)

JOYCE. A long time ago, before the time of the Great Flood, there were two brothers who lived with their grandparents. One was very dark. The other was very white. They fought all the time. This made their grandparents very angry. One day, their grandparents said to them—

GIRL TWO. "Now that you have grown into young men, it is time for you to leave."

JOYCE. To the dark brother, they said: "You must go toward where the sun sets and grow with the land. Make a good life. Be useful." Then, to the white brother, they said—

GIRL ONE. "You must go toward where the sun rises. Far from your dark brother. Make your life there."

JOYCE. Then, to both brothers, they said—

GIRL TWO. "Because of your fighting, you will never in your lifetime come together again."

JOYCE. "But someday, many years from now, your *children*—"

GIRL ONE. "And your *children's children*—"

GIRL TWO. "May find a way to come together."

JOYCE. "And on that day, and not before . . ."

(*JOYCE looks at the YOUNG GIRL, who has wiped away her tears.*)

YOUNG GIRL. "They may live together in peace."

JOYCE (*nods*). "The peace which you never found."

(*The LIGHTS SNAP ON in the room. FLUTE stops abruptly. The GIRLS leap up, the candle is blown out, the quilt, knife, and carving are hidden. MISS BRENNAN enters.*)

MISS BRENNAN. You should be asleep, girls. But . . . since you're up . . . I have a present for all of you. It's an anonymous gift to the school that came in the mail today.

(*MISS BRENNAN reveals FOUR SMALL GOLD CROSSES on CHAINS. She puts a CROSS around each of the GIRLS' necks, as the SINGING of a HYMN is heard coming from offstage: a youthful choir's slow, deliberate, beautiful rendition of "ONWARD CHRISTIAN SOLDIERS." MISS BRENNAN leaves. The GIRLS look at their CROSSES. They look at one another, as lights shift to the SCHOOLYARD. Day. A young Indian man, DARIN LONGFEATHER, is pushed onstage. He falls to the ground, hard. His arms are tied behind his back with rope. His clothes are torn and dirty. There is blood on his neck and face. MULLIN, the county sheriff, enters carrying a rifle. He grabs DARIN by his hair and pulls him to his feet. JOYCE watches all of this from a distance. They do not see her.*)

MULLIN. This is your new school, boy. And this one's not so easy to run away from as the last one. But I hope you try. I really do. Because when you do, I'll be waiting for you. (*yanks his hair hard*) Got me? (*DARIN nods. MULLIN sees JOYCE.*) Girl.

JOYCE (*quietly*). Yes, sir?

MULLIN. Where's the headmaster's house?

(*JOYCE points. MULLIN shoves DARIN off in that direction, following behind him.*

JOYCE watches, frightened and confused. The HYMN CONCLUDES. Lights shift to ANOTHER PART OF THE SCHOOLYARD. Morning. DR. BUCHANAN enters, his good clothes covered by a work apron of some kind, his sleeves rolled up. He carries a burlap sack and a small shovel. He is planting tulips. JOYCE stands near him, staring at him. After a moment, DR. BUCHANAN looks up at her.)

DR. BUCHANAN. Shouldn't you be in class, Joyce? (*JOYCE nods.*) Did you need to ask me something? (*JOYCE nods.*) Well, what is it?

JOYCE. Why did they beat that boy? He was all bloody. Why did they do that?

(DR. BUCHANAN looks at JOYCE, then slowly stands, facing her.)

DR. BUCHANAN. I'm sorry you had to see that.

JOYCE. Did you tell them to beat him?

(Silence. He moves closer to her, looks in her eyes.)

DR. BUCHANAN (*softly, firmly*). No, Joyce. I didn't.

JOYCE. But what did he do wrong?

(silence)

DR. BUCHANAN (*this is the truth*). I don't know. (*She puts her head against his chest, wiping away tears, frightened. He puts an arm around her, tentatively. Speaks softly.*) You should be in class, Joyce. (*She nods, still holding onto him.*) Well . . . would you like to help me plant some tulips? (*She nods slightly. During the following, he releases her, hands her a sack of tulip bulbs, kneels, and resumes his work. She joins him.*) Did you know the word "tulip" can be traced back to the Turkish word *tulbend*, meaning "gauze," which is also the root of the word "turban"?

JOYCE (*referring to the bulbs*). Like this?

DR. BUCHANAN. Give 'em just a little more room. (*She does, as the SUPERINTENDENT enters unseen, holding a small briefcase of some kind. The SUPERINTENDENT stands upstage watching JOYCE and DR. BUCHANAN plant.*) There you go. The people of the Ottoman Empire believed the tulip resembled a turban in the way its petals wrapped around one another. There are literally hundreds of varieties to choose from. The important thing is to plant them in the fall—

JOYCE (*busy working*). Before the first frost.

(These words slipped out. She quickly covers her mouth, fearful. DR. BUCHANAN looks at her.)

DR. BUCHANAN. What have you said? (*She looks away.*) Joyce. Tell me.

JOYCE (*pause*). *Before the first frost.*

DR. BUCHANAN (*firm*). In English, Joyce.

JOYCE. Before the first frost. (*pause*) Isn't that right?

SUPERINTENDENT. Dr. Buchanan.

DR. BUCHANAN (*turns to the SUPERINTENDENT and stands, startled*). Superintendent Lang. Hello. We weren't expecting you till next week.

SUPERINTENDENT. There was a change in my schedule.

DR. BUCHANAN. Well, we're thrilled you're here. Joyce, this is Mrs. Lang, the superintendent of Indian schools, visiting from Washington, D.C.

SUPERINTENDENT. I see we've added horticulture to our list of classes.

DR. BUCHANAN. Oh, I was just—

SUPERINTENDENT. Who authorized that purchase, Dr. Buchanan?

DR. BUCHANAN. Well, you did, Mrs. Lang. In your most recent report.

SUPERINTENDENT. I authorized the cultivation of local trees and plants, *not* tulips from Holland.

DR. BUCHANAN. I'll be glad to cover the cost myself, Mrs. Lang—

SUPERINTENDENT. The *cost* is only part of the issue.

The use of student time to plant flowers seems a willful extravagance. Why isn't this girl in class with the others?

DR. BUCHANAN. With all due respect, I don't feel that beauty is an *extravagance*. I feel these students have a right to live in a schoolyard that is as rich in beauty as the homes from which we took them.

SUPERINTENDENT (*sharp*). And are you in a position to *grant them rights*? Such as the right to speak their native language.

DR. BUCHANAN. I wanted to know what she said. Surely we can—

SUPERINTENDENT. Dr. Buchanan, the Indian language is not only discouraged, it is *forbidden*. (*puts her arm around JOYCE, speaks with compassion*) The way to care for this girl, Dr. Buchanan, is to give her useful knowledge and help her forget the pagan superstitions of her people.

(*A BELL rings. The OTHER GIRLS and BOYS enter in a line, followed by MR. CONRAD. They carry large baskets filled with berries.*)

MR. CONRAD. What have I told you, Richard? No cutting in line. Cutting in line will not be tolerated here.

(*They stop.*)

SUPERINTENDENT. Well, hello. What do we have here?

DR. BUCHANAN. Children, this is Superintendent Lang. Can you say hello?

STUDENTS. Hello.

MR. CONRAD. We've been out picking fall berries. Care for a taste?

SUPERINTENDENT. Certainly.

(*The SUPERINTENDENT takes a few berries in her hand and eats them, dropping a leaf or two to the ground in the process.*)

MR. CONRAD. Well?

SUPERINTENDENT. Absolutely delicious. Thank you. I'd like a photograph of all of you on the front steps of the school, for our files in Washington.

MR. CONRAD. We'll be waiting for you there. (*to the STUDENTS*) Let's go, now. And remember, Richard,

(*MR. CONRAD leaves, followed in a line by the other GIRLS and BOYS, who take their baskets of berries with them. NURSE WARNER enters and stands nearby.*)

SUPERINTENDENT. Dr. Buchanan, have I made myself clear on these issues?

DR. BUCHANAN. Yes.

SUPERINTENDENT. Good. (*holds out her berry-stained fingers*) I should wash up before our photo. The berries are delicious, but they do stain the skin. (*JOYCE kneels, picking up one of the dropped berry leaves. She hands it to the SUPERINTENDENT.*) What is this?

JOYCE. It's the leaf of that berry. It will remove the stain.

SUPERINTENDENT (*starting off*). I've learned to rely on soap and water.

DR. BUCHANAN. I'd do as she says. It's the best way we've found.

(*The SUPERINTENDENT stops and stares at DR. BUCHANAN.*)

JOYCE. Lick it with your tongue, then rub it on your fingers in a circle, slowly.

(*The FLUTE is heard, distant and soft. The SUPERINTENDENT looks at JOYCE. Then she uses the leaf as JOYCE suggested. The stains disappear. She looks at JOYCE.*)

DR. BUCHANAN. Amazing, isn't it? Her grandfather taught her that. We've also learned that madrona-leaf tea is good for ulcers; and as for high-blood pressure, the leaf of the huckleberry bush can—

SUPERINTENDENT (*firmly*). Let's take that photo, shall we?

(*THE SUPERINTENDENT leaves. After a look at JOYCE, DR. BUCHANAN follows her.*)

NURSE WARNER. Joyce, I've been asked to pick one of the girls to be my nurse's aide. We'll tend to cuts and scrapes. And we'll learn about treating illness and preventing disease. Are you afraid of blood?

JOYCE. No.

NURSE WARNER. Good. Because I've chosen you, Joyce.

JOYCE. But I've already been taught those things. My grandfather told me about remedies for fevers and illness—

NURSE WARNER. I know that. That's why I've chosen you. The things you learned at home will help us put the students at ease here. (*JOYCE stares at her.*) Now, why don't you tell me the Squaxin word for "doctor."

JOYCE. But we're not supposed to speak our language.

NURSE WARNER. I asked you something, Joyce.

(*JOYCE looks around to make sure no one's listening, then speaks softly.*)

JOYCE (*saying the word in her language*). Doctor.

NURSE WARNER (*awkwardly, trying to say it*). Do-ct-or. Close?

JOYCE (*with a bit of a smile*). Sort of.

NURSE WARNER. What about "medicine"?

JOYCE (*again, in her language*). Medicine.

NURSE WARNER (*trying it*). Me-di-cine. (*JOYCE shakes her head "no." NURSE WARNER tries again.*) M-edi-cin-e. (*JOYCE nods.*) Okay. One more. How about "remedy"? What is your word for "remedy"? (*JOYCE stares at her, then looks away. FLUTE BEGINS, quietly, distantly.*) Joyce? (*JOYCE keeps looking away.*) Well. Maybe there isn't one. Not all languages have words for the same things we do.

(*JOYCE looks back at NURSE WARNER.*)

ADULT JOYCE. There was a word for it. But no matter how long I stood there, I couldn't think of it. I couldn't remember it.

NURSE WARNER. Don't worry, Joyce. You're going to be a fine nurses' aide. And here. A letter came for you. It's from home.

(*NURSE WARNER gives JOYCE the letter and goes, leaving JOYCE alone. JOYCE watches her go. Then she looks down at the letter in her hands. During the following, JOYCE opens and reads the letter silently. Behind her, all the STUDENTS, the SUPERINTENDENT, DR. BUCHANAN, MR. CONRAD, and NURSE WARNER gather and pose for a group photo. The flag flies behind them. The FLUTE is joined by distant DRUMMING.*)

ADULT JOYCE. I'd never gotten a letter before. I knew it must be from Henry, since he knew how to write. It was a short letter.

(*A shaft of light on HENRY, opposite.*)

HENRY. Dear Joyce, I have news from home. Your grandfather, Mud Bay Sam, has passed on to the next world.

(*Behind those gathered for the photo, the SHADOW OF MUD BAY SAM paddling his CANOE is seen on the upstage wall.*)

DR. BUCHANAN. Joyce, we're waiting for you.

(*JOYCE moves and takes her place amidst the OTHERS, facing the camera. She still holds the letter. The SHADOW OF MUD BAY SAM remains.*)

HENRY. He loved nothing more than carving his cedar canoes. He spoke of one day paddling a new canoe across time.

SUPERINTENDENT. Look at the camera, everyone.

HENRY. We know in our hearts that he is doing just that, and that he will meet all of our cherished ancestors on his journey.

MR. CONRAD. Say "cheese."

ALL (*except JOYCE*). Cheese.

(*A crash of DRUMS and a flash of BRILLIANT WHITE LIGHT as the picture is taken. When the light recedes, a shaft of light illuminates only JOYCE, standing in the midst of the OTHERS, who are now in darkness. The SHADOW OF MUD BAY SAM is gone.*)

HENRY. And we know his thoughts are with you, Joyce. Because your day has come. You are now the Rememberer.

(*Lights fade on HENRY and ADULT JOYCE as the FLUTE concludes its SONG. Then a crash of DRUMS as the light snaps out on JOYCE.*)

END OF ACT I

ACT II

(*As the audience gathers for Act Two, DRUMMING, SINGING, and DANCING have already begun. This is a "Greeting Dance," led by ADULT JOYCE, that includes ALL of the native cast members, including JOYCE and the other BOYS and GIRLS. Each wears the decorative clothing of their particular tribe. [The CHILDREN wear blankets over their school clothes.] As the dance continues, the BOYS and GIRLS gradually exit, leaving the ADULTS to continue the dance. The group of ADULTS moves downstage and parts, revealing MISS BRENNAN and MR. CONRAD in their midst. They are teaching the BOYS and GIRLS to waltz. They count "one-two-three, one-two-three" as the BOYS and GIRLS emerge in their school clothes, paired off in groups of two, learning the dance. DRUMMING, SINGING, and DANCING continue, as the ADULTS dance offstage in one direction and the BOYS and GIRLS waltz offstage opposite. ADULT JOYCE is left alone at one side of the stage. JOYCE is left alone, opposite, holding a small, partially completed quilt.*)

ADULT JOYCE. It was winter now. I hadn't seen my family in six months. But I kept working on my salmon quilt, stitching it together in my room at night, when no one was around.

(*A TRUMPET plays "REVEILLE." Morning. Lights reveal the WASHROOM, again, as JOYCE enters in line behind the other three GIRLS. They bring their tin boxes with them, as before. NURSE WARNER, as before, walks down the line and gives them their tooth powder. They begin to brush their teeth, identically, as before. NURSE WARNER leaves. The GIRLS are alone. They immediately turn and start talking to one another, now brushing any way they want to.)*

GIRL TWO. *You were laughing, I saw you!*

JOYCE. You were laughing louder!

YOUNG GIRL. *Laughing at what?*

GIRL TWO. *At the fish oil!*

(JOYCE and GIRL TWO laugh, as GIRL ONE quiets them quickly.)

GIRL ONE *(in an urgent whisper).* Quiet. She's here—

(The GIRLS straighten up and brush their teeth very formally, as MISS BRENNAN looks in on them.)

MISS BRENNAN. No Indian words, girls. You know better. *(MISS BRENNAN checks her hair in their mirror quickly. She gives the perfume on her wrist a quick sniff. She smiles.)* I'll see you in class.

(MISS BRENNAN goes, the GIRLS relax.)

GIRL ONE. You did not!

GIRL TWO. Yes, I did!

YOUNG GIRL. What? Did what?

GIRL ONE. Who saw you?

GIRL TWO. Joyce saw me.

YOUNG GIRL. What? Saw what?

GIRL TWO. Tell her.

JOYCE. Yeah, I saw her.

GIRL ONE. Really?

JOYCE. Yeah.

YOUNG GIRL. What? Saw her do what?

GIRL TWO. Tell her, Joyce.

JOYCE. She found a bottle of Miss Brennan's perfume.

GIRL ONE. So?

JOYCE. And she dumped out the perfume and filled it with fish oil.

YOUNG GIRL. Really?

GIRL ONE *(to GIRL TWO).* Did she get mad?

JOYCE. She hasn't noticed!

(The GIRLS laugh heartily.)

YOUNG GIRL. When did you do this?

GIRL TWO. Two weeks ago!

(*The GIRLS laugh even louder. They finish brushing their teeth and hair during the following.*)

GIRL ONE. Darin Longfeather showed me the scars on his back.

(*The GIRLS laugh a bit.*)

JOYCE. What scars?

GIRL ONE. It's not funny. The scars from his other school. Where they whipped him with a belt.

(*The GIRLS are more serious now.*)

JOYCE. Why'd they do that?

GIRL ONE. I don't know. But they did. I *saw*. That's why he ran away.

JOYCE. They caught him and sent him here.

GIRL TWO. I bet he runs away again.

GIRL ONE. The sheriff'll kill him if he does. Darin said so.

JOYCE. Dr. Buchanan wouldn't let them hurt him.

GIRL TWO. They can do whatever they want, Joyce. It doesn't matter what the teachers say.

GIRL ONE. Darin said there's no way he'll get caught.

JOYCE. What do you mean?

GIRL ONE. He says he knows a trail. A secret trail that will get him home.

(*A BELL rings. The GIRLS file out in a line as the SHADOW OF THE PITCH WOMAN is seen upstage, briefly. She is wielding her walking stick as a weapon, swinging it around over her head. JOYCE stops and looks at the SHADOW. The SHADOW OF THE PITCH WOMAN is accompanied by quick bursts of DRUMMING and WAILING. After a moment, the SHADOW vanishes, the DRUMMING and WAILING fade as lights shift to a CLASSROOM. MR. CONRAD stands in front of ALL of the gathered BOYS and GIRLS, holding a history book. In groups of twos, the BOYS and GIRLS share history books and listen to MR. CONRAD. One of the BOYS is DARIN LONGFEATHER. JOYCE shares her book with OTIS, who still wears the pouch around his neck.*)

MR. CONRAD. Now, this period of history was preceded by what we call the Great Flood. Joyce, I believe it's your turn to read for us. (*JOYCE stands, holding her book.*) Why don't you begin with "God commanded Noah to build an ark . . ."

JOYCE (*reading*). "God commanded Noah to build an ark . . ."

(*OTIS raises his hand.*)

MR. CONRAD. Yes, Otis?

OTIS. What's an ark?

GIRL ONE. A boat.

MR. CONRAD. A very large boat. You'll see. Continue, Joyce.

JOYCE. "And God told Noah to fill the ark with two of every sp— (*trying to pronounce the word*). Every spec—

MR. CONRAD. *Species.*

JOYCE. "With two of every *species* of animal on the earth."

MR. CONRAD. Good. Keep going.

JOYCE. "Having done this, Noah and his—"

(*She stops.*)

MR. CONRAD. Go on, Joyce. "Noah and his family gathered with the animals on the ark."

JOYCE. But there aren't any animals yet.

MR. CONRAD. Sure there are. God created them on the sixth day. Noah has saved them, prior to the flood. He has brought them to the ark two by two. Now—

JOYCE. There are no animals until *after* the Great Flood.

MR. CONRAD. What did you say?

(*JOYCE hands the book to OTIS and continues.*)

JOYCE. During the Great Flood, some of the Indians made it safely to the top of a high mountain on rafts they had built of cedar logs. When the flood was over, some of the Indians were selected by the Great Spirit to carry on as people. Others were—

MR. CONRAD. Joyce, I won't have you telling those stories in this class.

JOYCE. It's not a story, it's the way the animals—

MR. CONRAD. This is history class, not story hour. Now, please sit down.

JOYCE. But you asked me to tell about the—

MR. CONRAD. *Sit. Down.* Otis, perhaps you can continue where Joyce left off. (*MR. CONRAD looks at OTIS. JOYCE looks at OTIS. The OTHERS look at OTIS. OTIS stands, holding the book. He looks at JOYCE. Then he faces MR. CONRAD.*) Well?

OTIS (*reads slowly, clearly*). "Having done this, Noah and his family gathered on the ark."

MR. CONRAD. Good. Keep going.

OTIS (*reads*). "The rains came and flooded the earth." (*He looks at JOYCE, then continues, not reading from the book.*) And then the Great Spirit chose *some* of the Indians to carry on as people—

JOYCE (*standing up next to OTIS*). And he made some of the other people into animals.

MR. CONRAD. That's enough—

JOYCE (*bolder now*). The Great Spirit said to one young man—

BOY ONE. "You are fleet of foot, but you are overly vain—"

GIRL TWO (*stands*). "So you shall be called 'Deer' and forever depend on your fleetness of foot to survive."

MR. CONRAD. Now, look here, I will not have—

GIRL ONE (*stands*). And to one cross old woman, the Great Spirit said: "You are a grumpy woman so you shall be known as 'Bear'—"

BOY TWO (*stands*). "And you will have to walk around forever on all fours—"

YOUNG BOY (*stands, smiling*). "And scratch around for your food."

MR. CONRAD. Sit down, all of you—

JOYCE. And that is why, to this day, our parents will say—

YOUNG GIRL (*stands, proudly*). "Be nice to bears in the woods—"

OTIS. "Because one of them might be your grandmother!"

(*The STUDENTS laugh, enjoying themselves.*)

MR. CONRAD. Sit down this instant!

(*They remain standing. The only student who is not standing is DARIN LONGFEATHER.*)

JOYCE. And the Great Spirit said: "Always respect the animals—for they once were your brothers and sisters, your aunts and uncles, your mothers and your fathers."

(*Silence. MR. CONRAD stares at JOYCE.*)

MR. CONRAD. As you can see, Darin Longfeather did not stand up. That's because he knew better. Now you're about to learn the same lesson he did. (*He slams his book shut with anger, causing EVERYONE except JOYCE to sit. MR. CONRAD and JOYCE stare at each other.*) Follow me.

(*Lights shift as JOYCE follows MR. CONRAD across the stage. A FLUTE plays.*)

ADULT JOYCE. As we walked across the schoolyard, I thought of the words of my father's grandfather, a Duwamish chief who has come to be called Chief Seattle.

(*CHIEF SEATTLE is seen in silhouette upstage. His VOICE is amplified.*)

VOICE of CHIEF SEATTLE. Your religion was written on tablets of stone by the iron finger of an angry god. Our religion is the tradition of our ancestors, the dreams of our old men, given to them in the solemn hours of night by the Great Spirit. And, it is written in the hearts of our people.

(*DR. BUCHANAN's OFFICE. It is designated by a high-backed leather chair and a small wooden chair. DR. BUCHANAN sits in the leather chair. JOYCE enters and sits in the wooden chair, followed by MR. CONRAD, who stands. ADULT JOYCE stands nearby, watching. The FLUTE fades away, as does the image of CHIEF SEATTLE.*)

DR. BUCHANAN. Joyce, Mr. Conrad has told me what happened in class today.

JOYCE. He's asking me to learn things that never happened!

MR. CONRAD. I will not stand for this impudence and—

DR. BUCHANAN. Enough, enough. (*to JOYCE, calmly but firmly*) Joyce, I expect you to respect your instructors here.

JOYCE. But I was—

(*DR. BUCHANAN raises his hand, and she stops immediately.*)

DR. BUCHANAN. This nation is currently governed on Christian principles. Those principles have found their way into the lessons that Mr. Conrad is hired to teach. There are, naturally, *differences* between our teaching and the teaching of your elders. But I require you to respect the difficult task that Mr. Conrad has been given. (*pause*) Is that clear?

JOYCE (*softly*). Yes.

MR. CONRAD. Thank you, Dr. Buchanan. Joyce, I'll see you in class.

(*MR. CONRAD starts to leave.*)

DR. BUCHANAN. Just a moment, Mr. Conrad. I'm not finished with you. (*MR. CONRAD stops.*) I have filed a request with the superintendent. That request asks that our students be allowed one hour a day in which to tell the stories of their culture. In this way, as we prepare them for the future, their lineage with the past will not be severed. (*pause*) I want your assurance that you will support my request.

MR. CONRAD. I most certainly will not.

DR. BUCHANAN. And why is that?

MR. CONRAD. We can't be expected to instill Christian and patriotic principles in these children while at the same time allowing them to retreat to their savage heritage.

DR. BUCHANAN. We are charged with giving them a humane, moral outlook.

MR. CONRAD. But we must not make them *self-consciously moral*—giving us only the answers they know we want to hear. We must, instead, make them *unconsciously, automatically moral.*

DR. BUCHANAN. And how do you propose to do *that*, Mr. Conrad?

MR. CONRAD. In the words of our superintendent: *"We must kill the Indian to save the man."* (*tense silence*) So *no*, Dr. Buchanan, I cannot support your request. It flies in the face of our mission here. If this gives you grounds to dismiss me, so be it. I have made my position clear.

(*MR. CONRAD leaves. DR. BUCHANAN watches him go, then returns to his chair and sits. Silence. JOYCE does not move.*)

DR. BUCHANAN (*simply*). It's time for your next class, Joyce. Don't be late.

(*JOYCE stands and looks at him. DR. BUCHANAN has taken out some work and is writing with a pen. JOYCE takes a few steps away. Then JOYCE stops and stares at the ground.*)

ADULT JOYCE. We don't always have the words when we're young. There were so many things I wanted to say. I wanted to say I was sorry. But I also wanted to tell him that I was now the Rememberer; I was now the protector of the past. I wanted to tell him I was afraid I'd fail. Both in his eyes and in the eyes of my tribe, my family. I looked at him. (*JOYCE looks at DR. BUCHANAN. DR. BUCHANAN looks up from his work, meeting her eyes. Silence.*) But no words came.

(*JOYCE leaves as lights shift to the SCHOOLYARD. As JOYCE walks, she is passed by DARIN LONGFEATHER, who is pushing a wheelbarrow filled with large feed sacks. JOYCE stops as DARIN goes past her. When he is nearly gone, she says —*)

JOYCE. Darin. (*He stops but does not turn to her. She looks around, then approaches him cautiously.*) I'm Joyce. (*He does not respond.*) I've never talked to you. (*He does not respond.*) Lillian said at your old school they beat you. (*He turns and looks at her. Long silence.*) Why?

DARIN LONGFEATHER (*softly*). What did you say?

JOYCE. Why? (*pause*) What did you do?

DARIN LONGFEATHER You're a stupid girl.

(*He grabs the handle of the wheelbarrow and prepares to leave.*)

JOYCE (*angry*). You must have deserved it.

(*DARIN immediately lets go of the wheelbarrow and walks up to JOYCE. He stands very close to her, frightening her.*)

DARIN LONGFEATHER. Do you want to know what I did? DO YOU? (*pause, softer now*) I said my mother's name. At night, *in my sleep*, I said my mother's name. And they heard me. "NO INDIAN NAMES," they said, "NO

INDIAN NAMES." So, the next night, they made me sleep on the wood floor, without a blanket. And they watched me. And I closed my eyes and I tried with all my heart to *forget my mother's name.* But in my sleep I said it again. So the next night they took me to the barn. And they stuffed cloth in my mouth. And they all stood around me while I slept. I tried to stay awake. I tried not to think about her, or her face, or her voice. *I tried to pretend my mother was dead.* But in the middle of the night, they woke me up and tied my hands to a post. They told me I'd said her name again in my sleep. And I swore I'd never do it again but they said it was too late. That I would have to be taught a lesson. (*pause*) They took off my shirt. (*pause*) One of the men took off his belt. (*pause*) And he started hitting me. (*Pause. Very distant sound of leather striking flesh.*) And I didn't cry. Because I could hear my mother's voice saying: *You'll be home soon, my beautiful boy.* (*pause, softly*) You'll be home soon. (*The sound of the whipping stops. DARIN stares at JOYCE. She says nothing. He walks back to the wheelbarrow, lifts it.*)

JOYCE. They say you know about a secret trail.

(*DARIN looks back at her as MR. CONRAD enters.*)

MR. CONRAD. C'mon, Darin. We're waiting. (*DARIN looks at JOYCE for another moment, then pushes the wheelbarrow past MR. CONRAD.*) Where are you supposed to be, Joyce? Do you know? (*JOYCE is looking off into the distance. She nods.*) Then go there.

(*MR. CONRAD leaves as lights shift to JOYCE's ROOM. JOYCE arrives and sits on the bed. She takes out her quilt and begins sewing, concentrating hard on her work. As she does this, she speaks to the empty room.*)

JOYCE (*Repeat and continue until noted*). Deeht was succeeded by his brother, Odiee. His descendants were Kat'hl-cheda, then Wa-wa-tsoo-pa, then Wat-lai-waih-kose, Klatch-tis-sub, How-e-sub, Ko-shah-sit, and then ... and then ... (*Repeat until noted.*)

(*DRUMMING begins distantly. The lights shift to NIGHT during the following. A shaft of MOONLIGHT comes through the window and illuminates JOYCE. The following cacophony of TAPED VOICES AMPLIFIED and DISTORTED begins softly, then builds to a deafening CRESCENDO. The VOICES overlap one another, forming a rush of language, distorted, echoing, filling the theatre.*)

MR. CONRAD. Kill the Indian to save the man—

DR. BUCHANAN. Joyce, I expect you to respect your instructors here—

EMILY SAM. Learn to accomplish one thing, Joyce—

DARIN LONGFEATHER. I tried to forget my mother's name—

(*JOYCE stops sewing and holds the quilt to her tightly. She looks in the direction of the WINDOW, still repeating the family names. DRUMMING grows very loud during the following. It is joined, at random intervals, by the sound of WAILING.)*

MUD BAY SAM. At twilight time, the Pitch Woman throws her basket over her back—

SUPERINTENDENT. The Indian language is not only discouraged, it is *forbidden*—

GIRL ONE. He says he knows a trail—

MUD BAY SAM. And goes forth looking for disobedient children—

EMILY SAM. You must account for yourself and your time on Earth—

NURSE WARNER. How about "remedy"? What is your word for "remedy"?

DARIN LONGFEATHER. "NO INDIAN NAMES—"

MUD BAY SAM. She is part of the black night now—

GIRL ONE. A secret trail that will get him home—

(JOYCE sets the quilt down. She moves to the WINDOW and looks out.)

DARIN LONGFEATHER. I tried to pretend my mother was dead—

MR. CONRAD. Kill the Indian to save the man—

EMILY SAM. You must learn to be useful—

MUD BAY SAM. She will never be seen again— *(HENRY's VOICE is heard, also AMPLIFIED and DISTORTED, SINGING the "HOO-HOO-HOO" song from Act One. This joins the ongoing DRUMMING and WAILING. JOYCE turns from the window. She looks at her quilt one more time, then hurries across the room to her chair. She picks up the chair and brings it across the room, setting it just below the window. She climbs up on the chair.)* The time will come, *little one*, when you will take my place—

SUPERINTENDENT. The way to care for this girl is to give her useful knowledge—

DARIN LONGFEATHER. "NO INDIAN NAMES"—

LONGHOUSE. *It's the only way that you'll learn, son*—

SUPERINTENDENT. And help her forget the pagan superstitions of her people—

(JOYCE opens the window and climbs onto the sill, looking out. DRUMMING, WAILING, and HENRY's SINGING reach a CRESCENDO.)

MUD BAY SAM. You will hold our history and our stories in your mind—

DARIN LONGFEATHER. "NO INDIAN NAMES"—

MR. CONRAD. Kill the Indian to save the man—

GIRL ONE. A secret trail that will get him home—

MUD BAY SAM. And you will pass them on—

(*JOYCE jumps out the window, and instantly there is SILENCE. DARKNESS. JOYCE's ROOM is gone. We are now in THE WOODS. It begins to RAIN. The SOUND OF RAIN is joined by occasional BURSTS OF THUNDER. As JOYCE fearfully navigates through this DARKNESS a BRANCH SNAPS. JOYCE stops, moves in another DIRECTION. But then, seemingly in front of her, ANOTHER BRANCH SNAPS. She changes directions as STILL ANOTHER BRANCH SNAPS. And ANOTHER. And ANOTHER. She does not know which way to turn. Suddenly there's a LOUD CRACK OF THUNDER, as JOYCE is enveloped in a BLACK SHAWL and "disappears." She SCREAMS. A shaft of MOONLIGHT slowly rises on AUNT SOPHIE, who has thrown her shawl over JOYCE.*)

AUNT SOPHIE. Quiet, *little one.* It's a cold night. I'm just trying to keep you warm. What are you doing out here?

JOYCE (*terrified, shaking*). Who are you?

AUNT SOPHIE. You'll come to know me.

JOYCE. You're the Pitch Woman! I knew it! (*JOYCE tries to run, but AUNT SOPHIE easily restrains her.*) Let me go! I want to go home!

AUNT SOPHIE. I know you want to go home, Joyce. That's why I'm here.

JOYCE. Let go of me!

AUNT SOPHIE. Is that what you want me to do?

JOYCE. Yes.

AUNT SOPHIE. Are you sure?

JOYCE. Yes.

AUNT SOPHIE. Then I will. Find your way now, Joyce. Find your way home. (*AUNT SOPHIE lets go of JOYCE. JOYCE turns to run as AUNT SOPHIE claps her hands once, and suddenly there is another loud crack of THUNDER. Instantly, the stage goes BLACK, except for a tight shaft of downlight on JOYCE. She is frozen with fear, staring front. The moonlight is mysteriously gone. The sound of RAIN grows louder. DRUMMING joins the rain, randomly, under. AUNT SOPHIE stands at a distance, watching.*) Why don't you go? There's no one to stop you.

JOYCE. The moon is gone. I can't see. (*looks around more*) I can't see anything at all.

(*JOYCE stares front in the tight shaft of downlight as the RAIN continues to fall.*)

AUNT SOPHIE. Did your grandmother tell you about "Taman'us"?

JOYCE. Yes.

AUNT SOPHIE. What did she say?

JOYCE. She said when I got old enough, I would go into the woods and pray
   to the Great Spirit—and I would be given power.

AUNT SOPHIE. You would be given "Taman'us."

JOYCE. Yes.

AUNT SOPHIE. How?

JOYCE. She said I would be given my song. And my song would give me direction. (*As the RAIN continues to fall, AUNT SOPHIE approaches JOYCE slowly,
   singing "JOYCE's SONG" to her. JOYCE watches and listens, carefully. After a moment, JOYCE speaks.*) Who are you?

AUNT SOPHIE. Sing with me.

(*AUNT SOPHIE sings the SONG, and gradually JOYCE joins in and sings with her.*)

JOYCE & AUNT SOPHIE. Hoo la chad sthloo la ha ha ob, Hoo la chad sthloo
   la ha ha ob, Ha woo, ha woo. ha woo, ha woo . . .

(*As they sing, the SHADOWS OF JOYCE's FAMILY are seen upstage. They, too, join
in the singing of "JOYCE's SONG." When the SONG has been learned, AUNT SOPHIE
steps away from JOYCE. The SHADOWS OF THE FAMILY continue SINGING softly.*)

AUNT SOPHIE. This is your song now. It's the voice of your ancestors speaking to you across time. And as you sing it, you will find direction.

JOYCE. But I'm lost. I don't know which way to—

AUNT SOPHIE. Close your eyes, Joyce. And sing your song.

JOYCE. Will it show me the way home?

AUNT SOPHIE. It will show you where you are *most needed.* It will show you
   how best to use your gift of life.

(*AUNT SOPHIE looks at JOYCE. JOYCE turns front, closes her eyes, and begins to
sing her SONG. The sound of RAIN continues. After a moment, JOYCE turns to speak
to AUNT SOPHIE.*)

JOYCE. But what is your name—?

(*AUNT SOPHIE is gone. The SHADOWS OF JOYCE's FAMILY are gone, also. JOYCE
stands alone. Then she begins once again to sing her SONG. And she begins to
walk . . .*)

ADULT JOYCE. I still didn't know where I was. But I sang my song . . . and I
   kept walking. I walked all night through the woods. And every time I got
   frightened, I sang louder. And as the sun rose, I hadn't found my way home.
   I had found myself . . . (*Distantly "REVEILLE" is heard.*) Back at the school, I still
   didn't know the name of that woman, but I remembered what she told me:
   that my song would lead me to where I was needed the most.

(*A BELL rings. Lights reveal the WASHROOM. The GIRLS enter in a line, as before,*

but this time there are only THREE of them: JOYCE, GIRL TWO, and the YOUNG
GIRL. GIRL ONE is not with them, though her TIN BOX is sitting on the counter,
unopened. As the GIRLS speak in their language, NURSE WARNER enters and
stands behind them, listening. They do not see her.)

GIRL TWO. One of the boys says it's a curse.

JOYCE. What are you talking about?

GIRL TWO. It's a curse on all of us here.

YOUNG GIRL. Why? What have we done?

GIRL TWO. We've forgotten our people, so we're being punished.

(NURSE WARNER steps forward. Seeing her, the GIRLS stop talking and ready
their toothbrushes. NURSE WARNER walks down the line with the tooth powder,
as before.)

JOYCE. Nurse Warner?

NURSE WARNER. Yes, Joyce.

JOYCE. Where's Lillian?

(The other GIRLS stop brushing and look at JOYCE. NURSE WARNER looks at
JOYCE for a moment, then turns to the other GIRLS.)

NURSE WARNER. Girls, finish up now. (GIRL TWO and the YOUNG GIRL finish
brushing and exit, taking their tin boxes with them.) Joyce, you're my nurse-
maid. And I'm going to need your help. Many of the children are getting
sick. We need to quarantine them—keep them away from the others—and
we've got to help them get better. (JOYCE nods.) It's called "influenza." We'll
do everything we can to fight it. (JOYCE is looking at GIRL ONE's abandoned tin
box.) Lillian got very sick. And she died. NURSE WARNER gently puts her arm
around JOYCE.) Have you known anyone who died, Joyce?

ADULT JOYCE. And I thought about Mud Bay Sam. I remembered how he
told us not to speak the name of someone who had died for one year after
their death, for fear we'd call them back to this world when they should be
moving on to the next.

NURSE WARNER. Can I count on you to help me?

(JOYCE nods. JOYCE and NURSE WARNER exit as the lights shift to a HOSPITAL
ROOM. NURSE WARNER and JOYCE move into the room, putting white masks
on to cover their noses and mouths. They encounter DR. BUCHANAN and MISS
BRENNAN each wearing heavy coats and pieces of fabric covering their noses and
mouths. They are carrying a stretcher. On the stretcher is the YOUNG BOY. He is
dead.)

ADULT JOYCE. This was the epidemic that would kill millions of people worldwide. It moved across the land like a plague. And we at Tulalip were not exempt.

NURSE WARNER. Who is it, Dr. Buchanan?

DR. BUCHANAN (*quietly*). It's Lucas.

(*NURSE WARNER kneels down to look at the YOUNG BOY. Then she makes a notation on her clipboard. JOYCE covers the YOUNG BOY's head with a sheet.*)

NURSE WARNER. When will the burial detail be here?

DR. BUCHANAN. They said Friday.

NURSE WARNER. We need them sooner. The disease is spreading. If we don't get the bodies buried, those still living won't stand a chance.

DR. BUCHANAN. I know that. I told them.

(*silence*)

NURSE WARNER. Take him to the basement with the others.

(*DR. BUCHANAN and MISS BRENNAN lift the stretcher and carry it off. During the following, NURSE WARNER and JOYCE take their positions behind a small cart which holds the medicinal drinks, as BOY ONE, BOY TWO, DARIN LONGFEATHER, GIRL TWO, the YOUNG GIRL, and OTIS enter in a line, waiting to receive their medicine. Everyone in line is wrapped in blankets or heavy coats.*)

ADULT JOYCE. I remember thinking how strange it was that we were staying in the same building where death had been. At home, when there was a death, often the building would be torn down, or left empty for a year until the spirit of death had passed. But that year, at Tulalip, there was nowhere to go. Death was in all the buildings.

(*MR. CONRAD enters, coughing, bundled in a blanket, very sick. He stands at a distance from the line of students.*)

NURSE WARNER. It's important that you abide by the quarantine. All of you. You must only leave your rooms to report here for your liquids and vitamins.

BOY TWO. Mr. Conrad. (*MR. CONRAD looks up. BOY TWO speaks gently.*) You can cut in line. (*MR. CONRAD stares at him.*) Right here. In front of me.

(*MR. CONRAD moves and takes his place in line in front of BOY TWO.*)

MR. CONRAD (*quietly*). Thank you.

(*The line begins to move. JOYCE hands out the medicinal drinks, one by one. NURSE WARNER makes notes on a clipboard.*)

JOYCE. Here you are. (*to the next in line*) Here you are. Make sure you drink all of it. (*The next person in line is MR. CONRAD.*) Hello, Mr. Conrad. How are you feeling? (*MR. CONRAD shakes his head no. JOYCE hands him a drink.*) Drink this. It'll help you feel better. (*MR. CONRAD takes the medicine and drinks, then moves on. BOY ONE hesitates as he approaches JOYCE. She offers him the drink. He shakes his head no.*) It won't hurt you. (*Again, he shakes his head no and steps out of the line. JOYCE moves close to him, speaks softly in her language.*) It will give us strength. The strength to go home.

(*He looks at her. Then he drinks the medicine. Looks at her.*)

BOY ONE. *Thank you.*

(*When the others have gone, OTIS, the last student in line, is handed his medicine by JOYCE.*)

JOYCE. Drink it all up, Otis. (*OTIS drinks, winces, and coughs a bit.*) Are you scared?

OTIS. No. (*OTIS shows JOYCE the pouch he still wears around his neck.*) You said this pouch will protect me.

JOYCE. And it will.

(*NURSE WARNER feels OTIS's forehead.*)

NURSE WARNER. Do you feel okay, Otis?

(*OTIS nods bravely, then walks off.*)

JOYCE (*looking in the direction of OTIS*). How is he?

NURSE WARNER. Not good. He's got a bad fever.

(*NURSE WARNER makes a note on her clipboard.*)

JOYCE. Nurse Warner?

NURSE WARNER. Yes, Joyce?

JOYCE. How many is it now?

(*NURSE WARNER lowers her clipboard and looks at JOYCE, but she can't find the words. She turns away and pushes the small cart offstage. JOYCE is left alone.*)

ADULT JOYCE. The epidemic was taking several children a day. Many teachers died, also. Nurse Warner carried her clipboard with her everywhere, keeping a record of the epidemic. (*A BELL rings. Lights reveal the WASHROOM, as before. A FLUTE begins to play, distant and melancholy. As ADULT JOYCE speaks, JOYCE enters and stands in front of her TIN BOX. She is alone. The BOXES of the OTHER GIRLS sit on the counter, unopened. The sound of DRUMMING, echoing quietly in the distance. JOYCE takes out her hairbrush and holds it in front of her. She does not brush her hair. She just stares front, alone.*) These were the coldest days of winter. And as the school waited for a military burial detail to arrive, they had only one place to store the bodies of the dead: in the freezing cold basement of the schoolhouse. As the winter wore on, the basement filled up with bodies.

*(The HOSPITAL ROOM, lit only by a few lamps. DR. BUCHANAN and DARIN
LONGFEATHER enter, carrying an empty stretcher. They wear cloth masks over their
noses and mouths. FLUTE and DRUMMING continue, under. JOYCE moves into the
room. DR. BUCHANAN removes his mask.)*

DR. BUCHANAN. Joyce, Nurse Warner has taken ill. She's been quarantined
with the others. She needs your help. *(JOYCE nods.)* The burial detail arrives
tomorrow. We need to have an accurate count before the bodies are taken
away. Nurse Warner needs you to find her clipboard and bring it to her.
Right away.

JOYCE. I'll look in her office.

DR. BUCHANAN. Thank you, Joyce.

(DR. BUCHANAN starts off. DARIN follows, then turns back to JOYCE.)

DARIN LONGFEATHER. I think I saw her clipboard tonight.

JOYCE. Where?

DARIN LONGFEATHER. At the schoolhouse. Downstairs.

JOYCE. In the basement?

DARIN LONGFEATHER. Yes.

*(DARIN leaves as JOYCE takes her lamp and leaves opposite. JOYCE descends a
small staircase into a dark, cold, musty room — the BASEMENT of the schoolhouse.
The floor of the room is covered with BODIES, most wrapped in dirty grey sheets or
blankets. The BODIES are only dimly visible in the foreboding darkness. The sound
of WATER DRIPPING. JOYCE wears a heavy coat and a hospital mask over her nose
and mouth. She carries the small lamp. She stops at the foot of the stairs and looks,
horrified and motionless, at the bodies. She coughs, wipes her eyes, and then begins
to walk amidst the bodies, slowly, looking for the clipboard. When she is surrounded
by the bodies, JOYCE stops. She has seen something. She bends down toward an
[UNSEEN] BODY in the midst of the pile. She covers her eyes with her hands, crying.
She reaches toward the BODY with her hand. She lifts something away from the
body and holds it to the light of her lamp. It is the small, leather pouch. She holds it
to her chest, crying. She stands. She looks again, back down at the [UNSEEN] BODY.
She wipes tears from her eyes. She continues on, moving through the bodies, looking
for the clipboard. Then, a very soft, frightened VOICE speaks.)*

VOICE. *Where am I? (JOYCE stops. She turns and looks in the direction of the
VOICE, which is coming from the pile of BODIES.) Hello?*

*(JOYCE looks around the room, too frightened to speak. Suddenly, a little boy's head
rises out of the pile of BODIES. It is OTIS.)*

OTIS *(very quietly, frightened)*. Where am I?

(*JOYCE sees him.*)

JOYCE. Otis!

(*She rushes to him and holds him, lifting him out of the pile of BODIES. He throws his arms around her and holds on tightly, crying.*)

OTIS. *Don't go. I'm scared. Don't go.*

JOYCE. It's all right. I'm right here. It's going to be all right.

(*They hold each other for a long time. Then JOYCE puts the pouch around OTIS's neck.*)

OTIS. I wore my pouch. Just like you said.

JOYCE. *Come on, Otis. Let's go.*

(*They leave the BASEMENT as lights shift to ADULT JOYCE.*)

ADULT JOYCE. He had been unconscious, with a bad fever, but they'd thought he was dead. They had mistakenly brought him to the basement with the others. I found him one hour before the burial detail arrived. He survived the epidemic and is alive to this day.

(*The SCHOOLYARD slowly fills with warm light. A FLUTE plays softly, beautifully. The FLAG flies at half-mast. DR. BUCHANAN enters, walking slowly to his flower box. He discovers several beautiful TULIPS. He kneels and views them quietly, joyously. JOYCE enters and stands near DR. BUCHANAN, looking at the tulips.*)

DR. BUCHANAN (*quietly*). Have you seen them, Joyce? (*JOYCE nods. DR. BUCHANAN speaks very quietly.*) Spring is here. And nature, once again, has healed the world.

(*A BELL rings. The STUDENTS enter and stand in a line, facing upstage, looking at DR. BUCHANAN. Their backs are to the audience. JOYCE joins them in line. MR. CONRAD and MISS BRENNAN walk behind them, placing small bundles in a row, downstage. The students do not see them. The FLUTE fades away.*)

ADULT JOYCE. And then, one day, without warning, they told us what we'd been waiting to hear.

DR. BUCHANAN. Have a safe trip home. I'll see you in the fall.

(*DR. BUCHANAN exits. MR. CONRAD and MISS BRENNAN exit opposite. The students, still in line, turn and face downstage. They see the bundles on the ground . . . their clothes. Their own clothes. A lost moment: They look at one another. They look at JOYCE. What now? Then some of the STUDENTS rush to their clothes, put on a shirt, etc. OTHERS stand, staring at the clothes, frightened. They look at one another. Some of them hug. Some of them walk off in groups, some alone. JOYCE stands, looking down at her clothes. OTIS stands next to her, doing the same. OTIS turns to JOYCE. He takes the pouch from around his neck. He puts it around JOYCE's*

neck. They embrace. OTIS smiles, grabs his clothes, and runs off. As JOYCE bends
down to pick up her clothes, she feels a tap on her shoulder. She turns and sees AUNT
SOPHIE holding a small suitcase. JOYCE screams and jumps back.)

AUNT SOPHIE. Did you miss me?

JOYCE. What do you want now?

AUNT SOPHIE. I came to say goodbye. My work is done. (*pause, a tender smile*)
   Joyce, I've been with you since you were given your name. (*pause*) You're a
   young girl. You don't have to understand it all, yet—but in time you will.
   (*A FLUTE begins to play "JOYCE's SONG" under the following.*) You're frightened
   about going home, aren't you? (*JOYCE nods.*) Remember your grandfather's
   words: We are never chosen for something that we don't have the power
   to do. (*AUNT SOPHIE goes to JOYCE and nearly touches her face.*) You have your
   song now, Joyce. It will give you strength. Never forget that.

(JOYCE looks at the suitcase. Then she quickly kneels and puts her own clothes in the
suitcase. AUNT SOPHIE smiles. JOYCE stands and speaks.)

JOYCE. But. I don't know your name—

(AUNT SOPHIE is gone. JOYCE finds herself in the midst of the YARD IN MUD BAY.
MOUNT RAINIER, once again, looms in the distance. The HOUSE POST is raised
back up, in place of the FLAGPOLE. A POTLATCH is in full swing: LOUD SINGING
and DRUMMING as a procession of GUESTS, young and old, enter. They carry a long,
wooden plank decorated with cedar boughs. In the midst of the cedar boughs lies the
FIRST SALMON of the year. JOYCE stands at the edge of the celebration, unseen. She
still wears her school uniform. She holds her small suitcase. ADULT JOYCE stands
opposite, watching. After parading the SALMON around the schoolyard, the GUESTS
place it downstage and gather around it. EMILY SAM looks up and is the first to see
JOYCE. SINGING and DRUMMING STOP abruptly. Everyone stands, motionless,
staring at JOYCE. After a long silence, EMILY SAM speaks quietly, simply.)

EMILY SAM. *My girl. You're home.*

(EMILY SAM walks to JOYCE, looks in her eyes, looks at her clothes, touches her
now-short hair, and then embraces her. They hold each other tightly. Silently. Still no
one else moves. When the embrace is over, LONGHOUSE, standing at the head of the
board containing the FIRST SALMON, speaks.)

LONGHOUSE. Joyce, we've caught the first salmon. (*pause*) Will you help us
   honor it?

(JOYCE stares at LONGHOUSE, and then at the OTHERS. JOYCE looks at EMILY
SAM, who nods. JOYCE walks very slowly through the GUESTS as they greet
her, embrace her, welcome her. Finally, she arrives in their midst, at the place of
prominence. When she is in place, LONGHOUSE looks at the others. The SINGING
and DRUMMING start up again.)

ADULT JOYCE. My people believe we must treat the first salmon with great respect and kindness—so the remaining salmon will continue to travel our way.

(*Two of the GUESTS conduct the ritual as it is described by ADULT JOYCE. The OTHERS look on. MUSIC and DRUMMING continue, under.*)

JOYCE. The Earth is a shrine.

ADULT JOYCE. We would lift the salmon from his bed of cedar boughs.

JOYCE. But it is a *borrowed* shrine.

ADULT JOYCE. We would take a cloth and wash the salmon's face.

JOYCE. It is loaned to us by the Great Spirit.

ADULT JOYCE. We would sing a song thanking the salmon for providing us with food today, and in years gone by.

JOYCE. We must use the gifts of the earth wisely, for they are sacred.

ADULT JOYCE. The salmon would be carried away and cooked.

JOYCE (*with a look at EMILY SAM*). We must account for ourselves and our time on Earth.

ADULT JOYCE. Its skeleton would be carefully preserved and returned to the water where it was caught.

JOYCE. We must learn to be useful.

(*EMILY SAM smiles. The GUESTS carry off the FIRST SALMON as the SINGING and DRUMMING fade into the distance. A FLUTE begins to play "JOYCE's SONG." HENRY walks up to JOYCE. He looks at her clothing. Smiles.*)

HENRY. Well, look at you.

(*They embrace.*)

JOYCE. I have something for you.

(*She opens her suitcase and hands him a book. He smiles.*)

HENRY. Welcome home, Joyce.

(*He follows the others off. EMILY SAM has remained behind. JOYCE removes her small, completed quilt from the suitcase. It has a "salmon" pattern. EMILY SAM looks at it, impressed.*)

EMILY SAM. It's beautiful.

JOYCE. *It's for you.* (*JOYCE wraps the quilt around EMILY SAM's shoulders. They embrace.*) I learned the stitching from Miss Brennan and Nurse Warner. But I learned the design from you.

EMILY SAM. *Thank you.*

JOYCE. Emily Sam, can I ask you something?

EMILY SAM (*nods*). *Of course.*

(*ADULT JOYCE gradually joins them, standing alongside JOYCE.*)

JOYCE. At the school, I met an old woman. She wore a long dress covered with a shawl and a kerchief on her head.

EMILY SAM. Did she carry a walking stick?

JOYCE. Yes. (*EMILY SAM looks at JOYCE, then laughs a bit.*) What's so funny?

EMILY SAM. That woman is your Aunt Sophie. She's an ancestor of ours who died many years ago. She came back to be my helping spirit when I was a young girl. You must have inherited her from me.

JOYCE. She gave me a song.

EMILY SAM (*smiles*). I was hoping she would. (*pause*) Joyce, your grandfather left something for you. (*EMILY SAM holds out a beautifully carved CANOE PADDLE. JOYCE looks at it. ADULT JOYCE reaches out her hand and takes hold of it.*) His spirit is still upon the waters.

(*EMILY SAM leaves, as JOYCE and ADULT JOYCE look at each other for a long time. Upstage, as before, is the silhouette of CHIEF SEATTLE. During the following, JOYCE takes the pouch from around her own neck and puts it around ADULT JOYCE's neck. They look each other in the eye. ADULT JOYCE hands JOYCE the CANOE PADDLE. JOYCE takes it from her, turns, and goes. FLUTE continues.*)

VOICE of CHIEF SEATTLE. There was a time when our people covered the land as the waves of a wind-ruffled sea cover its shell-paved floor. That time has passed away. But when your children's children think themselves alone in the fields, the store, the shop, upon the highway, or in the silence of the pathless woods, they will not be alone. At night, when the streets of your villages and cities are silent, and you think them deserted, they will throng with the returning hosts that once filled them. (*Lights rise on JOYCE paddling the CANOE toward us in the blue-lit water. MOUNT RAINIER looms behind.*) And I passed something else on to them, as well: the teachings of Mud Bay Sam. The history, the humor, the legends. The stories of our people. (*ADULT JOYCE watches JOYCE paddle the CANOE, then turns back to the audience. She smiles.*) There is a lot to remember.

(*Light fades slowly to black on ADULT JOYCE as the FLUTE continues to play. After a moment, light fades slowly on JOYCE paddling the canoe into the distance. The SONG ENDS as the stage goes to black.*)

END OF PLAY

Still Life with Iris

Steven Dietz

Premiere production, Seattle Children's Theatre, 1997

Production credits from the premiere of *Still Life with Iris* and details concerning performance rights are included in the acting edition of the play as published by Dramatic Publishing.

And she forgot the stars, the moon, and sun,
And she forgot the blue above the trees,
And she forgot the dells where waters run,
And she forgot the chilly autumn breeze.

John Keats

Cast of Characters

(doubling as indicated)

IRIS

MOM
MISS OVERLOOK

MAN / MISTER MATTERNOT
THUNDER BOTTLER TWO
DAD

LEAF MONITOR
ANNABEL LEE

THUNDER BOTTLER ONE
MOZART

MEMORY MENDER
RAIN MAKER
MISTER OTHERGUY
RAY

ELMER
HIS MOST EXCELLENT, GROTTO GOOD
THIRD STRING

HAZEL
HER MOST EXCELLENT, GRETTA GOOD
CAPTAIN ALSO

FLOWER PAINTER
BOLT BENDER
MISTER HIMTOO

ACT I

(*The MUSIC of Mozart fills the theatre as the audience arrives. MUSIC BUILDS as the theatre darkens, and then plays under as a shaft of LIGHT rises on a tall sign. The sign reads: "WELCOME TO NOCTURNO." Attached to the sign are arrows pointing in various directions. Written on the arrows are the following destinations: "Cloud Factory," "Bird Assembly," "Plant Plant," "Rain Storage," "Fruit Coloring," "Fish School — swimming classes nightly." Standing beneath the sign — his back to us — is a MAN in dark, somber attire. He wears dark gloves on his hands at all times. Unlike the residents of Nocturno, he is not wearing a PastCoat. He stands, reading the sign, as IRIS enters. She looks at the MAN's back for a moment, then speaks to him.*)

IRIS. Are you curious or lost?

MAN. Pardon me? (*When he turns, we see that he wears a weathered sort of tool belt around his waist, containing numerous objects of practical need. The MAN himself has an oddly sinister bearing.*)

IRIS. It's better to be curious than lost, don't you think? Which are you?

MAN. I'm new.

IRIS. Yes, I know. I can tell by your coat. Why have you come?

MAN. I'm looking for someone.

IRIS. Well, at this time of night, everyone's at work.

MAN. Doing what?

IRIS. You name it. Whatever you see in the world by day, it's made here by night. Like that fly on your nose — (*The MAN swats the unseen bug away.*) That fly was assembled right here in Nocturno. We crank those out by the millions and teach every one of them to fly. Plus, no two are the same. Our Bug Sculptors are very proud of that.

MAN (*catching on*). Just like snowflakes, then — no two alike?

IRIS. Actually — and this is privileged information — the snowflakes are made in *pairs*. But we separate them and load them into clouds bound for different locations. Don't spread that around.

MAN. I won't.

IRIS. So, you've never been here before?

MAN. Not that I remember.

IRIS. Oh, you'd remember. Unless you've got a tear in your coat. Who are you looking for?

(*LIGHTS EXPAND to reveal the Land of Nocturno, as HAZEL and ELMER — siblings, similar in age to Iris — rush on. HAZEL carries a large burlap sack marked "Spots." ELMER carries a wooden box.)*

HAZEL. I know you took them.

ELMER. I didn't take them.

HAZEL. Where did you put them?

ELMER. I didn't take them.

HAZEL. I bet you're hiding them.

ELMER. I DIDN'T TAKE THEM. Tell her, Iris —

IRIS. What is it, Elmer?

HAZEL (*before ELMER can answer*). We're almost done with our chores. All that's left is to put the spots on the Ladybugs —

(ELMER removes two large Ladybugs from the box. They're each bright orange and about the size of a cantaloupe. They are without spots.)

ELMER. But why do Ladybugs need spots, anyway? I think they look fine without them.

HAZEL. And I reach into the Spot Sack and it's filled with these —

(HAZEL reaches into the sack and pulls out several long black stripes, like those found on a zebra.)

IRIS. Stripes.

ELMER. There must have been a mix-up.

HAZEL. We can't put stripes on the Ladybugs.

ELMER. Why not? And then we'll put the spots on the zebras.

HAZEL (*to IRIS*). You're lucky you don't have a brother. It's like this all the time.

ELMER. Can you help us, Iris? No one can find things like you can.

IRIS. I'll help you as soon as I —

(She turns to the MAN.)

MAN (*interrupts her*). Your name is Iris.

IRIS. Yes. Why?

(The FLOWER PAINTER enters. He wears a beret and has a palette and brushes on a strap over his shoulder. He goes directly to ELMER, HAZEL, and IRIS as, at the same instant, the MEMORY MENDER enters, opposite, pushing a cart inscribed "Memory Mender" in large letters. The cart holds large spools of thread, extra-large buttons, scissors, etc. His hat looks like a thimble. He is a cranky but caring man, adamant about his work. Upon their entrance, the MAN turns and leaves.)

MEMORY MENDER (*calls out across the distance*). You there, sir — let me take a look at that coat! Sir, did you hear me?

(*But the MAN is gone. The MEMORY MENDER remains at a distance busying himself with the objects on his cart.*)

FLOWER PAINTER. Elmer, Hazel—are you finished with your chores?

HAZEL. We have a problem.

IRIS. The spots are missing.

ELMER. I didn't take them.

FLOWER PAINTER. Did you talk to the Spot Maker?

HAZEL. He sent them out, just like he always does.

FLOWER PAINTER. But the world requires Ladybugs, and Ladybugs must have their spots—

IRIS. Maybe you could paint them on.

(*ELMER holds the Ladybugs out to the FLOWER PAINTER.*)

FLOWER PAINTER. Out of the question. I'm a Flower Painter—nothing more. I wouldn't know the first thing about painting spots on bugs.

ELMER (*happily*). I guess our chores are done—

FLOWER PAINTER. It's not that simple, Elmer. Without us, the world would come to a standstill. If I abandoned my work, the flowers of the world would look like this. (*He produces a large, dull grey flower with a long stem.*) Instead of like this. (*A flourish of MUSIC as he makes several strokes with his paintbrush and produces [seemingly] the same flower—now bright yellow and red.*) Now, you are Spotters and you must do your work.

HAZEL. But we've looked everywhere—

FLOWER PAINTER. I'm sure Iris can find them. She's like her dad in that way. That man could find the moon on the blackest of nights.

ELMER. Then why has he never found his way back home?

HAZEL (*a reprimand*). Elmer—

ELMER. He's been gone forever.

FLOWER PAINTER. No one knows why, Elmer, and I think it's better left—

IRIS. Would you tell me if you knew? (*The FLOWER PAINTER stares at her.*) I was only a baby, then. Even my mom won't tell me why he left.

FLOWER PAINTER (*calmly, definitively*). Because she doesn't know, Iris. No one does. It was the night of the Great Eclipse, and the moon was particularly hard to find. He went out to bring it in . . . and he's never returned.

IRIS. There's an eclipse tomorrow.

FLOWER PAINTER. The first one since that night. I doubt we'll get to enjoy it, though—

IRIS. Why not?

FLOWER PAINTER. The order just came and it's a big one.

HAZEL. An order for what?

FLOWER PAINTER. A *storm*.

ELMER. And it's a big one?

FLOWER PAINTER. Huge. (*He starts off, saying his farewell.*) Now and again.

ELMER, HAZEL, IRIS. Now and again.

HAZEL (*gently, to IRIS*). Sorry about my brother. He says stupid things.

ELMER. I didn't mean—

IRIS. It's not stupid. I think about it all the time, too.

ELMER. I know what would make you feel better, Iris.

HAZEL. Helping us find those spots.

ELMER. Better than that. The order has come and a storm must be assembled. Now, what does this mean to people like you and me?

IRIS. It means that somewhere in this town . . . right now . . . just *waiting for us* . . . is a big . . . fresh . . . wet . . . batch of . . .

IRIS, HAZEL, ELMER (*a delicious whisper*). . . . rain.

(*They sigh with delight.*)

HAZEL. I bet the Rain Makers have been working nonstop—

ELMER. And it's just *sitting there*, and no one's—

HAZEL. Played in it, or—

ELMER. Tasted it, or—

IRIS. Race you there.

(*As they begin to rush off they are stopped by the MEMORY MENDER, who pushes his cart in their path.*)

MEMORY MENDER. Careful, now—or you'll trip and rip your coats. And if you rip your coats I'll have to sew 'em back up for you. And you know why, don't you?

IRIS, ELMER, HAZEL (*having heard this a million times*). Yes, we know why—

MEMORY MENDER (*quickly, quizzing them*). Hazel, who are the rulers of Nocturno, our home?

HAZEL. The Great Goods.

MEMORY MENDER. Iris, where do the Great Goods live?

IRIS. Across the water, on Great Island.

MEMORY MENDER. And Elmer, how deep is the water that surrounds Great Island?

ELMER. Umm—

IRIS. I know!

HAZEL. I know, too!

ELMER (*sharp, to the girls*). So do I.

MEMORY MENDER. Well?

ELMER. It's—umm—

MEMORY MENDER. You knew it when I asked you last week.

ELMER. It's—oh, I don't know. Why do I always get the hard questions?!

MEMORY MENDER. Let me see your coat. (*ELMER walks over to the MENDER, who discovers a tiny rip in the sleeve of ELMER's PastCoat. He sews it back up as he speaks.*) See there. A little rip in your coat and your memory is harmed. It makes me crazy. You've got to take care of your coat because your coat holds your *past*. Every stitch, every pocket, every button and sleeve—it's your whole life in there! Think you can just go out and get a past like you can get a glass of milk?! Think again. (*He is finished sewing Elmer's coat.*) There we are. Now, Elmer, how deep is the water that surrounds Great Island?

ELMER (*touching the new stitches in his coat*). Ninety-nine thousand and twenty-three feet.

MEMORY MENDER. Exactly. Now, don't trip and get a rip. (*To IRIS, referring to her coat.*) Iris, have your mom keep an eye on that button. It's getting loose.

IRIS. I will.

MEMORY MENDER (*taking IRIS aside*). And one thing more: The Fog Lifter is retiring today. After all these years, she can still set the fog down in the morning—but she just can't lift it up anymore. She'd like you to take her place, Iris.

IRIS (*honored*). Thank you.

MEMORY MENDER. Now and again.

IRIS, ELMER, HAZEL. Now and again.

(*MUSIC, as the MEMORY MENDER exits, pushing his cart, and LIGHTS SHIFT to reveal the LEAF MONITOR—Hazel and Elmer's mom—standing near a tree. She holds several large leaves and a clipboard. Near her are two large sacks with leaves protruding out of the tops of each. One is marked "OLD," one is marked "NEW." IRIS, ELMER, and HAZEL rush past her.*)

LEAF MONITOR. Hazel. (*HAZEL stops. ELMER and IRIS also stop, and stand behind her.*) Where are you going?

HAZEL (*innocently*). What, Mom?

LEAF MONITOR. You heard me. Where are you rushing off to? Did you finish your chores?

HAZEL. Why don't you ever ask Elmer that question?

LEAF MONITOR. Because you're the oldest.

ELMER. And you always will be. (*HAZEL glares at ELMER.*)

LEAF MONITOR. I need you to help me balance these books. I keep checking and double-checking, but I'm still *one leaf off.*

ELMER (*quickly*). I didn't take it.

LEAF MONITOR. In all my years as the Leaf Monitor, I've never encountered this. We must be certain that for every new leaf we put on a tree, an old one falls. (*to HAZEL*) But where could the missing one be?

(*The THUNDER BOTTLERS enter, pushing a tall crate on wheels marked "THUNDER." Stacked inside the crate are bottles sealed with bright red lids. Other bottles in the crate are empty and unsealed. The men are busy bottling the thunder: Holding bottles to their mouths, they use a funnel of some kind to make a loud, vocal SOUND OF THUNDER into the bottle. Then they quickly seal up each bottle with a red lid and place them inside the crate. They repeat this during the following.*)

THUNDER BOTTLER ONE. How many is that?

THUNDER BOTTLER TWO. That's thirty-four thunders.

THUNDER BOTTLER ONE. And that's not enough?!

THUNDER BOTTLER TWO. The order was for a forty-thunder storm.

ELMER. I've never seen so much thunder.

THUNDER BOTTLER TWO. We've been bottling it up all night.

THUNDER BOTTLER ONE. Gonna be a monster.

(*He thunders into a bottle.*)

THUNDER BOTTLER TWO. We gotta be ready.

(*He thunders into a bottle.*)

THUNDER BOTTLER ONE. Word is, the Color Mixer has outdone himself. For this storm, he's come up with a brand-new shade of *stormy sky blue-black.*

IRIS. Really?

THUNDER BOTTLER TWO. Gonna be something.

(*He thunders into a bottle.*)

THUNDER BOTTLER ONE. We gotta be ready.

(*He thunders into a bottle.*)

LEAF MONITOR (*to BOTTLER ONE*). Keep an eye out for a missing leaf.

THUNDER BOTTLER ONE. Did you take it, Elmer?

ELMER. Why does everyone always—

LEAF MONITOR. Once the storm comes and they start *swirling*, I'm afraid I'll never find it.

THUNDER BOTTLER TWO. It's not the BEST leaf that's missing, I hope.

HAZEL. Why not?

LEAF MONITOR. The BEST leaf must be sent to the Great Goods. You know that.

THUNDER BOTTLER ONE. Have Iris help you—if it's lost, she'll find it.

(*The BOLT BENDER enters carrying a piece of lightning about four feet long. He's bending it in various ways, trying to get the right shape. Other lightning bolts poke out of a quiver he wears over his shoulder.*)

THUNDER BOTTLER ONE (*greeting the BOLT BENDER*). Almost day.

BOLT BENDER (*nods, greets them ALL*). Almost day, indeed—and I can't get the lightning right. Even the best Bolt Bender gets tired of making the same old lightning bolt, over and over again.

IRIS. But when there's thunder, people expect lightning to go with it.

BOLT BENDER. But why couldn't it be something else?

ELMER. Like what?

BOLT BENDER. Open up one of those thunders and let's experiment. Instead of a *lightning bolt* lighting up the sky, maybe it's—(*The BOLT BENDER reaches into his quiver as BOTTLER ONE opens up one of the sealed bottles of thunder. A huge, quick crack of thunder fills the theatre as the BOLT BENDER produces a bolt in the shape of a cactus—or some other incongruous object—and holds it high above his head. If possible, it lights up.*)—THIS!

THUNDER BOTTLER ONE. That's a possibility.

THUNDER BOTTLER TWO (*holding up the original lightning bolt*). The Great Goods would never approve. As long as they've been our rulers, the lightning has always looked like *this*. (*with seriousness*) And, believe me, you don't want to get on the bad side of the Great Goods.

HAZEL. What can happen to you?

THUNDER BOTTLER ONE (*directly to HAZEL*). If you disobey the Goods, your punishment is great.

HAZEL. Mom. (*HAZEL reaches into her PastCoat and brings out a large, beautiful autumn leaf.*) I'm sorry. I didn't mean to offend the Goods. But it was so pretty.

ELMER. It's the best leaf of them all.

(*The LEAF MONITOR holds out her hand, and—reluctantly—HAZEL hands her the leaf. The LEAF MONITOR gently brushes a strand of hair from HAZEL's face.*)

LEAF MONITOR. Someday, Hazel, when *you're* the Leaf Monitor, you'll understand. Now, finish up your chores. It's almost day.

(*The LEAF MONITOR exits, as the BOLT BENDER lifts the lightning bolt, saying—*)

BOLT BENDER (*as he leaves*). It's gonna be huge.

THUNDER BOTTLER ONE & TWO (*as they leave*). We gotta be ready.

(*The BOTTLERS thunder into their bottles and leave with the BOLT BENDER.*)

ELMER (*whispers to IRIS and HAZEL*). Come on, it's our last chance before the storm.

(*The KIDS rush away and arrive at a very large rain barrel. It is wooden, with notches on its side [or a ladder] that enable it to be climbed. A large label on the barrel reads "RAIN. Batch #7893392." The KIDS see the barrel. They stop, stunned. ALL take a deep breath and are about to cheer loudly with delight but realize they might be heard and get caught, so they exhale while quieting one another.*)

IRIS, HAZEL, ELMER (*to one another*). SSSSSSSSShhhhhhhhhhhh! (*They approach the barrel, looking around to make sure they're not being seen. They each roll their pant legs up a little ways. They begin to climb up the side/ back of the barrel. Their voices remain soft, urgent.*)

HAZEL & ELMER (*to themselves, overlapping one another*). Please don't let my mom call my name, please don't let my mom call my name, please don't let my mom call my name, please don't let—

IRIS. Hey, Hazel.

HAZEL. Yeah?

IRIS. Why is that?

HAZEL. Why is what?

IRIS. Why is it that no matter how far away from our mom we get, if she says our name we can still hear her?

HAZEL. I don't know. But I wish we could change it.

ELMER. Let me ask you both a question: Are we going to gab . . . or are we going to splash?!

(*IRIS and HAZEL nod. ALL climb up and then stop, looking down into the barrel below them. They look at one another. They each pull back one of their sleeves, exposing the whole of their arm. They take a deep breath, then shove their arms down into the freezing cold water.*)

IRIS, HAZEL, ELMER (*a joyous scream*). AAAAAAAAAAAAUUUUUU-
UUGGGGGGGGGGGHHHHHHHHH! (*They laugh. They shiver. They cup
their hands and drink water [which we see] from the barrels. They laugh
and play some more, splashing a bit of water on one another, all the while
repeating under their breaths, overlapping.*) Please don't let my mom call
my name, please don't let my mom call my name, please don't let my—

(*Shafts of LIGHT discover Iris's MOM and the LEAF MONITOR, or their AMPLIFIED
VOICES are heard.*)

MOM (*simultaneous with LEAF MONITOR*). Iris!

LEAF MONITOR (*simultaneous with MOM*). Hazel and Elmer!

MOM & LEAF MONITOR. Time to come home!

(*The KIDS freeze, poised over the water, exasperated.*)

IRIS, ELMER, HAZEL. HOW DO THEY *DO* THAT?!

(*MUSIC, as the RAIN MAKER backs onto the stage, not seeing the KIDS. He wears a
long apron covered with bright raindrops. He holds bright orange batons in his hands
and uses them to direct an unseen approaching cloud into place.*)

RAIN MAKER (*backing in*). Okay, let's back her on in. Good. Little to your left.
Good. Man, they keep building these clouds bigger and bigger. I don't know
how they even get off the ground. Okay. Good. Keep her coming.

(*The KIDS have climbed down from the barrels, unseen.*)

IRIS (*whispering*). Now and again.

HAZEL & ELMER. Now and again.

(*They run off in separate directions and are gone.*)

RAIN MAKER. Okay, fellas. Let's load 'er up. We got some rain to drop.

(*MUSIC CHANGES to what will become recognized as the "Still Life" music, as
LIGHTS REVEAL Iris's home. It consists, in total, of a white wooden table with three
white chairs. On the table is a simple vase. Nothing else. IRIS arrives home. Just
before entering the scene, she stops and rolls her pant legs back down. As she does so,
she watches, unseen, as her MOM puts an iris in the vase and sets a steaming cup of
cocoa on the table. She pulls IRIS's chair away from the table. She goes to the middle
chair and touches it, looks down at it. Then she moves to her own chair, pulls it away
from the table, and sits. She looks at the iris in the vase, admiring it. Note: This is the
"Still Life"—the image that IRIS will remember throughout the play. IRIS stares at
this scene for a long moment as the music plays, then she enters.*)

IRIS. Hi, Mom.

MOM. How was the rain?

IRIS. What rain? (*MOM looks at her.*) Good. Cold. (*MOM smiles. IRIS sits, the cocoa in front of her.*) Mom, they asked me to be the Fog Lifter.

MOM (*knowing this in advance*). I'm very proud of you, Iris.

IRIS. And we saw all the thunder they're bottling up.

MOM. This storm means a lot of extra work for me. A lot of wind to be taught.

IRIS. Why doesn't the wind remember how to whistle?

MOM. The wind has no memory. Just like us if we lost our PastCoats. So every storm, I've got to start from scratch. And this being a big storm, I've got to teach not only whistling—but *howling.*

IRIS. Did Dad used to help you?

(*Silence. MOM stares at her.*)

MOM. Yes, in fact, he did.

IRIS. And did you ever help him?

MOM. Iris, I've told you, it's better forgotten, it's better not to think about—

IRIS. Did he leave because of me? (*Pause. MOM stares at her.*) Because he didn't want to be my dad?

MOM (*gently*). No.

IRIS. Why, then?

MOM. I wish I knew. On the night of the Great Eclipse he went in search of the moon—but it was so dark, Iris. I'm afraid he lost his way and was captured by that black night. I stood at the door, waiting for him, but all that arrived was the wind . . . moving through the house, not making a sound. Your dad was gone.

IRIS (*moving into the center chair*). I know you haven't forgotten him. I know he's still part of your coat. (*IRIS touches MOM's coat near her heart.*) Please, Mom. Tell me about him.

(*Silence. MOM looks at her, then speaks, a reverie.*)

MOM. Every night he roped the moon. And he pulled it down out of the sky. Then he'd give the signal—(*palm open, fingers spread, arm extended, she raises her hand slowly in front of her*)—to raise the sun into place. That was his job. He was the Day Breaker.

(*Silence, as IRIS smiles at the memory, then grows more serious.*)

IRIS. There's another eclipse tomorrow.

MOM. Yes, there is.

IRIS. And who will find the moon?

(*MOM stares at IRIS for a long moment.*)

MOM. He left something for you, Iris. A leather pouch. He wore it every night while he worked.

IRIS. Why haven't you ever given it to me?

MOM. I was afraid it would make you sad. All these years I've tried to protect you from that.

IRIS (*simply*). Please don't. Not anymore.

(*MOM stares at her, then gently touches IRIS's face.*)

MOM. You're right. It's time it was yours. (*MOM starts to exit, as IRIS lifts her cocoa from the table.*) Careful. That's hot.

(*IRIS nods and sips the cocoa. Then she speaks to MOM offstage.*)

IRIS. Sometimes I get mad at him, Mom. Sometimes I wish I could find him and make him tell me why he left. I've waited so long for him to come home.

(*MUSIC UNDER, as the MAN we saw earlier enters from the direction MOM exited. His name is MISTER MATTERNOT.*)

MISTER MATTERNOT. Your waiting is over, Iris. (*IRIS turns and sees MATTERNOT.*) You've been selected.

IRIS. Mom—?

MISTER MATTERNOT. You needn't call for your mother. You needn't think of your father anymore—

IRIS (*growing more frightened*). What are you doing here? You were lost—you were looking for someone—

(*MATTERNOT approaches IRIS.*)

MISTER MATTERNOT. And I've found her.

IRIS. But I don't know who you are—(*IRIS tries to run off to find her MOM. MATTERNOT stands in her way.*) MOM!

MISTER MATTERNOT. You're a special girl, Iris. I'm told you can find missing things.

(*IRIS is confused, scared, staring up at MATTERNOT.*)

IRIS. Yes, but I don't—

MISTER MATTERNOT. And because you are special, you've been chosen.

IRIS. Chosen by whom?

MISTER MATTERNOT. Why, by the rulers of Nocturno—the Great Goods. No one can travel to Great Island without their permission. But you, Iris, have been chosen to make the voyage.

IRIS. I don't want to visit Great Island. I want to know what's happened to my mom. Where did she—?

MISTER MATTERNOT. Listen to me, Iris, you have not been chosen to *visit* Great Island. You have been chosen to *live there.*

IRIS. Live there? What are—?

MISTER MATTERNOT. They have, you see, only the BEST of everything on Great Island—but until this moment they have never had a little girl. Now they will have you. You will be their daughter.

IRIS. I don't want to be their daughter! (*IRIS runs again in the direction her MOM left.*) I belong here with my mom!

(*As IRIS says this, MOM appears and faces her. She looks the same as before, except that she is not wearing her PastCoat. IRIS throws her arms around MOM, desperately. MOM does not respond at first, but then puts her arms gently around IRIS, sympathetically. IRIS is crying, holding tightly onto MOM as she speaks.*)

IRIS (*cont'd*). Make him go away! He's scaring me—I don't want to go to Great Island—please, Mom, make him go away!

(*MUSIC FADES OUT, as MOM continues to hold IRIS.*)

MOM (*to MATTERNOT, concerned*). Why is this girl calling for her mother? Isn't there something we can do? Where is her family? Where is her home?

IRIS (*pulling away*). What are you saying? What is—(*For the first time, IRIS notices that her MOM's PastCoat is gone. She speaks quietly.*) Mom. Where's your coat?

MOM. What's that?

IRIS (*to MATTERNOT*). Her coat—where is it?

MOM. What coat is she talking about?

IRIS. She went in there to bring me a pouch—a leather pouch—and now she—

MOM (*holds out the old and weathered leather pouch*). You must mean *this*. I found it in the next room. Is it yours?

(*MATTERNOT takes the pouch from MOM.*)

IRIS (*desperately*). Yes. It belonged to my dad—

MISTER MATTERNOT. Iris, listen to me, the Great Goods do not wish to cause you any pain. And so, to remove the heartache, we must remove the coats.

(*IRIS wraps her PastCoat tightly around herself. She backs away, crying.*)

IRIS. No. You can't. The Memory Mender said "Never let anything happen to your coat, or you'll be lost, you won't know who you are or—"

MOM (*overlapping, to MATTERNOT*). If the little girl wants to keep her coat, I think she should be allowed to—

MISTER MATTERNOT. Iris, I want to tell you something—

IRIS. Stay away from me—

MISTER MATTERNOT. Iris—

IRIS (*looking at MOM*). YOU'VE TAKEN AWAY HER COAT—

MOM (*to MATTERNOT*). We should find her mother. We should take her home.

IRIS (*crying*). LOOK AT HER! SHE DOESN'T KNOW WHO I AM!

MISTER MATTERNOT (*grabbing her, holding her*). IRIS. (*quieter now*) Listen to me. *This is what's done.* I don't like it, but it's what the Great Goods desire and therefore it must be done. Believe me, it's better to let me have your coat. If you keep it, you will be haunted by your past. You will think of your mother all the time. You will think of your home and your friends and your life here—and *you will never stop missing it.* It will be an ache that will never vanish from your heart. (*She looks up at him, holding her PastCoat tightly around her. MATTERNOT now reaches out his hands to her, asking for the coat.*) Now . . . please.

IRIS. But if you take my past, who will I be?

MISTER MATTERNOT. You will be Iris. You'll be the girl you are now, but you'll remember nothing that happened before this moment.

IRIS. I'll never think of my mother again?

MISTER MATTERNOT. And, therefore, you'll never be saddened by your loss. (*looking at MOM*) Nor will she. (*to IRIS*) It's the only way, Iris. It's the only way to make it not hurt.

IRIS (*stares at him*). Let me keep the pouch.

MISTER MATTERNOT. Iris—

IRIS. Please?

MISTER MATTERNOT. It will mean nothing to you once your coat is gone.

IRIS. *Please?* (*MATTERNOT hands her the pouch. She attaches it around her waist, or over her shoulder. Then she looks over at MOM, with some final hope of recognition.*) Mom . . . ?

MOM (*kindly*). I do hope you find her, Iris. Whoever she is. Wherever she's gone.

(*IRIS looks back at MATTERNOT. He holds out his hand, awaiting the coat. She stares at him. She looks down at her coat. She looks over at her MOM one final time. She wraps her PastCoat around herself very tightly for a moment . . . closing her eyes . . . and then, eyes still closed, she slowly removes her coat and holds it out away from her. A long, mournful gust of wind is heard as MATTERNOT takes the coat in his arms. He then goes to the table and removes the iris from the vase. The table and chairs are taken away. The sound of wind fades. IRIS's eyes remain closed. The three of them stand there in silence for a moment. Then, finally, MATTERNOT speaks.)*

MISTER MATTERNOT (*gently*). Iris. Open your eyes. (*IRIS opens her eyes. He stands before her, speaks kindly.*) My name is Mister Matternot.

IRIS (*pleasantly*). Hello.

MISTER MATTERNOT. And this is Miss Overlook.

MISS OVERLOOK [formerly MOM]. Hello, Iris. It's a pleasure to meet you.

IRIS. It's nice to meet you, too. Where are we?

MISTER MATTERNOT. A little girl and her mother once lived here. We came to visit them. But now we're on our way to Great Island.

IRIS. Why's it called that?

MISTER MATTERNOT. Because everything on the island—every single thing—is the BEST of its kind. And you, Iris, will continue that tradition.

IRIS (*looking at the pouch*). And what's this?

MISS OVERLOOK. That's your pouch, Iris. It belongs to you.

MISTER MATTERNOT. One thing more.

(*He holds up IRIS's PastCoat.*)

IRIS. What a wonderful coat. Is that mine, too?

MISTER MATTERNOT. It belonged to the little girl who lived here. (*testing her*) Would you like it?

IRIS. Really?

MISTER MATTERNOT. She won't be needing it anymore. Would you like to wear it?

IRIS. Is it cold where we're going?

MISTER MATTERNOT. Not at all. The temperature on Great Island is always perfect.

IRIS (*simply*). Then I won't need it. Thank you, anyway.

MISTER MATTERNOT (*smiles*). As you wish. (*to OVERLOOK*) Miss Overlook, I'll see you on Great Island.

(*MATTERNOT exits, taking the PastCoat with him. IRIS begins to follow him as OVERLOOK sees something on the ground. She reaches down and picks it up. It is a button from Iris's PastCoat.*)

MISS OVERLOOK. Iris? (*IRIS stops, turns back to her*) Did you drop this?

(*She holds up the button.*)

IRIS. What is it?

MISS OVERLOOK. It's a button.

IRIS. It must have fallen off that girl's coat.

MISS OVERLOOK (*hands IRIS the button*). Why don't you hold on to it. Maybe you'll find her in your travels.

IRIS. I'll put it in my pouch.

MISS OVERLOOK. I hope I see you again, Iris.

(*IRIS nods and watches MISS OVERLOOK exit. IRIS starts to put the button in her pouch. She stops, looks at the button, holding it in front of her. She closes her eyes. She rubs the button between her thumb and forefinger. As she does so MUSIC PLAYS—the same music we heard under the "Still Life" earlier—and LIGHTS SHIFT, isolating only IRIS and a [perhaps] miniature "Still Life," the table, cocoa, and the iris in its vase, suspended in mid-air above the stage. The rest of the stage is in darkness. IRIS does not look at the "Still Life." Instead, she closes her eyes, tightly, once again. As she continues to rub the button, the light on the "Still Life" grows brighter and brighter. Then, as she opens her eyes and puts the button back in her pouch, the "Still Life" goes suddenly black. It is gone. MUSIC OUT as MISTER MATTERNOT reappears quickly, saying—*)

MISTER MATTERNOT. We're due at one o'clock, Iris, and we mustn't be late. Are you ready?

IRIS. Ready!

(*IRIS runs off. MISTER MATTERNOT follows her as MUSIC PLAYS and LIGHTS REVEAL the Great Room of the Great Goods. HIS MOST EXCELLENT, GROTTO GOOD, stands in the room. His dashingly elegant clothes have one button, one pocket, one tassel of fringe. He wears one shoe only. He holds a monocle in his hand, which he uses from time to time. He speaks to his servant, MISTER OTHERGUY, who's dressed in the same somber manner as MATTERNOT and wearing a similar sort of tool belt. MISTER OTHERGUY is hurriedly dusting everything in the room with a single-feather duster. MUSIC UNDER and OUT.*)

GROTTO GOOD. But my fear is this—that I will handle it badly. I fear I don't know how to *maintain* a little girl. What do they *do*? What do they eat? And what will I do if she *says something to me*?

MISTER OTHERGUY. I'm sure you'll handle it well, Master Good.

GROTTO GOOD. Shouldn't they be here? It's nearly one o'clock.

(*HER MOST EXCELLENT, GRETTA GOOD, enters. She is dressed in a similarly elegant style as her husband. She, too, wears only one shoe. She has one ring on her finger. She is affixing her one earring as she arrives.*)

GRETTA GOOD. I must tell you, a terrifying thing just happened to me.

GROTTO GOOD. What was it, my dear?

GRETTA GOOD. I found a *second earring*. It was just lying there next to this one.

GROTTO GOOD. My good, what did you do?

GRETTA GOOD. I threw it away instantly.

GROTTO GOOD. Oh, thank good.

GRETTA GOOD. It set me back, I must tell you. A shock like that.

GROTTO GOOD. Don't think of it again. Now, Gretta dear, I've been assured by Mister Otherguy that I needn't be nervous about meeting a little girl.

GRETTA GOOD. We'll be fine, Grotto dear. We've chosen the best of the best.

GROTTO GOOD. But what do they *do*—these *children*? That's all I'd like to know. And what if she *says something to me*? (*GRETTA shrugs "I don't know."*) Mister Otherguy?

(*OTHERGUY shrugs, imitating GRETTA.*)

GROTTO GOOD (*cont'd*). Oh, my good.

(*The door flies open quickly, revealing IRIS. She now wears an overlayer of clothing that is similar to the Great Goods—elegantly eccentric, very different from her Nocturno attire. She wears one very shiny shoe. The GOODS gesture for her to take a step into the room. She does so. She stands stiffly, with a pleasant, forced smile on her face. The clock chimes once. For a moment, they all just stand and nod at one another. Finally, IRIS turns to GROTTO and speaks in as friendly a way as possible.*)

IRIS. Hello. I'm Iris. What an odd place this is.

(*GROTTO nods at her for a moment, then turns quickly to OTHERGUY.*)

GROTTO GOOD. My good, she said something to me. (*OTHERGUY gestures for GROTTO to respond. GROTTO looks at IRIS, looks at GRETTA, looks back to IRIS . . . then finally speaks, smilingly, definitively.*) You are a girl.

IRIS. Yes.

GROTTO GOOD (*smiling throughout*). And now you are here.

IRIS. Yes, I am.

GROTTO GOOD. And I am speaking to you.

IRIS. Yes, you are.

GROTTO GOOD (*still smiling*). And now I am finished. (*turns to his wife*) Gretta?

GRETTA GOOD (*walks toward IRIS, calmly*). You must forgive my husband. He's never spoken to a little girl before. You are the first one to ever arrive on Great Island.

IRIS. I see.

GRETTA GOOD. But you are welcome here, Iris. More than welcome, you are *treasured.*

GROTTO GOOD. You will now be the greatest of our goods.

GRETTA GOOD. Have you nothing to say?

IRIS. Umm . . . thank you . . .

GRETTA GOOD. And?

IRIS. And where's my other shoe?

GROTTO GOOD. Oh, my.

GRETTA GOOD. You are wearing the finest shoe under the sky. Have you *looked* at it?

IRIS. Yes, I have, and it's beautiful—maybe the most beautiful shoe I've ever seen but, still, one of them is missing and the one I'm wearing really hurts my foot. Is there another pair I could wear?

GROTTO GOOD. Oh, my.

IRIS. They don't have to be as nice as these—

GROTTO GOOD. Oh, my.

IRIS. Just a little more comfortable, so I can—

GRETTA GOOD. Iris.

IRIS. Yes, Mother Good?

GRETTA GOOD. There are no other shoes for you. We have only what's BEST on this island and to ensure the value and importance of each item, *we have only one of everything.* (*to OTHERGUY*) Bring her something to drink.

(*OTHERGUY nods and brings a goblet, as well as a small, sealed glass container on a tray to IRIS.*)

IRIS. One of everything—what do you mean?

GROTTO GOOD. Look around, Iris! Everything here is unrivaled in its goodness. Like, for example, our BOOK. Or this—our DRAPE. Or our CHAIR.

IRIS. You only have one chair?

GROTTO GOOD. Isn't it a beauty?

(*He brings it to her and insists she sit in it during the following.*)

GRETTA GOOD. So you see, Iris, that is why you have only one shoe.

IRIS. What happened to its mate?

GROTTO GOOD. It is now in the Tunnel of the UnWanted.

GRETTA GOOD (*sees that IRIS's drink is ready*). Oh, here we are. Thirsty?

IRIS. Very. (*OTHERGUY offers IRIS the goblet. She takes it and looks in it. It is empty.*

OTHERGUY opens the sealed glass container. He tips it over and pours its contents into the goblet: one long, slow, perfect drop of water. The GOODS nod approvingly as IRIS looks into the goblet.) What is this?

GROTTO GOOD. It's a perfect raindrop.

IRIS. This is all the water you have?

GRETTA GOOD. It's all we need. For, at daybreak, another perfect drop will arrive. There's a land near here, where they work all night to see to our pleasure each day.

GROTTO GOOD. So drink up!

(IRIS looks at them, looks at the goblet, then drinks. She, of course, barely tastes it. As she swallows, the GOODS sigh audibly, blissfully.)

GRETTA GOOD. Perfect, isn't it?

IRIS. I guess.

GRETTA GOOD. Now, Iris, we've heard you have a gift for finding things. Is that true?

IRIS. I don't know. Maybe. I don't remember finding *anything.*

GROTTO GOOD. You'll help us find PERFECT THINGS for the island, I'm sure. Now, we've prepared the best of the best for you—

IRIS. What exactly do you *do* here?

GRETTA GOOD. We enjoy our goods in the greatest of ways.

IRIS. Don't you work?

GROTTO GOOD. Certainly not.

GRETTA GOOD. But we are ever on the lookout for flaws. We mustn't let anything that is not the BEST invade Great Island. *(GRETTA sees the pouch that IRIS wears.)* Like *this*, for example. What is the meaning of this old pouch?

GROTTO GOOD. And what's inside?

IRIS. A button. It belongs to a little girl I'm looking for.

GROTTO GOOD. There are no other girls, Iris. You're the only one here.

GRETTA GOOD. Mister Otherguy, show Iris her toy box.

(OTHERGUY raises the lid of the toy box as IRIS continues to stare at GROTTO.)

IRIS. There's no one else to play with?

GRETTA GOOD. We're still searching for a little boy.

GROTTO GOOD. One who's perfect—like you.

IRIS. You brought me here because you think I'm perfect?

GROTTO GOOD. Of course we did.

IRIS. I'm not perfect.

GRETTA GOOD (*after a quick look at GROTTO*). *Really?*

IRIS. Not perfect at all.

GROTTO GOOD. Very well. Tell us something you've done that *wasn't perfect*. Some day when you did a bad thing. Something from your *past*, Iris. (*The GOODS look at her.*) Well?

(*Silence. IRIS thinks.*)

IRIS. I can't think of anything.

GROTTO GOOD. You see!

IRIS. But, I know I'm not—

(*The GOODS leave happily, in a flourish, saying—*)

GROTTO GOOD. Enjoy your toys, Iris!

GRETTA GOOD. And if you find anything that is not the BEST of its kind—

GROTTO GOOD. We'll discard and replace it immediately!

GRETTA GOOD. A great good pleasure to meet you!

GROTTO GOOD. A great good pleasure, indeed!

(*MUSIC, as LIGHTS shine DOWN to isolate IRIS near the toy box. The face of the clock remains lit. MISTER OTHERGUY lifts something out of the toy box: a doll encased in glass. On the side of the glass is a small lock. The doll is dressed identically to IRIS. OTHERGUY holds the doll out to IRIS. IRIS looks at him . . . then takes it from him. She looks at the doll, then tries to open the lock to take the doll from the case—but it won't open.*)

IRIS. It's locked. How can I play with her if she's locked inside?

(*MISTER OTHERGUY simply shrugs and exits. MUSIC builds as IRIS sits on the closed toy box, her hands pressed against the glass that houses the doll as the face of the clock grows brighter and brighter. The clock chimes once. LIGHTS RISE fully on the room once again as MISTER MATTERNOT enters.*)

MISTER MATTERNOT. Hello, Iris.

IRIS. What day is it today?

MISTER MATTERNOT. It's the BEST day of the week—just like it always is.

IRIS. And how long have I been here?

MISTER MATTERNOT. You've been on Great Island for one month—the BEST month of the year. (*IRIS is silent. She takes off her lone shoe and tosses it aside.*) Is something wrong? Are you unhappy?

IRIS. I don't remember being happier and I don't remember being sadder. But there must have been a time when I had someone to play with.

MISTER MATTERNOT. Iris, the Goods have filled your toy box with the finest toys under the—

(*IRIS finishes his sentence with him, as she goes to the toy box and pulls out the following items as she describes them.*)

IRIS (*simultaneously with MATTERNOT*). "—finest toys under the sky." Yes, I know—and maybe *you'd* like to play with them. Would you like to play cards, well . . . here's the CARD. Or maybe you'd like to do a jigsaw puzzle, well . . . here's the PIECE.

MISTER MATTERNOT. What is it you want to do, Iris?

(*She now begins to play "Jacks" with the ball and the one—very beautiful—jack.*)

IRIS. I want to, I don't know, I want to go fishing.

MISTER MATTERNOT. But the Goods have already *caught* a fish—a remarkable fish—

IRIS. I don't care! I wouldn't mind TWO of something. Like maybe two jacks instead of one. Or maybe two kids that I could play with.

MISTER MATTERNOT. Perhaps you'd like to go *find* something—the perfect leaf, the perfect stone?

IRIS. There's no need—(*She holds up a picture frame. Framed within it is the leaf we saw HAZEL give to the LEAF MONITOR.*) The perfect leaf arrived today. Where do these things come from?

MISTER MATTERNOT. A land near here.

IRIS. Is that where the little girl lived? The girl whose coat you offered me?

MISTER MATTERNOT. I don't recall.

IRIS. Of course you do. She lived there with her mother. May we go see her?

MISTER MATTERNOT. She's gone, Iris.

IRIS. Where did she go?

MISTER MATTERNOT. She can't be found.

IRIS. But I need to return something to her.

MISTER MATTERNOT. Put it out of your mind.

IRIS. Show me the way—I'll find her myself.

MISTER MATTERNOT. I've told you: No one leaves the island without the permission of the Goods.

IRIS. Then I'll—

MISTER MATTERNOT. And the Goods intend to keep you here.

IRIS. Here in this room? Forever?

(*MISTER MATTERNOT stares at her, saying nothing, as MISTER OTHERGUY and MISTER HIMTOO enter.*)

MISTER OTHERGUY. Iris, the Goods have denied your request.

(*IRIS lifts the doll still in the glass case and holds it.*)

MISTER MATTERNOT. What request?

IRIS. I asked for the key to unlock this case.

MISTER HIMTOO. She is to remain under glass.

MISTER OTHERGUY. It is the word of the Goods.

MISTER MATTERNOT (*attempting to cheer her*). I'm sure you'll find a way to play with her, Iris. She's the BEST doll under the—

IRIS (*simply*). My toy box does not suit me.

MISTER MATTERNOT (*thrown by this new tone in her voice*). I beg your pardon?

IRIS. I am a Good now and I deserve the best of the best, isn't that correct?

MISTER MATTERNOT. Well, yes, of course, but—

IRIS. This box is flawed and I can no longer abide it. I want it replaced.

MISTER MATTERNOT. If I may ask . . . what is wrong with it?

IRIS. It . . . has TWO handles! One on either side! It's intolerable! The Goods asked me to tell them if something was not satisfactory—and this, clearly, is not. I want it replaced immediately.

(*MATTERNOT stares at her, then turns to OTHERGUY and HIMTOO.*)

MISTER MATTERNOT. Inform the Goods.

(*OTHERGUY and HIMTOO exit.*)

IRIS. Mister Matternot?

MISTER MATTERNOT. Yes?

IRIS. Why are there three of you?

MISTER MATTERNOT. What do you mean?

IRIS. You all work for the Goods. And they have only one of everything. How come they have three of you?

MISTER MATTERNOT (*a fact, without pity*). Because we're ordinary. We're not special in the least. (*pause, going to her*) It's only been one month, Iris. In time, you'll come to love it here. (*She looks up at him.*) What better place could there be?

IRIS. I don't know. But there must be something. Somewhere. (*She removes the button from her pouch. As she rubs it, MUSIC PLAYS and LIGHTS rise on the miniature "Still Life" once again.*) Because when I hold this button in my hand and close my eyes . . . I see a picture in my mind. Why would that happen?

MISTER MATTERNOT. May I see that button?

(*IRIS holds the button out to him. He removes his gloves and takes hold of the button, inspecting it. The "Still Life" is now gone. The MUSIC FADES OUT.*)

IRIS. And why don't I know what that picture means?

MISTER MATTERNOT (*gently, close to her*). Iris. Some things are the way they are because the way they are is the least likely to bring sadness or bad memories.

IRIS. I don't have any bad memories. Do *you*? (*She sees the open palms of his hands—still holding the button. She touches one of his hands.*) You have scars on your hand. Long, red scars. Where did they come from?

(*MATTERNOT looks at her, then quickly hands the button back to her and pulls his gloves back over his hands. He exits as the GOODS' VOICES are heard, opposite.*)

VOICE OF GROTTO GOOD. OH, IRIS!

VOICE OF GRETTA GOOD. WE HAVE YOUR NEW TOY BOX!

(*IRIS looks off in the direction of their VOICES, then looks at the toy box next to her. An idea! She opens the toy box and climbs into it, closing the lid and disappearing just as the GOODS enter followed by MISTER OTHERGUY and MISTER HIMTOO, who carry a new, larger, more ornate toy box—with only one handle.*)

GROTTO GOOD. Here we are!

GRETTA GOOD (*looking around*). Iris?

GROTTO GOOD. She must be with Matternot. We'll leave it here and surprise her.

(*As GRETTA speaks, GROTTO gestures to OTHERGUY and HIMTOO, showing them where the new toy box should be placed. They follow his instructions.*)

GRETTA GOOD. I'm so proud of her, Grotto. She found fault with something! She's become a Good through and through.

GROTTO GOOD (*points to the "old" toy box*). Look at that—it's an abomination! Away with it this instant!

(*MISTER OTHERGUY and MISTER HIMTOO lift, or roll, the "old" toy box, exchanging a quick, curious look regarding its weight—and then exit, taking it away, as MISTER MATTERNOT enters, passing them.*)

GRETTA GOOD. Ah, there you are.

MISTER MATTERNOT. Where are they going?

(*GROTTO is putting IRIS's toys—the puzzle piece, the card, etc.—into the new toy box.*)

GROTTO GOOD. In with the best, out with the rest.

GRETTA GOOD. Is Iris with you?

MISTER MATTERNOT. No. I left her right here.

GRETTA GOOD. That's impossible.

(*GROTTO spots IRIS's shoe on the ground.*)

GROTTO GOOD. Gretta.

GRETTA GOOD. What? (*GROTTO lifts the shoe.*) Oh, my good.

GROTTO GOOD. I fear she's escaped.

GRETTA GOOD. Escaped? But where would she go?

GROTTO GOOD. Every inch of the island must be searched.

GRETTA GOOD (*to MATTERNOT*). Well, don't just stand there—

GRETTA & GROTTO GOOD. START SEARCHING!

(*MUSIC, as LIGHTS SHIFT to night. A beach on Great Island. One very large seashell, or stone, is prominent upstage. MUSIC FADES into the SOUND of waves. IRIS enters, exhausted, worried. She is barefoot. She looks around in all directions, calling out.*)

IRIS. Hello! (*no answer*) Is anybody out there, across the water?! (*no answer*) Can you tell me where I am?! (*IRIS climbs atop the shell and calls out.*) HELLLOOOOO!

(*An ECHO comes back to her from the water.*)

ECHO. HELLLOOOOO!

(*IRIS looks into the distance, trying to locate the ECHO. Note: If possible, both live and recorded voices are used to make the "echo" come from a variety of directions in the theatre.*)

IRIS. WHERE AM IIIIII?

ECHO. WHERE AM IIIIII?

(*IRIS gradually climbs down and approaches the water downstage. Liking the sound of the "IIIIII," she continues.*)

IRIS. IIIIII!

ECHO. IIIIII!

IRIS. I!

ECHO. I!

IRIS. IIIIII'M—

ECHO. IIIIII'M—

IRIS. IIIIIIIRIS!

ECHO. IIIIIIIRIS!

IRIS. IIIIII'M IIIIIIIRIS!

ECHO/VOICE OF ANNABEL LEE. IIIIIII'M ANNABEL LEE!

IRIS (*jumps back away from the water's edge*). Who's there?

VOICE OF ANNABEL LEE. An echo waiting to be free.

(*IRIS stares into the distance, still unable to locate the VOICE.*)

IRIS. Can you help me get away from here? I'm lost.

VOICE OF ANNABEL LEE. Yes, we both seem to be.

IRIS. Really? Where do you live?

(*ANNABEL LEE, a young woman of the sea, appears. She wears a tattered gown of dark blues and greens and the boots and belt of a pirate. Her belt holds a small telescope. Her hair is entwined with seaweed. And, most prominently, she has a long chain [or rope] attached to her wrist — or ankle — with a large padlock, which leads far out into the sea, offstage. IRIS stares at her, amazed.*)

ANNABEL LEE (*as she enters*). In a kingdom by the sea. Have you never seen an Annabel Lee?

IRIS. Never. How did you —

ANNABEL LEE. For years I've been locked away — held against my will — but now you, Iris, will set me free.

IRIS. How?

ANNABEL LEE. By loosing these chains that bind me to the sea.

IRIS. But how did you get here?

ANNABEL LEE. Through your wishing, I assume. What else could it be?

IRIS. I did wish for someone to play with. And I wished for someone to help me get across this water.

ANNABEL LEE. And I wished I would find my ship.

IRIS. You have a ship?

ANNABEL LEE (*looking through her telescope*). It's what I'm searching for, and my ship is searching for me.

IRIS. How do you know?

ANNABEL LEE. I listen at night, locked away, in my kingdom by the sea.

> And as the waves crash and fall —
> I can hear in the squall —
> My ship's voice calling to me —

IRIS. What does it say?

ANNABEL LEE. "For the moon never beams without bringing me dreams

Of the beautiful Annabel Lee;
And the stars never rise, but I see the bright eyes
Of my captain, Annabel Lee."

IRIS (*smiles*). Your ship really calls out to you?

ANNABEL LEE. I'm so close to finding it, Iris. It's just out of reach.

IRIS. I see a picture like that, sometimes. A picture of a room. But I don't know where it is.

ANNABEL LEE. What have you been using to navigate with? Have you been using the stars?

IRIS. There's more than *one*?

ANNABEL LEE. Of course there are. Look.

(*She hands IRIS the telescope, and IRIS looks through it at a sky full of stars.*)

IRIS. Oh, my. From the palace of the Great Goods, you can only see *one* star.

ANNABEL LEE. Why is that?

IRIS. It's the best one. They chose it.

ANNABEL LEE. There's no best in stars. They're like waves upon the sea. A multitude of many; far as the eye can see. (*shakes the chain with her arm*) Now, if you'll free me from this, I'll find my ship and together we'll sail away.

(*IRIS goes to her and tries to pry the lock from ANNABEL LEE's arm.*)

IRIS. It's locked shut. Maybe we could cut the chain.

ANNABEL LEE. It's too strong—I've tried.

IRIS (*looks closely at the lock*). Then we have to pick the lock. We need something long and narrow and flat.

(*IRIS looks around, but sees nothing that will work.*)

ANNABEL LEE. Maybe something in your pouch?

IRIS. No. (*showing her*) All I have is this button. (*still looking*) There must be *something* we can use—

ANNABEL LEE (*looking up to the sky*). I think I know what it is.

IRIS. You do? (*ANNABEL LEE nods.*) What is it?

(*ANNABEL LEE sits, leaning against the shell, looking up at the stars.*)

ANNABEL LEE. The same thing that brought me here to you.

IRIS. But that was just me—wishing.

ANNABEL LEE. Exactly. (*gestures for IRIS to join her*) C'mon, Iris. Your wishes will be our vessel. And the stars will be our map. And with courage and faith as our captain and mate, the ship I've lost and room you seek may fall into our lap.

(*ANNABEL LEE begins to whistle "Twinkle, Twinkle Little Star" softly and beautifully. After a moment, IRIS sits next to her and joins her. They whistle/hum the song together, happily. As they are about to repeat the song, they hear a PIANO playing the same melody nearby. They stop whistling/humming. They look around — not knowing where it's coming from. As they stand up and look around, the PIANO stops. IRIS and ANNABEL LEE whistle/hum a phrase of the song, and the PIANO echoes the phrase. Note: If possible, the PIANO phrases should come from a variety of directions in the theatre, similar to the echo earlier in this scene. IRIS and ANNABEL LEE look around. Then they rush downstage and whistle/hum a phrase of the song, and the PIANO echoes the phrase. Still looking for the source, IRIS and ANNABEL LEE rush upstage and whistle/hum the next phrase of the song, and the PIANO again echoes the phrase, and then, unseen — at first — by IRIS and ANNABEL LEE, MOZART, age eleven, appears downstage, at the edge of the water. He is playing a small piano, which is attached to his waist like a drum. The song is the "Twelve Piano Variations in C" [which we know as "Twinkle, Twinkle Little Star."] He is dressed in the clothes of his day. A white handkerchief cascades from his breast pocket. In between phrases, he repeatedly jumps back away from the unseen waves and shakes water from his shoes — all the while continuing to play, avidly. IRIS and ANNABEL LEE turn and stare at him, curiously. They've never seen a person like this before. MOZART finishes the song with a flourish as ANNABEL LEE and IRIS — behind him — applaud. MOZART turns, surprised.*)

MOZART. *Guten tag! Bon jour!* Good day! (*a quick look up at the stars, speaks urgently*) Or *night*. Why is it night? How long has it been night? And how close are we to morning? It's crucial that I find out. Can you tell me?!

IRIS. Who *are* you?

MOZART. Oh. Yes. Where are my manners? I must have left them in Vienna where manners seem to be all that matters. (*steps toward them, bows*) I am Mozart. Wolfgang Amadeus Mozart.

(*IRIS and ANNABEL LEE mimic his bow, as they speak simultaneously.*)

IRIS. Hi.

ANNABEL LEE. Hello.

MOZART. But you can call me Motes. I prefer that. Where are we?

IRIS. On the shores of Great Island.

ANNABEL LEE. Isn't it a beautiful beach?

MOZART (*sincerely, wiping away some water*). Yes — but why must it be so close to the water?

IRIS (*smiles*). I'm Iris. And this is Annabel Lee.

MOZART. Are you a pirate?

ANNABEL LEE. My mother was.

MOZART. Your *mother* was?

ANNABEL LEE. And my father was the sea.

MOZART. And I thought *my* family was strange.

ANNABEL LEE. Why must you know when the night ends?

MOZART. I've been searching for something. Something that's *just out of reach.* (*IRIS and ANNABEL LEE look at each other.*) It's a song I work on at night. Only at night. (*With one finger, he plays the first few phrases of the Serenade in G — the Allegro movement from Eine kleine Nachtmusik. He stops abruptly, one note prior to completing the second phrase. He looks back at them.*) But that's it. I can't seem to finish it, because when the sun rises . . . the melody vanishes. If only I could stop time — if only I could find a way to make the sun wait *just a few seconds more before rising* — I think the song would come to me.

ANNABEL LEE. I know that feeling. Something just out of reach, like my ship —

(*IRIS removes the button from her pouch and shows it to them.*)

IRIS. Like when I hold this button in my hand. (*She closes her eyes as the "Still Life" is illuminated once again. The MUSIC that accompanied it plays softly, under, as IRIS describes it.*) There is a table. And on the table, a vase. And in the vase, an iris.

MOZART. Is it a memory?

IRIS. I'm not sure. This button belonged to a little girl. If I can find her, maybe she'll tell me.

(*The "Still Life" vanishes. The MUSIC FADES.*)

ANNABEL LEE. Is she on this island?

IRIS. I've looked everywhere, and I've found a lot of things for the Great Goods and I found the two of you, but I can't find that little girl.

MOZART (*as he searches once again for the final note of his melody*). If she's that elusive, she must be worth the search. Like a melody that hovers in the ether — anonymous and unknown — until it is captured and rendered unforgettable.

IRIS (*looking at MOZART's tiny piano*). That's it.

ANNABEL LEE. What?

(*IRIS approaches MOZART and points to something on his piano.*)

IRIS. May I see that note?

MOZART. That is not, technically, a *note*. It is rather a *key*.

IRIS. Then it's perfect. May I have it?

MOZART. *Have it?*

IRIS. Just for a moment—yes.

ANNABEL LEE. Iris, what are you—

MOZART. But I may need it. It may be part of the melody I'm searching for—

IRIS (*pointing to another one*). Then give me that one—or that one—or that one. Surely you can do without one of your notes.

(*MOZART looks at her, then chooses a key from the piano and hands her the thin, ivory top of it, saying—*)

MOZART (*reluctantly*). Here. (*reprimanding*) And, as I said, it is not, technically, called a *note*. It is—rather—

(*IRIS inserts the piano key into ANNABEL LEE's lock and frees her from the chain, saying—*)

IRIS.—a *key*.

ANNABEL LEE (*happily tossing the chain aside*). Thank you, Iris! And thank you, Motes! Now, if we find my ship, we can go in search of that little girl.

MOZART. Did you say "ship"?

ANNABEL LEE. Yes.

MOZART. As in wood that floats precariously over deep, freezing water?

ANNABEL LEE. Yes.

MOZART (*moving away*). Could you point me to Vienna?

ANNABEL LEE. Are you afraid of the water?

MOZART (*taking his "key" back from IRIS*). I prefer to be anchored to a piano bench.

ANNABEL LEE. But water is like a rush of music—it is the common language of the world. (*to IRIS*) Isn't that right, Iris?

IRIS. Well, I don't remember if—

ANNABEL LEE. When you're on the water, your heart pounds with delight. And your past is a tide which crashes inside and you speak aloud the story of your life. (*to IRIS*) Isn't that so, Iris?

(*Silence. IRIS stares at ANNABEL LEE.*)

IRIS. I can't say.

ANNABEL LEE. But, Iris—

IRIS. I have no story to tell.

MOZART. But what about your past? What's the first thing you remember?

IRIS. The face of Mister Matternot. A woman standing with him. And this button.

ANNABEL LEE. And that's all?

IRIS. That's all.

(*A huge crash of thunder/crack of lightning, followed by the SOUND of rain. IRIS, ANNABEL LEE, and MOZART stare at the sky in wonder.*)

MOZART. Look at that.

ANNABEL LEE. I've never seen the sky that color. What would you call that?

IRIS. Stormy sky blue-black.

ANNABEL LEE. It's so lovely.

MOZART. And so . . . *wet.*

(*IRIS and ANNABEL LEE are about to playfully grab MOZART and push him toward the water as a VOICE is heard nearby.*)

VOICE OF MISTER MATTERNOT. IRIS? IRIS, IS THAT YOU?

(*They freeze. ANNABEL LEE and MOZART turn to IRIS.*)

MOZART (*whispers*). Who's that?

IRIS (*whispers*). They'll take me back to the Great Goods.

ANNABEL LEE. Hide, Iris. We'll take care of it.

MOZART. We will?

(*ANNABEL LEE gestures for MOZART—who's still wearing his piano—to run offstage. She then exits, opposite. IRIS hides behind the large shell as MISTER MATTERNOT and MISTER OTHERGUY rush on, looking around.*)

MISTER OTHERGUY. I heard her voice. I know I did.

MISTER MATTERNOT (*calling out*). THE GOODS ARE VERY DISPLEASED WITH YOU, IRIS. (*no response*) If you don't let me bring you home, I'm afraid they'll punish you. They'll throw you into the Tunnel of the Un-Wanted and you'll never be found again. (*no response*) IRIS?

(*OTHERGUY realizes IRIS must be behind the shell. He signals to MATTERNOT and they begin to approach the shell, slowly, from either side. As they are about to look behind it and find IRIS, a VOICE comes from a distant place, offstage.*)

VOICE OF ANNABEL LEE. Here I am!

(*MATTERNOT and OTHERGUY turn in the direction of the VOICE. IRIS, too, peeks up briefly from behind the shell.*)

MISTER OTHERGUY. Over there!

(*MATTERNOT and OTHERGUY start to rush off in the direction of the VOICE as a PIANO plays a quick phrase of MUSIC from a distant place, offstage, opposite. MATTERNOT and OTHERGUY stop, turn in the direction of the piano.*)

MISTER MATTERNOT. What was that?

(*As MATTERNOT and OTHERGUY start to rush off in the direction of the PIANO, the VOICE OF ANNABEL LEE calling "Here I am!" and the line of Mozart MUSIC begin to repeat and overlap each other, coming from seemingly every possible direction all at once. MATTERNOT and OTHERGUY freeze, trying to decide which way to go. They look at each other. They decide to split up and head off in opposite directions. They rush off, calling out as they go.*)

MISTER MATTERNOT & MISTER OTHERGUY. IRIS!

(*As they disappear, the VOICE and PIANO fade away and are gone. Silence as IRIS slowly emerges from behind the shell. She walks downstage, calling off to either side of the stage in a whispered voice.*)

IRIS. It's safe. They're gone. (*Silence. IRIS looks around for them.*) You can come out now. (*Silence. She continues to look.*) Motes? Annabel Lee? (*Silence. She stares in disbelief, heartbroken.*) Oh, no. I made you up. (*IRIS sits on the ground, sadly.*) I made you up, and now you're gone —

(*MUSIC UP as suddenly ANNABEL LEE and MOZART are revealed standing in the back of the theatre [or pop up from behind the shell]. They call out to IRIS, gesturing for her to follow them.*)

ANNABEL LEE. Come on, Iris!

MOZART. Off we go!

(*IRIS stands and breaks into a big smile as MUSIC CRESCENDOS and LIGHTS SNAP OUT quickly.*)

END OF ACT I

ACT II

(*MUSIC, as LIGHTS REVEAL a small downstage area. MISTER MATTERNOT leads IRIS, MOZART, and ANNABEL LEE onstage. They stand in a line, facing the audience, as MATTERNOT addresses them.*)

MISTER MATTERNOT. The Goods will be with you in a moment. Please — for your own safety — wait here until they're ready for you. Great Island can be a dangerous place to get lost.

IRIS. We weren't lost, we were curious. And how can that be dangerous? If everything here is the BEST under the sky, what harm can befall us?

MISTER MATTERNOT. The Goods only allow the best of things to be *seen*.

But elsewhere on the island, hidden away in the Tunnel of the UnWanted, are all the OTHERS—all the angry, forgotten, discarded things that are common and unremarkable. You must take care to avoid them.

ANNABEL LEE. You don't understand. All she wants to do is—

MISTER MATTERNOT. Are you her friend?

ANNABEL LEE. Yes, I am.

MISTER MATTERNOT. Then convince her of this: (*approaches IRIS and speaks to her*) The Great Goods are willing—as you might expect—to forgive you . . . *once*. But after that, they may lock you up behind glass.

IRIS. Like a decoration.

MISTER MATTERNOT. Wait here.

(*MATTERNOT exits.*)

MOZART. I know the feeling, Iris. Everyone just stares at you all the time like you're perfect and you'll never change and you'll never make a mistake—

IRIS. And everyone makes mistakes—

MOZART (*simply*). I don't. But I'm *afraid* I might. I'm afraid I'll disappoint my father and never amount to anything and just be another guy in Vienna named Wolfgang Amadeus Mozart.

ANNABEL LEE. If you hadn't been so afraid of the water, we'd have gotten away. There was only that ONE wave.

MOZART. But it was HUGE! Crashing and returning—over and over again.

IRIS. And the wind was so strong—but you couldn't hear it whistle. It was completely silent.

ANNABEL LEE. And the fog—thick as cotton—blanketing the horizon in every direction. I think that fog has captured my ship.

IRIS. I wonder when it will finally lift?

MOZART. I miss Vienna. I miss the little streets. I miss the way my sister makes me hot cocoa. I *adore* hot cocoa, don't you?

(*LIGHTS EXPAND to reveal the Great Room of the Great Goods. The GOODS enter, followed by MISTER MATTERNOT and MISTER HIMTOO. GRETTA GOOD is carrying a candelabra—with one candle, of course—which she sets on a beautiful piano that has been added to the room. GROTTO GOOD walks down the line past IRIS, MOZART, and ANNABEL LEE—as though inspecting them.*)

GROTTO GOOD (*with typical definitiveness*). Well, here we are—gathered and assembled and brought together here in the very midst of each other—right now, presently, at this time. Gretta?

GRETTA GOOD (*to MATTERNOT*). The shoe. (*MATTERNOT produces IRIS's tight, shiny shoe and places it on her foot during the following.*) We're glad to see it restored to your foot, Iris. And as for your clothes, which became quite disheveled during your misadventure on the beach—a tailor is on his way to the island to sew you a new, best outfit.

(*MATTERNOT gives IRIS a look which prompts her to say—*)

IRIS (*quietly*). Thank you.

GROTTO GOOD (*to MOZART*). You, young man, will be staying with us.

GRETTA GOOD. We've been looking for a little boy.

GROTTO GOOD. We think you'll do nicely.

(*GRETTA removes the tiny piano that MOZART wears and hands it to HIMTOO.*)

GRETTA GOOD. And you won't be needing this—

MOZART. But that's my piano—

GROTTO GOOD (*standing by the new piano in the room*). From now on THIS is your piano.

MOZART (*excitedly, seeing the other piano*). May I play it?

GROTTO GOOD. Not now, son.

GRETTA GOOD (*to ANNABEL LEE*). And as for you, Miss Lee, the numbers are not in your favor. (*indicating IRIS*) For you see, we already have a girl on Great Island.

GROTTO GOOD. You're superfluous and we're sorry.

ANNABEL LEE. But I'm helping Iris find her home—

GROTTO GOOD. And you've succeeded. Now—

(*GROTTO GOOD claps his hands. HIMTOO takes hold of ANNABEL LEE.*)

GRETTA GOOD. You'll be shown to the Tunnel.

GROTTO GOOD. The Tunnel of the UnWanted.

(*HIMTOO begins to pull ANNABEL LEE away.*)

ANNABEL LEE. Don't worry, Iris. I'll find my ship and I'll—

(*MATTERNOT steps in and stops them.*)

MISTER MATTERNOT. Is this truly necessary, Master Good?

GROTTO GOOD. Did you just *speak to me without consent?!*

MISTER MATTERNOT. My apologies, Master Good. But perhaps we can make room for another—

GROTTO GOOD. Perhaps we can make room for *you* in the *Tunnel.*

GRETTA GOOD. Off with you, now.

(*MATTERNOT and HIMTOO lead ANNABEL LEE offstage. The following three speeches are spoken simultaneously.*)

ANNABEL LEE. Have courage and faith, Iris—

IRIS. Please—don't do this!

MOZART. Let her stay!

(*ANNABEL LEE is gone. Smiling widely, the GOODS put their arms around IRIS and MOZART, as if posing for a quick photograph.*)

GROTTO GOOD. And now here we are, a FAMILY at last!

(*The clock chimes once. The GOODS step away, admiring their children.*)

GRETTA GOOD. Do you like spaghetti?

GROTTO GOOD. We've procured the BEST noodle in all the world!

MOZART (*whispers quickly to IRIS*). One noodle?

IRIS (*whispers quickly to MOZART*). I told you.

GRETTA GOOD. What a special treat it is to welcome our new son!

GROTTO GOOD. The newest of our Goods!

GRETTA GOOD (*to MOZART*). Your father and I want you to know that you mean the world to us, and we shall provide for your every happiness here on Great Island. The tailor will measure you for your new, best clothing.

GROTTO GOOD. A perfect room shall be prepared for you.

GRETTA GOOD. And we shall employ the best piano teacher in the world to come and give you lessons.

IRIS. Motes doesn't need a piano teacher. He's pretty good at it already.

GRETTA GOOD. He is not a "Pretty Good." Nor are you, Iris, a "Pretty Good." We are—all of us—*Great Goods*. And that must never be forgotten!

MOZART. May I play the piano?

GROTTO GOOD. Not now, son.

MOZART. But it's *night*—and I need to play as much as I can. The song that I'm searching for can only be captured at night. So please, Father Good— may I play? Would that be all right?

(*GROTTO looks to GRETTA. She does not have an answer. She stares right back at him. He's on his own.*)

GROTTO GOOD. Well—I'm not sure if it *is* all right—I've never had a little boy—or a piano—so, I don't—YES—absolutely—that would be fine—I mean—actually—in fact—NO—certainly not. Is that clear?

(*MOZART just stares at him.*)

IRIS. I want to see the Tunnel.

GROTTO GOOD. That's out of the question.

IRIS. Mister Matternot told us about it. He said—

GRETTA GOOD (*looking to GROTTO*). Mister Matternot will be reprimanded.

GROTTO GOOD. You don't want to see the Tunnel, Iris. I assure you.

IRIS. Why not?

GROTTO GOOD. Because— (*looking at GRETTA*)

GRETTA GOOD. Because— (*looking at GROTTO*)

IRIS. Yes?

GROTTO GOOD. Because . . .

GRETTA GOOD. . . . you're *afraid of the Tunnel.*

IRIS. I am?

GRETTA & GROTTO GOOD. Yes.

(*Silence. IRIS looks at them, curious and hopeful.*)

IRIS. So, I've been there before?

GRETTA GOOD. Yes. *Many times*—when you were younger.

GROTTO GOOD. And you asked us to never show it to you again.

IRIS. I did?

GROTTO GOOD. Yes.

IRIS. Why don't I remember that?

(*Silence. The GOODS stare at her, then look away.*)

MOZART. Iris, ask them about the room.

IRIS. Did we have a white table with three chairs? And on the table was there a—

GROTTO GOOD. I think you know that *three chairs* would be out of the question.

GRETTA GOOD. Yes, now let's—

IRIS. *Tell me things.* Please. Tell me things that happened when I was little.

GRETTA GOOD. But why, Iris?

IRIS. Because I don't remember. I want you to tell me about when I was a baby. (*The GOODS look at each other.*) Please? Tell me anything—even if it's little. Tell me what my first word was. Or what my favorite toy was. Or what games we used to play. (*Silence. The GOODS stare at her. Her tone becomes more serious.*) Did we used to be happy? If we were, please tell me about that. What did that feel like?

(*The GOODS stare at her for a long moment, saying nothing. Then GROTTO turns quickly to MOZART, saying—*)

GROTTO GOOD. It's time to play the piano, son.

GRETTA GOOD. A great, good idea.

(*MOZART is still looking at IRIS, as GROTTO seats him at the piano bench.*)

GROTTO GOOD. You mustn't dawdle. You mustn't hesitate. You must do what you're asked when you are asked to do it.

(*The GOODS prepare to listen.*)

GRETTA GOOD. Ah, the delights of a castle above us and our family around us, and now the sweet caress of music, like water from a distant well, filling our—

(*MOZART begins to play: It is, once again, the beginning of the serenade from "Eine kleine Nachtmusik." He plays it with a huge, pounding rhythm—loud and showy—but stops briefly at the end of his incomplete phrase each time . . . and then immediately starts into the opening notes again, louder still, avidly searching for the song. The GOODS' reaction is horrified and immediate.*)

GROTTO GOOD. Oh, my.

GRETTA GOOD. Oh, my good.

GROTTO GOOD. Oh, good help us.

IRIS. I told you he was pretty good!

(*MOZART does not hear them, does not stop playing. They step toward the piano and exclaim—*)

GRETTA GOOD. Great good son—

GROTTO & GRETTA GOOD. STOP THIS INSTANT!

(*MOZART looks up at them, stops playing.*)

MOZART (*innocently*). What is it, Mother Good?

GRETTA GOOD. Grotto?

GROTTO GOOD. My son, you are now a Good. And a Good must be . . . *selective*. A Good must not fritter away his time in a variety of directions. A Good must always gravitate to that which is great.

MOZART. I'll show more respect, Father Good.

GROTTO GOOD. I knew you would.

(*MOZART begins to play again. He plays the identical, still incomplete passage, but this time with a languorous, melancholy feeling. Again, after a few notes, the GOODS step forward. They each take hold of one of his hands, stopping him.*)

GROTTO & GRETTA GOOD (*firmly, not with anger*). No, son.

(*MOZART looks up at them as they hold his hands.*)

IRIS. Why did you stop him? He's playing for you, he's—

GROTTO GOOD. Quiet, Iris.

GRETTA GOOD. You are very talented, my son. This talent gives you many choices.

GROTTO GOOD. And so, you must *make one.*

MOZART. Make one *what?*

GRETTA GOOD. Make one choice.

GROTTO GOOD. You must pick the Greatest Note and play *only* it.

(*MOZART looks up at them. They release his hands. He looks back down at the keyboard, then back up at them.*)

MOZART. One note?

GROTTO & GRETTA GOOD. Yes.

MOZART. And *only* one? (*They nod. MOZART smiles.*) Surely you're joking!

GROTTO & GRETTA GOOD. No.

(*MOZART stops smiling. The GOODS move away and prepare to listen once again. MOZART removes one of the keys—as he did earlier with his tiny piano—and holds it up, offering it.*)

MOZART. What if I gave you one and kept the rest?

(*The GOODS shake their heads. MOZART returns the key to the keyboard as the GOODS wait expectantly.*)

GRETTA GOOD. Now, our great good son, we are ready.

MOZART. But may I say, that is not music. Music is the sound of many things coming together.

GRETTA GOOD. We await your note.

MOZART (*standing*). But there are eighty-eight keys, there are—

GROTTO GOOD. And ONE of them must be the best of all!

IRIS (*at MOZART's side*). *Why?* Why must everything have a "best"? With so many things in the world, it makes no sense to—

GROTTO GOOD. I warn you to say no more—

IRIS. This island is not great—it is *small.*

GRETTA GOOD. Iris!

IRIS. A "great" island would have *hundreds* of things and not just ONE!

GROTTO GOOD (*forcefully, to IRIS*). You must be silent.

GRETTA GOOD (*forcefully, to MOZART*). And you must *choose.*

(*Silence. MOZART looks at them, then sits back down at the bench, solemnly. He looks at the GOODS. They nod. Then they close their eyes expectantly, awaiting the playing of the "note." MOZART looks at the keyboard. His hands move tentatively up and down the keys looking for the "perfect" place to land.*)

GROTTO GOOD (*whispers*). Oh, the expectation!

GRETTA GOOD (*whispers*). Quiet!

(*After another moment of searching, MOZART slowly lowers his finger to the keyboard and plays a note, a beautiful, low A-flat. The GOODS sigh, rapturously, and speak simultaneously.*)

GROTTO GOOD. Oh, my good . . .

GRETTA GOOD. Yes, that's it . . .

MOZART (*lifts his finger from the keyboard, looks back at the GOODS, and tries to smile*). Are you pleased?

GROTTO & GRETTA GOOD. Oh, yes.

GRETTA GOOD (*to GROTTO*). Shall we hear it again?

GROTTO GOOD (*deliciously*). Do you think we *dare*?

GRETTA GOOD. Yes, let's do!

(*The GOODS close their eyes again and wait, expectant, as MOZART turns back to the keyboard and looks down at the "note." He pauses . . . then plays the same note again. Then he plays the incomplete phrase of "Eine kleine Nachtmusik" using only the ONE note. The GOODS sigh again, audibly.*)

IRIS. Motes . . .

MOZART (*broken, looking down at the keys*). It's over. I've failed. I'm never going to find that song.

(*MISTER HIMTOO enters and announces—*)

MISTER HIMTOO. Master Good, the tailor has arrived.

(*The MEMORY MENDER enters. He does not have his cart. He has, instead, a leather case that has "Memory Mender" printed on the outside. He looks around with part dread, part curiosity, having never been to Great Island before. He does not immediately see IRIS.*)

GRETTA GOOD (*approaching the MEMORY MENDER*). We require measurements of our new son—

GROTTO GOOD (*also approaching*). And a garment made for him that will be the finest under the—

MEMORY MENDER (*having just seen IRIS*). Iris?

IRIS. How do you know my name?

GRETTA GOOD. Yes, that is—in fact—our daughter, Iris.

GROTTO GOOD (*a firm threat*). And beyond saying her name, you will say *nothing more*. Do you understand?

(*The MEMORY MENDER looks at them, looks at IRIS.*)

GRETTA GOOD (*coldly*). There is a place for people who *speak more than they should*. Do you know of it? (*The MEMORY MENDER nods.*) Splendid. We have an understanding.

(*GROTTO GOOD snaps his fingers, and HIMTOO brings the piano bench to center. The MEMORY MENDER gestures for MOZART to stand on the stool. During the following, the MEMORY MENDER measures MOZART with a brightly colored measuring tape.*)

IRIS. Father Good, I wonder if I could ask the tailor a question.

GROTTO GOOD (*after a look at GRETTA*). Very well.

IRIS (*pointing to his leather case*). What do these words mean? What is a "Memory Mender"?

MEMORY MENDER. Well, Iris, where we—(*quickly corrects himself, looking at the GOODS*) where *I* come from, our memories are—

GRETTA GOOD. Your memory is perfect, Iris. It holds nothing but the best of thoughts.

IRIS. Yes, but I—

GROTTO GOOD. We've arranged for you to have an unblemished past—free from sadness, free from—

IRIS. But it's not free. It's *incomplete*.

MOZART. There's a picture in her mind, and she doesn't know what it—

GROTTO GOOD. The mind plays tricks!

GRETTA GOOD. That's it!

GROTTO GOOD. Tricks and nothing more!

GRETTA GOOD (*firmly, to the MEMORY MENDER*). *Tell her.*

MEMORY MENDER (*choosing his words carefully*). Well—as they say—the mind can be mistaken. If one's memory is harmed—or lost—or *taken*—

GROTTO GOOD (*stepping in very close to him*). You've said *enough*.

IRIS (*to the MEMORY MENDER*). May I look at your buttons? (*IRIS looks at the buttons on the MEMORY MENDER's PastCoat.*) I'm looking for a girl who had a coat like yours. (*IRIS reaches into her pouch and removes the button. She hands it to the MEMORY MENDER.*) And she lost this button. Do you know where I might find her?

GROTTO GOOD. Of course he doesn't know! He's not from this island! He's a common tailor, for good's sake!

IRIS. I want him to answer me!

GRETTA GOOD. Iris—

IRIS. Why are you so afraid of him?!

GROTTO GOOD. Afraid of him?!

GRETTA GOOD. Don't be silly—

IRIS. He's a common tailor—or so you said—so why won't you let him answer me?

(*The GOODS look at IRIS. Then they turn and look at the MEMORY MENDER threateningly.*)

GRETTA GOOD (*quietly, firmly*). He will *answer you*—

GROTTO GOOD (*quietly, firmly*). —*carefully.* Won't you?

(*The MEMORY MENDER nods. He turns to IRIS.*)

MEMORY MENDER. I know the girl of whom you speak. I made her this button myself.

IRIS. You did?

(*The GOODS step in, looking at the MEMORY MENDER.*)

MEMORY MENDER (*looking into IRIS's eyes*). But . . . I don't know where she is now. She should be very nearby . . . but I'm afraid that that girl—as I knew her—is gone. (*The GOODS smile, relieved. The MEMORY MENDER leans in more closely to IRIS and hands her the button, saying—*) I will tell you this, though: If you find her coat . . . you will find *her.*

(*IRIS looks at him. MOZART has heard this as well. The GOODS now begin to rush the MEMORY MENDER out of the room with HIMTOO's help.*)

GROTTO GOOD. Is your measuring complete?

MEMORY MENDER. Well, yes, but I—

GRETTA GOOD. We expect the garment to be the best of the best.

MEMORY MENDER. Good luck, Iris—

GROTTO GOOD. Off we go now—

IRIS. Goodbye.

(*The MEMORY MENDER and HIMTOO are gone.*)

GRETTA GOOD (*happily, to MOZART*). And now, son, before supper, why don't you play us another note?

(*MOZART stares at her as LIGHTS SHIFT to a dark, forgotten room on Great Island.*

All that is required is a dirty old brown table with one chair. Nearby are two other dirty chairs, lying about, broken. MISS OVERLOOK sits at the table. She wears dark clothing, similar to MISTER MATTERNOT, MISTER OTHERGUY, etc. She is busy polishing several dark, dirty pots and pans with a wire brush. It is filthy, tedious work. MATTERNOT enters, carrying a large box. He speaks, officiously.)

MISTER MATTERNOT. Miss Overlook, the supplies for the island have arrived from Nocturno.

MISS OVERLOOK. And the paint I requested? Did it arrive?

MISTER MATTERNOT. Your request was denied by the Goods.

MISS OVERLOOK. I only wanted to give this dark room some light.

MISTER MATTERNOT. There is, however, paint which was ordered by the Goods that — due to a flaw in its creation — will be of no use to them. It was to be thrown into the Tunnel. You're welcome to it.

MISS OVERLOOK. What flaw?

MISTER MATTERNOT. It is white. All of it. Each and every can.

MISS OVERLOOK. Why is that?

MISTER MATTERNOT. An accident in Nocturno. The Color Mixer has died. He fell from his Color Wheel during last night's storm — thrown to the ground by a great rush of wind.

MISS OVERLOOK. That's terrible.

MISTER MATTERNOT. He was given no warning. The wind, it is said, remained perfectly silent as it blew through the town. *(He sets the paint in front of her.)* You're an excellent worker, Miss Overlook. The Goods are pleased with you.

MISS OVERLOOK. I've never even met them.

MISTER MATTERNOT. That is a sign of their satisfaction. *(He starts to leave.)* Have a great good evening.

MISS OVERLOOK. Mister Matternot.

MISTER MATTERNOT. I've work of my own to do, excuse me —

MISS OVERLOOK. You once told me that I'd always lived here and always done this work. Is that true?

MISTER MATTERNOT. That is the word of the Goods.

MISS OVERLOOK. I'm not asking the Goods. I'm asking *you*. Is it true? Have I truly spent my life in this dark, musty room. Have I never seen the sky, never felt the wind?

MISTER MATTERNOT *(challenging her)*. What sky are you speaking of? What wind do you remember?

MISS OVERLOOK (*a pause as she thinks, then quietly*). None. None at all.

MISTER MATTERNOT. Then you have your answer.

MISS OVERLOOK. But I've dreamt of such things. And my dreams hold a picture—a picture of a family, a house, a table set for three.

MISTER MATTERNOT. I am a worker, Miss Overlook. I do not dote on wishes and dreams. Nor should you. Be thankful for the *generosity* of the Goods—that they have provided you with a room and a function. Better that than to be thrown into the Tunnel—the home of the angry, forgotten, unremarkable things. At least you and I are *needed* here. (*She stares at him . . . and then nods.*) You have the paint you requested. But as for seeing the sky, don't think of it again.

(*MISTER MATTERNOT turns to leave, just as IRIS and MOZART appear at the entrance to the room.*)

MISTER MATTERNOT. What are you doing here?

IRIS. We were just . . .

MOZART. . . . *looking.*

MISTER MATTERNOT. For what?

IRIS. For the way to the Tunn— (*stops*)

MISTER MATTERNOT. The way to the what?

MOZART. *Cocoa.* The way to the cocoa.

IRIS. Yes.

MOZART. Is it through here?

MISTER MATTERNOT. I'll have Miss Overlook find you some cocoa.

MISS OVERLOOK. I'd be happy to.

MISTER MATTERNOT. This room is not for the children of the Goods; it is for workers.

MISS OVERLOOK (*to IRIS*). Did you ever find your mother? Your name is Iris, isn't it?

IRIS. Yes.

MISS OVERLOOK. I met you once. You were looking for your mother.

MISTER MATTERNOT. And she found her. The Goods are her parents. Now, it's time to—

IRIS (*opens her pouch and removes the button*). I just remembered, you gave me this button. It had fallen off a little girl's coat. It's my oldest memory.

MISS OVERLOOK. I remember that as well. And you put the button in your pouch.

IRIS. Yes—

(*MATTERNOT removes one of his gloves and reaches out his hand toward the button.*)

MISTER MATTERNOT. It's time you gave me that, Iris. It doesn't belong to you.

IRIS. But it's my—

MISTER MATTERNOT. I'll return it for you.

IRIS. Do you know where that little girl is?

MISTER MATTERNOT. Yes, I do.

IRIS. Then why won't you tell me?

MOZART. We needn't ask his help, Iris. If we find that coat, we'll find her.

(*IRIS puts the button back in her pouch.*)

MISTER MATTERNOT. Who told you that?

MOZART. My tailor, if you must know.

MISTER MATTERNOT. Enough, now. There is to be no more discussion of coats and button and—

MISS OVERLOOK. But you were there, Mister Matternot. I remember that as well. You were there the day it happened.

MISTER MATTERNOT (*forcefully*). *Do you not know what can happen to you?* (*He points in a specific direction—which IRIS and MOZART observe.*) Do you not know what awaits you in the Tunnel if you displease the Goods?!

IRIS. But she didn't—

MISTER MATTERNOT. Iris, you are *never to come to this room, again.* You don't belong here. (*indicating OVERLOOK*) This woman is ordinary—just as I am—and you're not to trouble yourself with that which is ordinary. Now, return to your parents—both of you! (*IRIS and MOZART exit—but MATTER-NOT does not see that they exit in the direction of the Tunnel.*) Miss Overlook, have I made myself clear?

MISS OVERLOOK. You were there. I saw you. (*As MATTERNOT puts his glove back on, OVERLOOK takes hold of his ungloved hand, saying.*) Your hands. There are long red scars on the palms of your hands. Why is that?

MISTER MATTERNOT. Excuse me, I need to—

(*She holds tightly to his hand, not letting him leave.*)

MISS OVERLOOK. Have you always been here, as well?

MISTER MATTERNOT. Yes.

MISS OVERLOOK. And these scars on your hands. Where are they from?

MISTER MATTERNOT (*pause, simply*). I don't remember.

MISS OVERLOOK (*quietly*). It's terrible, isn't it? To forget so much. What would
cause that, I wonder?

(*MUSIC PLAYS, as LIGHTS SHIFT quickly to the Tunnel. The MUSIC under the scene
is joined by the SOUND of the angry, forgotten things that live in the Tunnel—the
random cries of people and animals and discarded objects. The SOUND of water
dripping is heard as well. Note: A live hidden microphone causes all the following
dialogue to reverberate as a slight ECHO. IRIS and MOZART are crawling on their
hands and knees. IRIS has abandoned her shoe once again and is barefoot.*)

IRIS (*whispering*). How much farther?

MOZART (*also whispering*). I wish I knew.

IRIS (*calling out*). ANNABEL LEE!

(*A frightening ECHO comes back at them—filled with the SOUND of the angry,
forgotten things.*)

MOZART. What are those noises?

IRIS. The angry, forgotten things, I guess.

MOZART. I had no idea there'd be so many of them. Is that what will happen
    to us, someday? Discarded and forgotten—known only for the noise we
    once made? (*sees something*) Iris?

IRIS. Yes.

MOZART (*lifting it*). Here's your other shoe.

(*It is, indeed, the mate to the fancy shoe she wore earlier.*)

IRIS. I don't want it.

MOZART. No one does. (*MOZART tosses the shoe aside. As it lands, a NOISE is
    heard: the rolling of wheels, the clanging of metal.*) What was that?

IRIS. I think *someone's coming*—

(*another, louder noise*)

MOZART. Or *some* THING—

(*Another, still louder noise is heard.*)

IRIS. Motes, c'mon. We've got to get—

(*As they start to stand and run, they immediately encounter a rusty, beat-up metal
shopping cart. The cart is filled with discarded items. On the side of the shopping cart
is a hand-lettered sign that reads "Your Name Here." Sitting in the shopping cart is
CAPTAIN ALSO—she wears dark, raggedy clothing with a huge number "2" on her
chest. She wears a colander as a hat and mismatched gloves on her hands. Pushing
the cart is THIRD STRING, a man in similarly raggedy clothing with hundreds of*

"Third Place" ribbons pinned to his clothing. He wears an old football helmet with no facemask and holds a single ski pole in his hand. With them is RAY, who wears a long, dark, raggedy coat with a small, battered black umbrella attached to his head as a hat. He also wears dark sunglasses. Note: The effect of these individuals is that of a strange, eccentric menace.)

CAPTAIN ALSO. — OUT OF HERE? Is that what you started to say? You've got to get OUT OF HERE?! Well, fat chance there is of THAT. You're DOWN UNDER, now. You're in the middle of the mediocre middle. (*IRIS and MOZART try to turn and run the other way, but RAY intercepts them and blocks them.*) And now that you're here, you've got to answer to ME.

IRIS. Who are you?

CAPTAIN ALSO. I'm Captain Also, the Dean of the Discards, the Chairman of the Abhorred. I'm second best to all the rest. And this is Third String—

THIRD STRING (*menacingly*). Have a nice *grey*.

CAPTAIN ALSO. Third String is not a winner and he's not a loser. He is undeniably *average*. So I made him my CEO.

THIRD STRING. Chief *Extra* Officer.

CAPTAIN ALSO. We are the Top of what's on the Bottom, the most Famous of the Forgotten! (*CAPTAIN ALSO reaches into the shopping cart and pulls out some items, tossing them at IRIS and MOZART.*) You want a TOASTER? — we got millions of 'em. HANGERS, PLASTIC TUBS, BRIDESMAID DRESSES — we got *millions of 'em*. Everybody wanted 'em ONCE—

THIRD STRING. — and nobody wants 'em NOW.

CAPTAIN ALSO. We are the Orphans of the Ordinary!

THIRD STRING. Unexceptional—

CAPTAIN ALSO. — and Unnecessary!

MOZART. And who's that?

THIRD STRING. That's Ray.

IRIS. Is he ordinary, too?

CAPTAIN ALSO. No, he's displaced. Ray used to work for the Sun. He did outreach. Show 'em, Ray—(*RAY opens his coat to reveal its brilliant yellow lining.*) You ever wonder what happens to the Sun when you shade your eyes or step under a tree to cool off? Ever wonder where those Rays of Sun end up once they're not needed anymore? (*RAY closes his coat.*) You got it. They end up right here. Just like the two of you.

THIRD STRING. What's your business here? Who threw *you* out?

IRIS. Nobody threw us out.

CAPTAIN ALSO. What?!

THIRD STRING. Then what are you doing in the Tunnel?!

MOZART. We're searching for our friend.

RAY. "Friend"—what's that? Won't find any of those down here.

IRIS. Why not?

RAY. If you're a friend, somebody wants you. There's no one like that down here.

MOZART. You see, we were living with the Goods, but we—

CAPTAIN ALSO. The GOODS?! We've got a couple of GOODS here?! Get 'em! (*THIRD STRING surprises IRIS and MOZART from behind, putting his ski pole under their chins, trapping them in place. RAY moves in on them as well.*) Oh, we've been waiting for this moment. Haven't we, Ray?

RAY. Since the day they turned me into shade.

CAPTAIN ALSO. And we're not alone. Do you hear them? (*The SOUND of the angry forgotten things begins to grow louder and louder.*) Do you hear all the angry, forgotten things? They've been waiting for you and now they'll have their revenge!

(*CAPTAIN ALSO gestures, quickly and dramatically, and the SOUND of the angry forgotten things stops, instantly.*)

THIRD STRING. Tell us your story, so we can devise your punishment.

CAPTAIN ALSO. Yeah—tell us what makes you SPECIAL. (*to MOZART*) You first.

MOZART. Me? Oh, nothing, really. Nothing in the least.

THIRD STRING. C'mon. You're a Good. Spill the beans.

MOZART. I've just written a few songs.

THIRD STRING. A few?

MOZART. Well, ten sonatas and three symphonies by the age of nine—

CAPTAIN ALSO. I see.

MOZART. But there's a song—or part of a song—that I'm still looking for.

RAY. You won't find it here. People *want* music—so, there's no music down here.

THIRD STRING (*to IRIS*). And what about you?

CAPTAIN ALSO. Yeah—what's your *story*?

IRIS. I don't have one.

THIRD STRING. Sure you do. Everybody's got a story. Even Ray.

RAY. It all started on a sunny day in a—

CAPTAIN ALSO & THIRD STRING. Shut up, Ray.

IRIS. I wish I had one. But I don't.

THIRD STRING. She's lying.

IRIS. All I have is a picture in my mind.

CAPTAIN ALSO. A picture of when you were *wanted?* A picture of your home?

IRIS. Yes, I think so—

CAPTAIN ALSO. Well, FORGET ABOUT IT. Because you'll never get back to it.

THIRD STRING. Nobody ever leaves the Tunnel.

MOZART. But, why?

CAPTAIN ALSO. Because *the only way out of here is to be* WANTED—

THIRD STRING. To be USEFUL—

RAY. So, we're TRAPPED—

CAPTAIN ALSO. Just like *you.*

(*They tighten their grips on IRIS and MOZART as ANNABEL LEE enters holding a wooden ship's wheel in her hand. Strapped over her shoulder is what appears to be a large fabric satchel of some kind. She goes directly to CAPTAIN ALSO, THIRD STRING, and RAY.*)

ANNABEL LEE. Unhand them this instant and prepare to set sail!

MOZART (*simultaneously*). Annabel Lee!

IRIS (*simultaneously*). There she is!

CAPTAIN ALSO. You know her?

ANNABEL LEE. There's a speedy escape should you do what I say—Or a watery grave should you me disobey.

RAY. Who are you?

ANNABEL LEE. When the fog is lifted and the tide is high—we will sail our ship and bid the Goods goodbye!

THIRD STRING. Ship? What ship?

ANNABEL LEE. Now, unhand them and see to your duties!

CAPTAIN ALSO. We don't answer to you, Miss WhoeverYouAre. These Goods are our prisoners here, and—

ANNABEL LEE. And I am your *captain.*

(*She tosses the ship's wheel to CAPTAIN ALSO, who catches it and holds it proudly. Silence, then—*)

THIRD STRING. You mean . . .

CAPTAIN ALSO. . . . . you *need us?*

ANNABEL LEE. I can't sail without you.

THIRD STRING. You mean . . .

RAY. . . . you'll *free us from the Tunnel?*

ANNABEL LEE. If you'll unhand my friends and serve as my crew—your discarded days will vanish from view. (*CAPTAIN ALSO, THIRD STRING, and RAY release their grip on IRIS and MOZART.*) *Now, fall in.* (*THIRD STRING and RAY line up next to CAPTAIN ALSO's shopping cart forming a line. ANNABEL LEE walks past them, taking stock of her new crew.*) The ship waits—trapped in fog—at the far end of this Tunnel. There are sails to mend, rigging to ready, and provisions to load.

> Are you able, willing, and sufficiently brave—
> To conquer the sea and make fear your slave?

CAPTAIN ALSO, THIRD STRING, RAY (*saluting*). We are!

ANNABEL LEE. Now, to the ship!

(*ANNABEL LEE gestures off, and the three of them rush off, pushing CAPTAIN ALSO, who steers with the ship's wheel. IRIS and MOZART approach ANNABEL LEE.*)

IRIS. How did you find the ship in all that fog?

ANNABEL LEE. I was looking for parts of your picture—the table, the flower, the vase. So, I kept following the Tunnel, on and on. And I saw something shining in the distance—a shimmering patch of light—and when I reached it—(*She removes the satchel from over her shoulder, and we see that it is actually a faded and weathered PastCoat, which she has used to carry an object. She unwraps the object. It is a vase—identical to that in the "Still Life."*) I found vases. Hundreds of them. Discarded in a huge pile.

(*ANNABEL LEE hands the vase to IRIS.*)

IRIS. Just like the picture in my mind.

ANNABEL LEE. And there the Tunnel empties into a cove shrouded in fog. And when I lifted this vase, the light cut through the fog and there it was . . . my ship, awaiting me.

(*IRIS has discovered the weathered PastCoat.*)

IRIS. Motes, look.

MOZART. Is that the coat you're looking for? Is it missing a button?

IRIS (*looking closely at the coat*). No. And it's too big to be a little girl's.

ANNABEL LEE. There are hundreds of those coats, piled up at the far end of the Tunnel.

IRIS. We'll need to get all of them. (*to ANNABEL LEE*) Can you make it back there?

ANNABEL LEE (*nods*). I found a shortcut through the water.

IRIS. Good. And take Motes with you.

(*IRIS takes the vase and rewraps it in the old PastCoat.*)

MOZART (*to ANNABEL LEE*). Wait . . . did you say *water?*

ANNABEL LEE (*tossing him a discarded life preserver*). It's an easy swim. There's only that ONE wave—

MOZART. I would like to rethink our entire plan—

(*ANNABEL LEE ushers MOZART off, and IRIS exits opposite as LIGHTS SHIFT to Miss Overlook's room. The table is now white. One of the chairs is painted white. Another is half-painted. The third remains a dirty brown. An open can of paint sits nearby. MISS OVERLOOK enters and sets a steaming cup of cocoa on the table in front of the one painted chair. She looks down at the table for a moment, touching the back of the white chair, as IRIS enters carrying the wrapped vase.*)

IRIS. Miss Overlook—

MISS OVERLOOK. Is Mozart with you? I have his cocoa for him.

IRIS. He'll be here. I wanted to ask you something.

MISS OVERLOOK. What do you have there?

(*IRIS unwraps the vase and sets it on the table. However, her focus is clearly on the PastCoat.*)

IRIS. It's something we found in the Tunnel. Would you hold on to it for me?

MISS OVERLOOK. By all means.

IRIS. What I wanted to ask you about was *this*. (*IRIS holds up the PastCoat, showing it to OVERLOOK.*) Have you ever seen this before?

(*Silence, as OVERLOOK looks at the coat.*)

MISS OVERLOOK. Not that coat, Iris. But one like it. On the day I met you.

IRIS. Yes, I remember that as well. It belonged to a little girl.

MISS OVERLOOK. It belonged to you. (*pause*) You had a coat like this.

IRIS. What happened to it?

MISS OVERLOOK. It's better that you don't know, Iris. That's what Mister Matternot said and I see now that he was right.

IRIS. But why would he say that?

MISS OVERLOOK. He took your coat from you. I watched him as he did it. (*pause*) At the time, I thought he was very kind. For before he took your coat, you were very upset—you were calling for your mother.

IRIS. My mother?

MISS OVERLOOK. Yes. But then, a moment later, he took your coat from you . . . and you were fine. (*pause*) He did it to protect you.

IRIS. I don't want that. Not anymore.

(*IRIS stares at her, then rushes out of the room, taking the coat with her.*)

MISS OVERLOOK. Iris—!

(*As LIGHTS SHIFT quickly to the Great Room, MISTER OTHERGUY and MISTER HIMTOO are putting a large, ornate glass case in place. It is an exact replica of the small case that held Iris's doll, including the lock on one side of it. MISTER MATTERNOT enters, watching, as GRETTA and GROTTO GOOD enter opposite.*)

MISTER MATTERNOT. Master Good, if I may ask, what is the meaning of this?

GROTTO GOOD. You may not ask. You may not ask it at all.

GRETTA GOOD. You were given a task, Matternot. You were told to bring us a little girl and make certain that she felt at home.

GROTTO GOOD. You were to remove any vestige of her past.

MISTER MATTERNOT. And that's what I did!

GROTTO GOOD. To the contrary—this girl, Iris, has grown curious about her before-Good life.

GRETTA GOOD. You have displeased us—

GROTTO GOOD. And we have your Fate under consideration.

MISTER MATTERNOT. And Iris—what of her? You can't hope to keep her here. Now that she is curious, she will—

GROTTO GOOD. It's no longer your concern.

GRETTA GOOD. We've found a fine place for her.

GROTTO GOOD. A fitting home for the greatest of our Goods!

(*The GOODS start off as IRIS enters carrying the old, tattered PastCoat and goes directly to MISTER MATTERNOT. Seeing IRIS, the GOODS stop at a distance, listening. MISTER OTHERGUY and MISTER HIMTOO stand on either side of the glass case.*)

IRIS. Mister Matternot—

MISTER MATTERNOT (*seeing the coat in her hand*). Iris, what do you have in your—

IRIS. The coat you showed me. It was *mine*, wasn't it? Tell me the truth. It was mine and you took it from me.

MISTER MATTERNOT. You had been *chosen*, Iris. The Great Goods had—

IRIS. You lied to me—

MISTER MATTERNOT. I was trying to save you—

IRIS. Save me?

MISTER MATTERNOT. From your sadness. From the loss of your home. Believe me, it was the only way I could—

IRIS. But why would you take my coat?

MISTER MATTERNOT. It holds your *past*, Iris—it holds the story of your life.

GROTTO GOOD (*stepping in*). Matternot—!

IRIS. Take me back there.

MISTER MATTERNOT. I can't—

IRIS. Take me back to that room—

MISTER MATTERNOT. That room is gone. (*forcefully*) Just like your mother. It is gone and you must forget about it.

IRIS. Who was she? *Tell me.*

(*The GOODS approach IRIS.*)

GRETTA GOOD. Your life is here with us, Iris.

GROTTO GOOD. We've given you the BEST things in all the world—

IRIS. You've given me everything but the thing I want most: *the story of who I am*. Even the common, forgotten things know where they came from—but I don't. I wish I was one of them.

GRETTA GOOD (*simultaneously*). Don't say that—

GROTTO GOOD (*simultaneously*). Iris, that's enough—

IRIS (*to MATTERNOT, desperately*). *I want you to take me to that room!*

MISTER MATTERNOT (*simultaneously*). But, Iris, I—

GRETTA GOOD. (*simultaneously*). Put it out of your mind.

GROTTO GOOD. We have a greater place for you, Iris!

(*GROTTO and GRETTA clap their hands, and OTHERGUY and HIMTOO step forward and grab IRIS. The old, tattered PastCoat falls to the ground.*)

MISTER MATTERNOT. What are you doing?

IRIS. Let go of me—

GRETTA GOOD. You will be the glory of Great Island!

(*MUSIC, as MATTERNOT runs toward IRIS but is restrained by OTHERGUY as*

HIMTOO takes IRIS to the glass case. The GOODS remove the lock and open the door to the case.)

MISTER MATTERNOT. You can't do this. You must tell her—you must tell her the truth!

GRETTA GOOD. Had you done your job well, this could have been avoided—

IRIS (*cries out*). No—please don't do this!

GRETTA GOOD. But now she must pay for your mistakes—

MISTER MATTERNOT. No, listen to me—

GROTTO GOOD. Her pain is your doing, Matternot. Her sadness is your curse.

(IRIS is placed inside the glass case. The lock is attached by GROTTO, who holds the large key ring with the one key aloft, proudly. IRIS stands, trying to plead with the GOODS through the glass: "Why are you doing this?" "Please, don't leave me in here!" etc., but she cannot be heard. The GOODS exit, followed by OTHERGUY and HIMTOO. IRIS stares out, helplessly, as MATTERNOT tries to talk to her through the glass.)

MISTER MATTERNOT (*painfully, from his heart*). I was afraid, Iris, afraid of the wrath of the Goods—that they'd send me to the Tunnel and I would die alone and forgotten. But worse than the Tunnel is what I've done to you; given you glimpses of your home and nothing more. (*pause*) What our memory leaves unfinished, our heart completes with ache. (*MATTERNOT puts his ungloved hand up and presses it against the glass. IRIS looks at him, then matches his gesture with her hand.*) Forgive me, Iris.

(ANNABEL LEE and MOZART rush on. MOZART carries a huge bundle of PastCoats in his arms.)

ANNABEL LEE. What have you done with her?!

MISTER MATTERNOT. I was trying to—

MOZART (*dropping the coats to the ground*). You've locked her up behind glass.

MISTER MATTERNOT. No, it was the Goods who—

(The GOODS rush on, followed by MISTER OTHERGUY and MISTER HIMTOO.)

GRETTA GOOD. What is all the motion and commotion?!

GROTTO GOOD (*seeing ANNABEL LEE*). And what are you doing here?! You were discarded!

ANNABEL LEE. Well, I'm *back.*

(MATTERNOT is now standing near the pile of PastCoats.)

MISTER MATTERNOT (*forcefully, to the GOODS*). Now I see what you've done! (*He kneels amid the coats, lifting armfuls of them as he speaks.*) All these years—I had no idea!

GROTTO GOOD (*simultaneously*). What is that?

GRETTA GOOD (*simultaneously*). What's there?

MISTER MATTERNOT. *Coats*. Look at all of them!

GRETTA GOOD. We've given each of them a Great Good life.

MISTER MATTERNOT. You told me there were only *two*. Only Iris and her mother. But there have been HUNDREDS!

GROTTO GOOD. Not another word, Matternot—

MISTER MATTERNOT (*referring to HIMTOO and OTHERGUY*). You've done this to *all of us*, haven't you?!

GROTTO GOOD (*throwing the key ring to OTHERGUY*). Lock him away as well!

(*As OTHERGUY catches the key ring and starts toward MATTERNOT, MATTERNOT throws one of the PastCoats from the pile to OTHERGUY, saying—*)

MISTER MATTERNOT. You've ripped the past from each and every one of us!

(*Upon catching the coat, OTHERGUY stops. He looks down at the coat, holding it tightly in one hand, the key ring in the other, then he looks at the GOODS—puzzled, wanting an answer.*)

GRETTA GOOD. You've been given an order, Mister Otherguy—

MISTER MATTERNOT (*to OTHERGUY*). That's not your name. Your name was stolen from you by the Goods—

GROTTO GOOD. Mister Himtoo—take that coat from him!

(*As HIMTOO rushes at OTHERGUY, MATTERNOT throws a coat from the pile to HIMTOO, who, upon catching it, immediately stops. He, too, looks at the coat, then up at the GOODS—puzzled, wanting an answer.*)

MISTER MATTERNOT. It's too late—now they know the truth.

(*OTHERGUY and HIMTOO look at their coats, at each other. Then they put their coats on and approach the GOODS with menace.*)

GROTTO GOOD. This, Gretta, is a great good problem.

(*MATTERNOT lifts the pile of PastCoats from the ground—inadvertently leaving behind the single, tattered PastCoat, which is laying elsewhere, and rushes off, saying—*)

MISTER MATTERNOT. Soon everyone will know!

GROTTO GOOD (*simultaneously*). NO—

GRETTA GOOD (*simultaneously*). MATTERNOT—

(*The GOODS start to rush off after MATTERNOT but are stopped by OTHERGUY and HIMTOO. ANNABEL LEE takes the key from OTHERGUY and opens the glass case, freeing IRIS, saying—*)

ANNABEL LEE. Don't worry, Iris. My ship is rigged and ready—

MOZART. And her crew is second to none—

ANNABEL LEE. And the moment the fog is lifted, we shall sail away and be gone.

IRIS. Thank you both.

(*OTHERGUY and HIMTOO begin to place the GOODS inside the glass case.*)

GROTTO GOOD (*to OTHERGUY and HIMTOO*). You wouldn't dare!

GRETTA GOOD. Grotto, dear, what will become of us?!

(*ANNABEL LEE tosses the key back to OTHERGUY, and the GOODS are locked inside, silently pleading for help.*)

MOZART. Now, let's get off this island before being a Good gets any worse.

(*ANNABEL LEE sees the tattered PastCoat that was left behind. She lifts it.*)

ANNABEL LEE. Mister Matternot left this behind—the old and tattered one.

IRIS (*taking it from her*). I'll bring it with me. C'mon—

(*IRIS rushes off, followed by ANNABEL LEE and MOZART, as the MUSIC CHANGES to that of the "Still Life," and LIGHTS SHIFT to Miss Overlook's room. MISS OVERLOOK holds a paintbrush in her hand, making a few final brush strokes on the third and final white chair. The table and chairs in the room are now all painted white. She positions the vase in the center of the table. She moves the cocoa slightly so that it is now in the exact position seen in the "Still Life." The "Still Life" is now lacking only the iris. OVERLOOK takes a long look at the table, then exits—exactly as she did in Act One—as MISTER MATTERNOT enters opposite. He now carries only one PastCoat in his arms. He stops when he sees the white table and vase.*)

MISTER MATTERNOT. Miss Overlook?

(*No response. MATTERNOT takes a long look at the table. Then he lowers the coat, revealing something he is holding in his hands . . . it is an iris. He places the iris in the vase. The "Still Life" is now complete. MUSIC CONTINUES as MATTERNOT steps away from the table, and IRIS enters, carrying the old, tattered PastCoat. IRIS stops when she sees the "Still Life." She steps toward the table and walks around it slowly. IRIS takes the button from her pouch. She closes her eyes and rubs it in her hand as the LIGHT on the table grows brighter and brighter. She opens her eyes and compares the picture in her mind with the picture in front of her. They are identical. The MUSIC FADES away.*)

IRIS (*quietly*). That's it.

(*IRIS moves to the table. She pulls "her" chair back from the table, exactly as she did in Act One. She sits. She looks at the vase, the flower, the cocoa in front of her. Then, just as she did in Act One, she begins to reach for the cocoa, as MISS OVERLOOK enters.*)

MISS OVERLOOK (*simply*). Careful. That's hot.

IRIS (*Looks at her. Then, simply, quietly*). Mom.

MISS OVERLOOK. Yes, I know, Iris. I know you miss her. Whoever she is, wherever she's gone. (*MATTERNOT takes the PastCoat and walks toward OVER-LOOK. She looks at him, puzzled.*) Mister Matternot?

MISTER MATTERNOT. I'd like you to meet someone.

(*MATTERNOT helps OVERLOOK put on the coat — her PastCoat. When it is on, she looks first at the table . . . and then at IRIS.*)

MOM [formerly MISS OVERLOOK] (*quietly*). Iris. (*IRIS and MOM embrace.*) Oh, Iris, I'm right here. And now, wherever you are, no matter how far away —

IRIS. —when you call my name, I'll hear you.

MOM. Thank you, Mister Matternot. (*MOM turns and looks at MATTERNOT. Then she approaches him.*) I'd like to see your hands, if I could. (*MOM helps MATTER-NOT remove his gloves. He stares at her, puzzled. MOM hands the gloves to IRIS. IRIS takes them, confused.*) Here, Iris. These gloves belong in your pouch. (*MOM touches the palms of MATTERNOT's hands as she looks into his eyes, speaking softly.*) These scars on your hands. They belong to the man who roped the moon every night, and hauled it down out of the sky. And then he'd give the signal for the sun to rise . . .

IRIS (*looking at MATTERNOT*). . . . . and the day to break.

(*MOM holds out her hand, and IRIS hands her the tattered PastCoat. MOM helps MATTERNOT put his PastCoat on.*)

MOM. Do you remember us?

DAD [formerly MISTER MATTERNOT] (*quietly*). Yes.

MOM. Even with your coat tattered and torn?

DAD. Your name is Rose.

MOM. Yes. (*pause*) And this is your daughter, Iris.

(*IRIS and DAD stare at each other.*)

IRIS. I thought you left us.

DAD. The Great Goods took me away, Iris. Just like you.

IRIS. Do you remember me?

DAD. You were just a baby. And my coat is old and worn —

IRIS. Don't worry, Dad — we'll be your coat. We'll tell you everything you missed.

(*DAD and IRIS embrace as ANNABEL LEE and MOZART enter. ANNABEL LEE is carrying a smaller PastCoat in her arms.*)

MOZART. The coats have all been returned, Iris.

ANNABEL LEE. We've given everyone back their Pasts.

MOM. And what of the Goods?

DAD. The Goods' reign is over. They work for *us* now.

ANNABEL LEE. They're loading Motes's piano onto my ship.

MOZART (*deliciously*). *One note at a time.*

ANNABEL LEE (*holding up the coat*). There's one coat left, Iris.

(*DAD takes the coat from ANNABEL LEE. MOM and DAD put the PastCoat on IRIS, and then stand, holding each other, arm in arm.*)

IRIS. Thank you. (*turning to ANNABEL LEE and MOZART*) I hope you find your song, Motes.

MOZART. I'll try again tonight. Perhaps I'll find it just before the sun rises.

IRIS (*giving ANNABEL LEE the button*). Annabel Lee, this is for you.

ANNABEL LEE. But this button—it's part of your coat—

IRIS. And now I'm part of yours. (*ANNABEL LEE smiles.*) I'll lift the fog for you as soon as I get home.

(*ANNABEL LEE and IRIS embrace.*)

MOZART. Hey, Iris—

IRIS. What?

MOZART. Are you going to drink that cocoa?

IRIS (*smiles and hands the cup of cocoa to MOZART*). Take it with you, Motes.

(*ANNABEL LEE and MOZART leave, saying—*)

ANNABEL LEE (*simultaneously*). Good sailing, Iris!

MOZART (*simultaneously*). Adieu!

(*IRIS looks at her MOM and DAD, who have taken their places at the table. IRIS joins them.*)

IRIS. But how will *we* get home?

DAD (*simply*). By *remembering*.

MOM (*quietly*). What do you see, Iris?

IRIS (*slowly, quietly*). I see an iris in a vase. And the vase is on a table. And the table is in a house. And the house is—

(*A flourish of MUSIC, as LIGHTS REVEAL the Land of Nocturno, once again—identical to the beginning of the play. The "WELCOME TO NOCTURNO" sign is there. The rain barrel is there, marked with the number of a new batch. And approaching the table from a distance are HAZEL and ELMER, each holding a still-spotless Ladybug, and the FLOWER PAINTER, painting a rose.)*

IRIS (*opens her eyes*). —in Nocturno, our home!

ELMER (*simultaneously*). Hazel, look—

HAZEL (*simultaneously*). Iris!

FLOWER PAINTER (*simultaneously*). Here they are!

(*IRIS, MOM, and DAD step away from the table.*)

IRIS. Does it look the same to you, Dad?

DAD (*looking around*). Some of it does . . .

(*The FLOWER PAINTER gives the rose to MOM as HAZEL and ELMER approach IRIS.*)

FLOWER PAINTER. Welcome home, Rose. The wind's been silent without you.

MOM (*smiles*). You'll hear it again in no time.

HAZEL (*to IRIS, like she never left*). Did you find the spots, Iris?

IRIS. The what?

ELMER (*holding up his Ladybug*). For the Ladybugs?

(*IRIS reaches into her PastCoat and removes one large black spot. She hands it to ELMER.*)

IRIS. Where I was, Elmer, they only had *one.*

(*HAZEL smiles and embraces IRIS as ELMER looks puzzled, and the MEMORY MENDER pushes his cart into the midst of the celebration, cranky as ever.*)

MEMORY MENDER. Well, look at this, a bunch a people huggin' and pattin' each other on their coats—when they oughta be takin' care of each sleeve and button and—

DAD (*approaches the MEMORY MENDER with a smile of recognition*). Well, one thing in Nocturno hasn't changed. You're still as cranky as ever!

(*A pause while the MEMORY MENDER stares at DAD, trying hard to place him in his memory. The others look on. The MEMORY MENDER looks hard at DAD while at the same time touching various parts of his own coat, saying —*)

MEMORY MENDER. Wait—wait—wait—don't tell me—(*After a few tries, the MEMORY MENDER touches a small button at the end of his sleeve, saying —*) The Day Breaker! Husband of Rose, father of Iris.

DAD (*shaking his hand*). That's me.

MEMORY MENDER. I gotta tighten that button down before I *lose you completely.* (*to IRIS*) I see you found your coat, Iris. Welcome home.

IRIS. Thank you.

MEMORY MENDER (*to DAD*). And you know, I had to rope the moon for you every night while you've been gone. It's awful hard on the hands—

DAD. Yes, it is.

MEMORY MENDER. In fact, I just now put her away for the day.

DAD. Have you given the sun her signal to rise?

MEMORY MENDER. Have at it. I got coats to sew. (*He moves away, still talking.*) People 'round here think the past's just some kind of toy that their mind plays with, but you gotta take care of it or you'll trip and get a rip—(*The MEMORY MENDER moves upstage and looks on as he sews. The others turn and look at DAD.*)

DAD (*turning to IRIS and MOM*). Ready?

(*From a great distance MUSIC PLAYS the first few phases of the Serenade in G from "Eine kleine Nachtmusik," as before. DAD reaches out his arm in front of him, preparing to raise it, as IRIS steps in, interrupting him.*)

IRIS. Wait, Dad. Wait one . . . more . . . moment. (*As soon as IRIS has said this, the full Mozart serenade continues and plays on—uninterrupted—for the first time. IRIS nods to her DAD, smiling. EVERYONE looks out at the horizon. IRIS stands next to her DAD, as he reaches his arm out in front of him, preparing to give the sun its "signal," preparing to break the new day.*) Almost day.

DAD. Almost day, indeed.

(*DAD lifts his arm dramatically in front of him, as upstage a huge sun lifts into place and a brilliant orange glow illuminates all of them. The MUSIC BUILDS and fills the theatre as the people of Nocturno gradually return to their work, except for IRIS, who stands front, home at last, looking up into the glorious morning light as the LIGHTS FADE to black.*)

END OF PLAY

Honus & Me

Steven Dietz

Premiere production, Seattle Children's Theatre, 2006.

Production credits from the premiere of *Honus & Me* and details concerning performance rights are included in the acting edition of the play as published by Dramatic Publishing.

When I was a boy growing up in Kansas, a friend of mine and I talked about what we wanted to be when we grew up. I told him I wanted to be a real major league baseball player, a genuine professional like Honus Wagner. My friend said that he'd like to be president of the United States. Neither of us got our wish.

Dwight D. Eisenhower

Cast of Characters

(6m., 2w., doubling as indicated)

JOEY STOSHACK: a 10-year-old boy (played by an adult actor).
MOM / FIRST LADY FAN
DAD / AUCTIONEER / FRIENDLY FAN
MISS YOUNG / SECOND LADY FAN
BIRDIE / BLUEBIRDS TEAMMATE / PIRATES TEAMMATE
RAVENS PITCHER / TIGERS PITCHER
HONUS WAGNER / SILHOUETTE FIGURE
HAWKS PITCHER / CHUCK / TY COBB / RAVENS CATCHER
COACH / MR. MENDOZA / SPORTSWRITER / HECKLER

Others:

BLUEBIRDS TEAM
HAWKS TEAM / HAWKS TEAMMATE 1 / HAWKS TEAMMATE 2
VOICE OF UMPIRE
ANNOUNCER'S VOICE
SINGING BOSTON FANS
RAVENS TEAM

Character Notes

MOM: Wears a jacket over the uniform of a registered nurse.
DAD: Dressed casually, wearing a Pittsburgh Pirates baseball cap.
COACH: Wears a baseball cap and a whistle.
BIRDIE: Attire is part jock, part biker, part bouncer. He wears a huge jeweled wrestler belt around his waist.
CHUCK: An odd, laconic, slightly menacing teenager.
MR. MENDOZA: Wears a suit.
RAVENS TEAM: Their baseball caps are black and their black jerseys have sweatshirt-type hoods, which they wear over their caps in Grim Reaper fashion.

Time and Place

The present and 1909. Pittsburgh.

Setting

An open playing space that will depict a variety of locales. The central arena for the play is that of a baseball diamond, which should only be suggested, not depicted in a realistic manner. Other small units include:

LITTLE LEAGUE BASEBALL FIELDS

MISS YOUNG'S YARD

MISS YOUNG'S ATTIC: A small area with an eccentric collection of odds and ends such as rusty birdcages, broken chairs, old lamps, vintage suitcases, bundled papers, and boxes.

BIRDIE'S HOME RUN HEAVEN SHOP: A glass case filled with baseball memorabilia serves as the counter. A small cash register or cash box sits atop it.

A LIBRARY

JOEY'S ROOM: A small bed and a nightstand. On the nightstand is a small lamp and a modern, digital clock.

JOEY'S FRONT YARD

A HOTEL ROOM

BENNETT PARK: The former ballpark in Detroit.

Note on Pronunciation

Despite the popular notion that Honus Wagner's first name rhymed with "bonus," his biographers and the National Baseball Hall of Fame have established that it is pronounced "Hawn-ess," a variation of "Hans." Stoshack is pronounced "Stow-shack." "Stosh" rhymes with gosh.

Note on Updating

The year mentioned in the text (2006), as well as the names of contemporary ballplayers, may be updated as needed.

ACT I

(Music plays and the CAST enters from various directions. They are seen in silhouette against the blue sky. They take their positions facing upstage and remove their caps, as though gazing at a distant, unseen flag. Farthest downstage is JOEY STOSHACK, facing front. After a moment, his DAD taps JOEY on the shoulder, reminding him to remove his cap. JOEY does. He turns and faces upstage like the others. A moment of stillness and expectation as the music reaches a crescendo. Then the VOICE OF UMPIRE calls out "Play ball!" Lights shift to reveal a Little League baseball field. JOEY is isolated in light downstage in the batter's box, facing the audience. His uniform says "BLUEBIRDS." He speaks to the audience between pitches. The HAWKS PITCHER is behind JOEY on a raised mound facing offstage left, to where he'll pitch. The BLUEBIRDS TEAM and the HAWKS TEAM might occupy benches to either side of the stage, or their voices can be heard as a recording.)

JOEY. OK. It makes no sense. Let me tell you that right away. It makes no sense
    at all. But still, the thing is —

(The pitch comes in. JOEY takes it. The sound of a ball hitting a mitt.)

VOICE OF UMPIRE. Strrrieeeeeeeeeek.

JOEY *(prepares for the next pitch)*. See, there's this thing — this thing that hap-
    pens whenever I hold a baseball card in my hands. It's happened since the
    first time I ever touched one. My hands, well, my hands start to . . . *tingle.*
    And if it's a really *old* card, well . . . my whole body starts to tingle. *(beat)* See,
    I told you it makes no sense.

(Another pitch comes in. JOEY takes it. The sound of a ball hitting a mitt.)

VOICE OF UMPIRE. Strrrieeeeeeeeeeeeeeeeeeeke!

JOEY *(steps out of the box, speaking to the unseen UMPIRE)*. Time out! *(to audience)*
    It's kind of like static electricity shooting through me. Like all of a sudden I
    have this . . . power. This *magical power.* But on the baseball field —

HAWKS TEAM. Sto-shack, Sto-shack —

JOEY. I don't have these powers.

HAWKS TEAM. — he's a no-hack!

(laughter)

JOEY. I'm an OK player, but under pressure — I freeze up.

HAWKS TEAMMATE 1. Hey No-Hack — could your ears be any bigger?!

HAWKS TEAMMATE 2. It looks like your head is growing wings!

HAWKS TEAMMATE 1. He looks like Dumbo!

VOICE OF UMPIRE. Batter up!

HAWKS TEAM. BATTER UP, DUMBO!

(*More laughter as JOEY's COACH appears, in the middle of a cell phone call.*)

JOEY. Whenever I look back to my coach, he just says something like—

COACH (*looks up, briefly*). Remember, Joey, even a blind squirrel can sometimes find a nut!

JOEY. It's not encouraging.

(*JOEY steps into the batter's box.*)

HAWK TEAM (*chanting*). STRIKE HIM OUT! STRIKE HIM OUT! STRIKE HIM OUT!

JOEY. See, we're down by one run in the bottom of the sixth—and I'm our last chance. Two outs. Two strikes. I've already struck out *three times* this game, and the only thing worse than the other team making fun of me is the sound of the guys on my team *packing up our equipment* 'cause they know it's over.

BLUEBIRD TEAMMATE. We're *hungry*, Joey. Just swing and *get it over with*.

(*The pitch comes in. JOEY swings and misses, badly. The sound of a ball hitting a mitt, as before.*)

VOICE OF UMPIRE. Strrrike threeee! Youuu'rree ooouuuuutt!

(*cheers and groans from the respective teams*)

COACH (*walking past JOEY*). Hey, Stoshack—how's your handwriting?

JOEY. My what?

COACH. I'm thinkin' you might make *oneheckuva good scorekeeper*. (*into cell phone*) Yeah, four times—he's the Strikeout King, that kid.

(*COACH goes as the HAWKS PITCHER approaches.*)

HAWKS PITCHER. Nice try, No-Hack.

JOEY. It's *Stoshack*.

HAWKS PITCHER. Yeah, whatever. Don't worry about it. Seriously. (*puts a consoling arm around JOEY's shoulder*) I didn't used to be able to hit, either.

JOEY. Really?

HAWKS PITCHER. Yeah.

JOEY. Then what happened?

HAWKS PITCHER. My mommy changed my diaper and everything was fine!

(*The HAWKS PITCHER shoves JOEY down and runs off, laughing with the HAWKS TEAM as JOEY's DAD appears. He hands JOEY his mitt.*)

DAD. It's OK, Joe. Don't listen to these jokers.

JOEY. Hi, Dad.

DAD. You'll get 'em next time. I just know it.

JOEY (*glum*). Thanks. (*JOEY's MOM appears opposite, holding JOEY's backpack.*) Hi, Mom.

MOM. You're not the only one who struck out, Joey.

JOEY. But I was the *last* one. I'm always the last one.

(*Silence. JOEY is waiting for his MOM and DAD to say something, anything, to each other. They don't.*) Mom, I'd like you to meet *Dad*. Dad, this is Mom.

MOM (simultaneously). Very funny—

Dad (simultaneously). Look, Joey—

JOEY. Would it, like, *kill you* to say something to each other? (*More silence.*) OK. Forget it.

DAD (*to MOM*). I thought we might go get some pizza.

MOM. Not tonight, Tom.

DAD. Oh, come on—

MOM. He has homework.

DAD. What's it going to hurt, Beth? We won't be late.

MOM (*simultaneously*). See, this is the thing. This is the thing you—

DAD (*simultaneously*). Can we not do this.

MOM. When I *call you*, when I try to make some *plans* for the two of you—

DAD. Forget it.

MOM. —some night when it would help me out, because I'm working *sixty-some hours a week*—

DAD. I said *forget it*.

MOM. —but on *those nights* when I really need you, where are you then?!

DAD. It's *pizza*. I'm not taking him *across the country*—I'm talking about PIZZA. I'm talking about spending one hour with my son!

(*This lands. She stares at him.*)

MOM. Ask him, then. It's his decision.

(*beat*)

DAD. Whaddya say, Joe? Want to grab a slice down at Angelo's?

JOEY. Mom—

MOM. You're old enough to make this decision on your own, Joey. It's up to you.

(*silence*)

JOEY. Sure.

DAD. Great.

JOEY. But can we—

DAD. Anything.

JOEY. —can we *all* go? All three of us?

(DAD gives MOM a long look.)

DAD *(quietly)*. I don't think so, Joe.

(pause)

JOEY. Then . . . maybe another time, OK?

(pause)

DAD. OK.

JOEY. Thanks for coming, Dad.

DAD. Hey, you did great. *(takes JOEY's bat and demonstrates)* Remember what we talked about. Keep your knees bent, your head down and your hands just a little bit apart—like this . . .

JOEY *(eager to learn)*. What does that do?

DAD. Gives you a little more bat speed.

JOEY. OK. Thanks.

DAD. Hey—did you get any new baseball cards?

JOEY. I've got my eye on a David Eckstein rookie card—and maybe an Omar Vizquel.

DAD. You love those shortstops.

JOEY. That's my position, you know that. Even though I usually just ride the bench.

DAD *(warmly)*. Come here. *(DAD gives JOEY a hug.)* I'll see you Friday.

(MOM mouths the words "thank you" to DAD. DAD goes.)

MOM. You OK?

JOEY *(regarding the backpack)*. You bring snacks?

MOM. Yep.

JOEY. Then I'm OK. *(JOEY sits near his MOM. He opens his backpack and munches on a snack during the following.)* You got off early.

MOM. I traded with Vicki.

JOEY. Why do you do that?

MOM. I wanted to see your game.

JOEY. Yeah, and then you'll have to work a *double shift* tomorrow and you'll be exhausted and your feet will hurt and you'll say, "When I win the lottery, I'm never setting foot inside that hospital again!" (*MOM laughs, enjoying this.*) It's not funny.

MOM (*mock serious*). No, not funny.

JOEY. Mom—

MOM. It's serious. Very, very serious.

JOEY. Stop it.

MOM. The first thing I'll do with my lottery money is buy you some new shoes.

JOEY. I like these shoes.

MOM. I can see your socks.

JOEY. It's just a little hole—

MOM (*repeating*). *I can see your socks, Joey.*

JOEY. —and it's nothing to worry about because I filled it with a baseball card. Look. (*Joey removes his shoe, from which he removes a baseball card.*) It works perfect.

(*JOEY hands the card to MOM.*)

MOM (*regarding the card*). *Larvell Blanks?*

JOEY. Utility infielder. Nine seasons. Two-fifty-three average. Twenty home runs. His nickname was "Sugar Bear."

MOM. Never heard of him.

JOEY (*taking the card back*). Me neither, but he keeps my feet dry. So when you *do* win the lottery, you can buy me a whole bunch of new baseball cards and get us a great big house with a yard for *my new dog* and lots of rooms—

MOM (*dryly*). With a *maid* to clean them.

JOEY. Yes, of course, and a big kitchen with a built-in TV for me and Dad to watch the ball games—one of those TVs that has a *split screen* so we can watch one game on *this side* and the other game—

MOM. Money doesn't solve everything, Joey.

JOEY. It would get you and Dad back together.

MOM. That's not true, honey—

JOEY. All those arguments, I heard them, you know, and at least HALF of them were about money—Dad losing a job, you working too much at the hospital . . .

MOM. Joey, look—

JOEY (*sharp*). Mom, it's TRUE. (*beat*) You know it's true.

(*pause*)

MOM. It's not going to happen. So let's not worry about it. OK? (*stands, gathers their things*) I got you a job to make a little spending money.

JOEY. What kind of job?

MOM. Miss Young on the corner. She needs her attic cleaned out. She'll pay you $10.

JOEY. Mom, Miss Young is like a *hundred years old*.

MOM. Well, yes.

JOEY. Or *older.* I think she's even *older.* I think she'll never die. And you know why, Mom? She's a *witch*.

MOM. Joey —

JOEY. Ask anyone! Old Miss Young is a witch who rides around on a broomstick.

MOM. She does not ride around on —

JOEY. What do you want to bet that when I go over there she's holding a BROOM?! And I bet her house is filled with the bodies of kids who went there to clean out her attic! (*scary sound*) Whawhahwhahwhwhahwhwhah whwhaa!!!

MOM (*starts to leave*). C'mon, kiddo, you've got homework to do.

JOEY (*scooping up and flinging imaginary grounders*). I'm not your kiddo. I'm Jeter! I'm Jimmy Rollins! I'm Miguel Tejada! (*Lights isolate him. To audience.*) Miss Young lives at the end of our street, in an old dark house with peeling paint — and big trees that scrape against the walls when it's windy. And it's *always windy* at that house.

(*MISS YOUNG's yard. MISS YOUNG appears, holding a broom. Nearby is an old garbage can.*)

MISS YOUNG. Joey Stoshack, you're shootin' up like a weed. (*beat*) What? You've never seen a *broom* before?

JOEY. Uh, yeah, sure.

MISS YOUNG. Your mom told you I had $10 for you, huh?

JOEY. Well, she said —

MISS YOUNG (*overlapping*). Better in your pocket than in mine. I got no use for money. But you, you could buy yourself some new shoes.

JOEY. I *like* these shoes.

MISS YOUNG. Maybe you'll see some up in the attic. Anything you want up there, Joey — *take it*. I just want it gone.

JOEY. OK.

MISS YOUNG. Still playing ball?

JOEY. Yeah.

MISS YOUNG. Who's your team? The Pirates?

JOEY. No. My dad's a Pirates fan, but I kind of like the Red Sox—

MISS YOUNG. Oh, Joey, *don't do that*—

JOEY. And the Cubs—

MISS YOUNG. Oh, *stop right there*—

JOEY. And the Mariners.

(*beat*)

MISS YOUNG. The who?

JOEY. The Mariners. Seattle. *Seattle, Washington?*

MISS YOUNG. They have a team way out there?

JOEY (*disbelieving*). Yeah, sure.

MISS YOUNG. That's still Indian country, isn't it?

JOEY. Well, *no*, Seattle's a pretty big—

MISS YOUNG. Well, good for them. You know, there's two kinds of people in this world: people who like baseball and people who *will* like baseball when they stop being *idiots*. My papa took me to my first game, right here in Pittsburgh at Exposition Park. In those days, the team was called the *Alleghenys*, named after the river. But the next year they stole away a second baseman from the Athletics, who were mad as heck about it, and took to calling the Pittsburgh team a bunch of "pirates." The name stuck.

JOEY. I never knew that.

MISS YOUNG. Oh, I was just a little girl, but I still remember those player's names: Ducky Hemp and Doggie Miller, Phenomenal Smith and Peek-A-Boo Veach. (*Off JOEY's look*) You don't believe me?

JOEY. Well—

MISS YOUNG (*sharp*). *Look 'em up*—you'll see. Heck, it was a manager of the Pirates who invented those flip-up sunglasses that the players wear.

JOEY. Really?

MISS YOUNG. Fred Clarke. He's in the Hall of Fame. And you've heard of Forbes Field?

JOEY. My dad told me about it.

MISS YOUNG. I was there when Babe Ruth hit a ball over the right-field roof. That was never done again.

JOEY. Babe Ruth . . . ?

MISS YOUNG. *And it was the last home run he ever hit. (Pause. He is staring at her.)* What is it?

JOEY. Nothing.

MISS YOUNG. You want to ask me something?

JOEY. No, I don't.

MISS YOUNG. Better ask it now, kid. Next time you're here I might be dead.

JOEY. Well . . . *how old are you?*

MISS YOUNG. You know what Satchel Paige said about that, don't you? "How old would you be if you didn't know how old you were?"

JOEY. You mean you don't know how old you are?

MISS YOUNG. I mean I'm as old as I *feel*, Joey. And right about now, that's pretty darn old. But, let me tell you, once upon a time . . . *(reaches into the garbage can. Music of a solo trumpet playing a slow, lovely version of "Take Me Out to the Ball Game.")* Here. Take a look. *(hands him a small photograph that has been torn in half)* See that fella? He was a ballplayer. And my, oh my, Joey, we were *young*. Someone took our picture in a garden on a Sunday afternoon.

JOEY. But why's it torn?

MISS YOUNG. When he left for spring training, he tore it in half so he could have my picture till we saw each other again. *(pause)* Throw it away, Joey. It's useless.

(music out)

JOEY. But what happened—didn't he come back?

MISS YOUNG. Like all the rest of that junk. *Useless.*

(And MISS YOUNG is gone.)

JOEY *(to audience)*. But I didn't throw it away. I'm a *collector.* I never throw *anything* away—especially a picture of a ballplayer. *(lifts the broom and drags the garbage can with him)* As I walked up to the attic, I looked into Miss Young's rooms. The walls were covered with old hats and dried flowers . . . and *guns.* Old shotguns. A lot of them. I pushed open the door to the attic, and right away I knew . . . *(MISS YOUNG's attic. The SOUND OF WIND begins to be heard, growing in intensity.)* I'd made a terrible mistake. This was gonna take me all day and night! *(beat)* But then—right there in my brain—I heard my mom's voice.

(A light on MOM. She speaks as JOEY mouths her words.)

MOM. Nothing gets finished until you make a start.

(And MOM is gone.)

JOEY. How does she *do* that? It's *sneaky.* *(lifts a large old box)* I worked for a couple hours, then decided to carry one more box downstairs and take a break. *(The box breaks — CRASH! He stares at the mess. Beat.)* Break time! *(Plops down in the midst of the mess. As he speaks, he rummages through the items on the ground around him.)* The junk in the box was mostly papers. *(wadding up the papers, tossing them into the trashcan)* Old bank statements and letters, faded old magazines and telegrams. And then, all of a sudden . . . *(He stops and stares down near him, on the ground. He lifts something. It is a small piece of cardboard about 1.5 by 3 inches. Music under the following.)* My hand started to *tingle.* It was a tiny piece of cardboard. On one side was printed the words "Piedmont. The Cigarette of Quality. Baseball Series. 150 Subjects." *(slowly turns the card around and looks at the front)* And now my whole *body* was starting to tingle. Because when I turned the card around, I saw . . . *(Upstage a huge replica of the famous card is slowly revealed.)* A *ballplayer.* Brown hair parted down the middle. Uniform buttoned to the top. The letters on his chest spelled out "Pittsburg," *without the "h" at the end.* And beneath his picture . . . the greatest thing of all — his name. *(lets out a joyous whoop)* WAA-HOO! *(and then instantly panics)* OH, NO! *(looks down at the card)* Fingerprints! Got to be careful! *(locates a vintage lace handkerchief and wraps the card in it)* Can't get any smudges or creases or anything on this card, because . . . *(pulls a small Tupperware container from his backpack, quickly dumps the sandwich it contains into the trash and places the wrapped card carefully inside the container)* This . . . baby . . . is . . . *MINT.* *(looks up at the audience)* Do you have any idea what something like this is *worth?*

(An AUCTIONEER appears. He stands before the huge replica of the card, addressing a crowd.)

AUCTIONEER. The Honus Wagner T-206 baseball card is, indisputably, the most valuable baseball card in the world. Unlike every other major league player of his day, Wagner objected to having the American Tobacco Company print and distribute a card bearing his likeness. And thus, only about 40 cards survive.

JOEY. Make that *41.*

AUCTIONEER. Our bidding today will start at 500 —

JOEY. Five hundred — is that all?

AUCTIONEER. —*thousand* dollars. Do I have an initial bid of 500,000? *(His patter begins.)* Yes! Five hundred thousand — do I have 550? Five-fifty? Yes! Do I hear six? Six hundred thousand?

JOEY. Oh.

AUCTIONEER. Yes! I have six. Do I hear seven?

JOEY. My.

AUCTIONEER. Yes! I have seven. Do I have 750?

JOEY. Gosh.

AUCTIONEER. Yes! Seven-fifty. Do I hear eight? Eight hundred thousand for the "Honus Wagner T-206."

(*The AUCTIONEER is gone.*)

JOEY (*pacing, excited*). OK. Well. Here we are. We've got the attic pretty clean. And we've had a little break. And, um, let's see, what else? Oh, yeah, right — we are RICH! (*JOEY places the card inside his backpack. Then he steps forward into a downstage area as the attic fades away.*) And not only are we rich — now *all of our problems are solved*! Mom can quit her job at the hospital and she and Dad can get back together and find a new house for all of us to —

(*MISS YOUNG appears.*)

MISS YOUNG. Stop right there!

JOEY (*startled*). Huh?

MISS YOUNG. Thought you'd just a *walk away* without sayin' a word to me, is that it?

JOEY. Umm . . .

MISS YOUNG. Well you got another thing comin'. (*JOEY's face goes blank. He slowly begins to open the backpack, presumably to give back the card, just as MISS YOUNG holds out a $10 bill.*) Ten bucks — wasn't that the deal?

JOEY. Yeah, I think it was.

MISS YOUNG. I'm not happy with it. Let me tell you that. I'm not a bit happy about you leaving here with my $10 in your pocket.

JOEY (*handing the money back to her*). Oh, OK. That's OK —

(*MISS YOUNG takes the money, adds another bill, and hands it right back to JOEY.*)

MISS YOUNG. How 'bout 15? That's much better, don't you think? I told you, I've got no need for money. Kid like you probably feels *rich* right about now, don't you? (*JOEY is speechless.*) Good. Now, get out of here. Kids are like tornadoes. They belong outside, throwin' things around.

JOEY. Thank you, Miss Young.

MISS YOUNG. And learn to root for the Pirates, or I might just *put a spell on you*.

(*And MISS YOUNG is gone.*)

JOEY (*to audience*). As I started to walk home, I knew exactly what my mom was going to say when I told her.

(*light on MOM*)

MOM. I am so proud of you, Joey. This is the answer to our prayers!

JOEY. And I imagined my dad would say something like—

(*light on DAD*)

DAD. You're going to be on *SportsCenter*!

(*MOM and DAD are gone.*)

JOEY. And I kept walking, right past my house, just walking on air. And as I walked, I started to have *other* feelings—and these were *sinking feelings*—like maybe my mom would say—

(*light on MOM*)

MOM. That card doesn't belong to you, Joey. You know that.

JOEY. But Miss Young said I could take anything I wanted.

MOM. And did you tell her you took that card?

JOEY. Well, no, but—

MOM. If it's worth as much as you say, don't you think she'd want to know that?

JOEY. She doesn't need any money. She told me that!

MOM. Joey, that card belongs to Miss Young.

JOEY. She would have just thrown it away!

MOM. Can you *look me in the eye* and tell me there's nothing wrong with you taking that card?

(*JOEY turns and stares at her for a long moment. Then he turns back to the audience in frustration.*)

JOEY (*regarding MOM*). *I HATE when she does that!* When she makes me look her in the eye. Because when I do that, I *know*, deep inside, I *know* that the right thing to do would be to give that card back to Miss Young. (*MOM is gone.*) OK, I thought. That's what I'll do.

(*Light on DAD.*)

DAD. You're going to be on *SportsCenter*!

JOEY (*to audience*). Or maybe I *won't*. (*DAD is gone.*) Before I told anyone about the card, I decided I better be sure, *absolutely sure*, that it was authentic. And I knew the one guy who could tell me. (*Birdie's Home Run Heaven Shop. Behind the counter, reading a magazine, is CHUCK. He does not look up from his magazine.*) Hey, Chuck.

CHUCK. Joey *No-Hack.*

JOEY. Is Birdie here?

CHUCK. Joey the *Strikeout King.*

JOEY. I need to see Birdie. Is he around? It's *important.*

CHUCK. Oh, gee, *I bet it is.*

(*BIRDIE comes barreling into the shop. He is being followed by MR. MENDOZA.*)

BIRDIE (*hot*). No way—huh-uh—I'm not listenin' to this!

MR. MENDOZA. I ran the numbers, Birdie, you can't argue with the numbers.

BIRDIE. Oh, yeah? Just *watch me.*

MR. MENDOZA. You're three months behind on the rent and this is *the last chance I'm gonna give you.*

BIRDIE. Now, wait a minute—

MR. MENDOZA (*overlapping*). You come up with your rent money by Friday—or you're OUT!

JOEY. Birdie, can I talk to you?

BIRDIE (*to MR. MENDOZA, ignoring JOEY*). You know what? When I wrestled, I used to throw guys *twice your size* outta the ring and into the fifth row! And you know what the crowd would holler?

CHUCK (*up from magazine, chants*). BYE-BYE-BIRDIE! BIRDIE. So, if anyone's gonna do some *throwin' out* around here, Mr. Mendoza, it's gonna be me!

JOEY. Birdie, it's important—

MR. MENDOZA. You think you're sittin' on some kinda *gold mine* here? Is that it? You really think the world needs another BASEBALL CARD SHOP?

BIRDIE. Hey, you watch what you're—

MR. MENDOZA (*overlapping*). Well the world needs another baseball card shop like it needs another DESIGNATED HITTER, OK? Your shop's not worth *squat.* You're a *small-market team.* You're the Pirates or the Royals or the Twins—

BIRDIE. Yes, AND?

MR. MENDOZA (*putting on his previously unseen Yankees cap*). And pretty soon you're gonna get swallowed up by the YANKEES!

BIRDIE. Don't say that word in my shop! GO OUTSIDE IF YOU'RE GONNA USE THAT WORD!

MR. MENDOZA. Have the money by Friday—or I'll lock these doors for good.

BIRDIE. *Where am I gonna get that money?!*

MR. MENDOZA. Borrow it. Steal it. I don't care—just GET IT!

(*MR. MENDOZA goes.*)

BIRDIE (*calling off*). Yeah, I'll borrow it, all right! And while I'm at it, can I borrow your FACE when my BUTT goes on vacation?! (*wheels on JOEY*) And what do YOU want?

JOEY. I want to show you a card.

(*BIRDIE goes behind the counter. JOEY opens his backpack and begins to take out card.*)

BIRDIE. I can't wait to see what you've got, Stoshack. Did you bring me another one of your "great finds?" Like maybe another Frank Snook. Or a Floyd Wicker. Or, hey, maybe a mint condition Robbie Wine. (*Beat. Scathing.*) Oh, look at your little hanky. Isn't that sweet? (*Now BIRDIE'S eyes land on the Honus Wagner card. He freezes.*)

JOEY. Well?

BIRDIE (*cool, noncommittal*). Huh.

JOEY. What?

BIRDIE. I said huh.

JOEY. What's that mean?

BIRDIE. Huh? Oh, huh just means, you know. Huh. (*whispers*) Chuck, look at this.

(*CHUCK joins BIRDIE in looking at the card.*)

CHUCK (*in awe*). Duuuuuuuuude.

JOEY (*regarding CHUCK*). What's that mean?

BIRDIE (*nervous*). I think what Chuck means when he says—

CHUCK (*still looking at card*). Duuuuuuuuuuuuude.

BIRDIE. —is that the card you got there is sort of . . .

CHUCK. Mythic. Historical. Totally, like . . . old.

JOEY. Hey, Birdie.

BIRDIE. What?

JOEY. Your head is sweating.

BIRDIE (*wiping his head*). What? Me? My head? Oh, Stoshack, you're a character. Isn't he a character, Chuck?

CHUCK (*nods, playing along*). Character with a capital "K."

BIRDIE. Mind if I take a closer look? (*lifts the card with a pair of tweezers and inspects it with a magnifying glass*) Oh, gee . . .

JOEY. What?

BIRDIE. That's a shame.

JOEY. What is?

BIRDIE. You're thinkin' this is a T-206. The famous Honus Wagner card. Am I right?

JOEY. You tell me.

BIRDIE. Well, it's an old card, that's for sure. And this player here—he's a Wagner, all right. Real name was Charles but everyone called him "Heinie." That's who you got here, kid, Mr. Heinie Wagner. No relation to Honus, who actually did have a brother that played in the "bigs," but his brother's name was Albert. People called him "Butts." Didn't they, Chuck?

CHUCK. Butts. Totally.

BIRDIE. Now, you'd think they woulda called the guy named *Heinie* "Butts" and called the guy named *Albert*, I don't know, something like "Al" or "Bert," but in point of fact—

JOEY. Birdie?

BIRDIE. Yeah?

JOEY. Your head's sweating again.

BIRDIE. What—this? That's not sweat! That's generosity. (*indicating his head*) It just bubbles right up out of me! Now, Stoshack, tell you what I'll do. I don't want you to go home all sad and disappointed, so I'm gonna give you 20 bucks for that Heinie Wagner card. (*holds out a bill*) What do you say, Joe? We got a deal?

JOEY. Twenty bucks is a pretty good price for a Heinie Wagner—

BIRDIE. That it is.

JOEY. But can I ask you something?

BIRDIE. Fire away, buddy.

JOEY. Why do you suppose he's got the word "Pittsburg" on his chest?

BIRDIE. Oh, gee, they must have been wearin' their road uniforms that day. (*offering the money again*) Now—

JOEY. It just seems a little odd to me.

BIRDIE. Yeah, sure—

JOEY. Since we both know Heinie Wagner played for *Boston*.

(*BIRDIE just stares at JOEY as he lifts the card and starts to go.*)

JOEY (*cont'd*). I think I'll hold onto it. Thanks.

BIRDIE (*quickly*). Wait. I'll give you a hundred bucks.

JOEY. You said it was worth 20.

BIRDIE (*jumping over the counter*). A *thousand*. I'll give you one thousand dollars! Cash!

JOEY (*putting the card in his backpack*). No, thanks.

BIRDIE. *TWO thousand*. C'mon, kid—I've got it in back!

JOEY. Just one card holder. Fifty cents, right? (*takes a card holder and drops two quarters down on the glass*) See you later.

(*JOEY dashes out as BIRDIE grabs a well-used baseball bat from behind the counter and wields it, threateningly.*)

BIRDIE (*yelling off*). You're makin' a big mistake, kid! Do you hear me?! 'CAUSE I KNOW WHERE YOU LIVE! (*Furious, BIRDIE turns back into the shop. CHUCK is staring at him.*) WHAT?!

CHUCK. Your head, dude. Totally sweating.

JOEY (*alone, to the audience*). Now that I knew the card was for real, I wanted to find out everything I could about Honus Wagner. (*A LIBRARY. JOEY sits down at a computer table.*) So I went to the library and I sat down in the midst of all those books. And I Googled Honus Wagner. (*beat*) Three hundred thirty-five thousand items came up! (*A turn-of-the-century SPORTSWRITER appears. He speaks in a broad, buoyant voice as music from the era is heard under.*)

SPORTSWRITER. If a man with a voice loud enough to make himself heard all over the United States should stand on top of Pike's Peak and ask, "Who is the greatest ball player?" untold millions of Americans would shout back, "WAGNER. HONUS WAGNER!"

JOEY. Every article said that Wagner was the best shortstop ever. (*looks up*) Better than *Ozzie Smith*?

(*His eyes go back to the computer screen.*)

SPORTSWRITER. Johannes Peter Wagner grew up working in the coal mines of Pennsylvania. He was hoping to one day become a barber. But, when he was 18, a pro scout saw him throwing rocks clear across a train yard. The scout signed him up on the spot.

(*An old-time ballplayer, a PIRATES TEAMMATE, appears.*)

PIRATES TEAMMATE. Honus was not only our best shortstop, he was our best first baseman, second baseman, third baseman, and our best outfielder. And, of course, *no one* was a better hitter.

JOEY (*amazed, reading*). Wagner batted over .300 for *15 straight years*.

(*A silhouette of HONUS WAGNER begins to appear, his back to us. During the following, HONUS turns, straightens his cap, taps dirt from his cleats, spits on his hands, and steps into the batter's box.*)

PIRATES TEAMMATE. Big Wag had hands bigger than most other player's *mitts.*

SPORTSWRITER. He is so bowlegged, it's said he couldn't catch a pig in an alley.

PIRATES TEAMMATE. He had a massive chest that looked like it came from a barrel maker's shop—

SPORTSWRITER. His movements call to mind those of a stumbling elephant.

PIRATES TEAMMATE. And shoulders broad enough to serve dinner on.

JOEY. They called him "Hans," "Honus," "The Flying Dutchman."

SPORTSWRITER. "The Hercules of the Diamond."

PIRATES TEAMMATE. "The Mayor of the Bleachers."

SPORTSWRITER. "The Idol of Rooter's Row."

(HONUS is now awaiting the pitch as TY COBB appears, looking at HONUS.)

JOEY. Wagner's career batting average is better than Joe Dimaggio's, he scored more runs than Mickey Mantle, had more hits than Willie Mays, more doubles than Hank Aaron—and, even though he had 200 more at-bats than Babe Ruth, he struck out *1,000 times less.*

PIRATES TEAMMATE. Oh, for nine men like Wagner!

(HONUS swings his bat and—SMACK! The sound of the ball being crushed as TY COBB watches it sail into the distance with admiration.)

JOEY. Even the famous and feared Ty Cobb, when asked about Honus Wagner, said this—

TY COBB. He's the greatest ballplayer that ever lived.

JOEY. When the baseball writers of America selected the *first five players* for the Hall of Fame, Ty Cobb got the most votes—only four short of being unanimous.

TY COBB *(turns to the SPORTSWRITER, with menace).* I'll find those four guys. You bet I will.

(The SPORTSWRITER rushes off, and lights fade on TY COBB and the PIRATES TEAMMATE.)

JOEY. As for the second-most votes, that was a tie. Between Babe Ruth . . . and Honus Wagner. *(The HONUS silhouette is gone.)* The last thing I typed in was "Honus Wagner T-206" and when the screen filled, I couldn't believe my eyes—

(The AUCTIONEER appears.)

AUCTIONEER *(as before).* I have eight, do I hear nine? Nine hundred thousand dollars?

JOEY. NO—

AUCTIONEER. YES, I have nine! Do I have one million?

JOEY. WAY!

AUCTIONEER. YES! I have one million! I have ONE POINT TWO! Aaaaannnnnddddd—SOLD for $1.2 million!

(*The AUCTIONEER hits his gavel. The light on him snaps out.*)

JOEY. I was right! ALL our problems are solved! (*beat*) Now all I had to do was tell my mom.

(*JOEY'S ROOM. MOM enters, still wearing her work clothes.*)

MOM. Hi, buddy. I didn't even hear you come in.

JOEY. Oh, just wanted to get started on my homework.

(*takes a book out of his backpack and pages through it, intently*)

MOM. School was OK?

JOEY. Yep.

MOM. And then you went over to Miss Young's?

JOEY. Yep.

MOM. Did you finish your work for her?

JOEY. Yep.

MOM. And she paid you?

JOEY. Fifteen bucks.

MOM. She told me 10.

JOEY. It's really no big deal.

MOM. Well, yes, that's very nice of her.

JOEY. 'Cause the thing to remember is *she has no use for money.*

MOM. Is that so?

JOEY. She told me that.

MOM. I see. (*beat*) Your dad called. He'll be at your game tomorrow. He asked if you were playing the Ravens.

JOEY. Yep.

MOM. Is that the Ritz Funeral Home team? The ones that bring their equipment in that little coffin?

JOEY. That's them.

MOM. That team is creepy.

JOEY. And they kill us. Every time.

MOM (*stares at him, leaning in*). Are you OK, Joey?

JOEY. I'm great. Why?

MOM. Well, I don't know. All of a sudden you're reading books *upside down*— (*JOEY immediately turns his book right-side-up, continues reading.*) And you don't seem to be able to look me in the eye. (*JOEY tries to look at her, but turns away, reading more.*) So, what are you going to do with *all that money?*

JOEY (*quick, nervous*). All *what* money?!

MOM. The $15.

JOEY. Oh, I don't know. I went down to Birdie's and looked around.

MOM. Joey Michael Stoshack, please don't spend all the money you earn on *baseball cards.*

JOEY. I was maybe going to sell a card. A *really* old card. Birdie offered me a hundred bucks for it.

MOM. Who would pay a hundred dollars for an old piece of cardboard?

JOEY. Mom, you have *no idea.*

(*staring at his backpack*)

MOM. Joey, is there something you want to tell me?

JOEY. I just wanted to tell you that . . . Miss Young said I could keep *anything* I found in her attic.

MOM. That's nice of her. Did you find anything you wanted?

JOEY (*looks her in the eye, then turns quickly to the audience, exasperated*). How does she DO THAT? It's like she's shining a big flashlight down into the *basement of my brain.* (*turns back to his MOM, opens his backpack and reaches inside*) OK. All I found in that attic was just this really . . . old . . . *handkerchief.* Here you go.

MOM (*holding it*). It's lovely.

JOEY (*no big deal*). Those're little flowers.

MOM. Roses. And it's hand stitched. Joey, that's so thoughtful.

JOEY. Yeah, well.

MOM. I'll see you downstairs. Dinner in 15.

(*MOM goes.*)

JOEY (*to audience, defensively*). Yeah, yeah—I know. I should have *told her.* But what if she *made me give the card back?* I couldn't take that chance. (*During the following, JOEY puts on his favorite baseball jersey of some well-known major league shortstop. The adult-size jersey is way too big and very long on him.*) Before I got in bed, I snuck downstairs and made sure all the doors to the house were double locked. Birdie was right—he *did* know where I lived. And he knew I had this card. And I knew he had that *bat*. (*climbs into bed*) I really needed a *plan*. And the only plan I could think of was to go to sleep and hope I woke up with a *perfect plan* in which I didn't have to tell Mom about the card until after we were already RICH. (*gets the card out of his backpack and turns off the lamp*) As soon as I held it, my hands stated to tingle. (*music under*) I thought of all those writers who called Wagner the greatest of all time. And I thought of the other thing they always said—that he was kind of funny-looking, sort of odd and awkward, not your typical ballplayer— and I realized that he kind of *reminded me of me!* And I fell asleep wishing I could meet him . . . and talk to him . . .

(*Now only the moonlight is seen streaming through a window. JOEY falls asleep, holding the card. Music and a series of odd, ominous late-night sounds, as a SILHOUETTE FIGURE of a man holding a baseball bat gradually appears. The SILHOUETTE FIGURE grows larger and larger, until it seems to be hovering over JOEY's bed.*)

SILHOUETTE FIGURE. Kid. (*JOEY stirs a bit, still asleep. SILHOUETTE FIGURE, louder*). Kid. (*JOEY stirs again, covering his head with his blanket. SILHOUETTE FIGURE, louder still*). I SAID—

(*JOEY sits bolt upright and sees the SILHOUETTE FIGURE with the bat.*)

JOEY (*screams*). AAUAUAUAUGHGHGHGH!!!

SILHOUETTE FIGURE. What is it, kid? (*beat*) What are you saying?

JOEY. BIRDIE, LEAVE ME ALONE! I MEAN IT, BIRDIE, GET OUT OF HERE OR I'LL CALL THE POLICE!

SILHOUETTE FIGURE. Listen, now—

JOEY. BIRDIE, PUT DOWN THAT BAT!

SILHOUETTE FIGURE (*lowers the bat*). Sure, kid. Whatever you say. You know, I've been called a lot of things in my day, but I'm sure I've never been called Birdie.

(*JOEY suddenly turns his lamp on. Standing there in his room is a large, powerfully built man in a Pittsburg Pirates uniform. It is, of course, HONUS WAGNER. JOEY stares at him in disbelief as HONUS looks at the strange room he is standing in.*)

HONUS. *What is this place?* (*moves cautiously, curiously into the room and sees his baseball card lying on JOEY's bed*) And where'd you get that?

(*reaches for the card*)

JOEY (*grabbing the card*). Leave that card alone!

HONUS. That's my baseball card.

JOEY. It's *my* baseball card. And I don't know who you are, but you can tell Birdie that I'm NOT SELLING HIM THIS CARD.

HONUS (*regarding the card*). That's my picture right there!

JOEY (*disbelieving*). Yeah, right. I bet Birdie sent you here to scare me, didn't he?

HONUS. Look—

JOEY. Or to steal the card!

HONUS. The only thing I've ever stolen is second, third, and home. Now, tell me the truth. *Where'd you get that card?*

JOEY. I found it!

HONUS. *I told that company to stop makin' 'em!*

JOEY. They did stop makin' 'em.

HONUS. I told 'em that kids shouldn't be spendin' money on tobacco just to get a picture of a ballplayer.

JOEY. What do you mean *you* told them?

HONUS. I'm the guy on that card!

JOEY. Yeah, and I'm Babe Ruth.

HONUS. Who?

JOEY (*quickly*). OK. Prove it.

HONUS. *What?*

JOEY. Show me some ID. Something in your wallet with your name on it.

HONUS (*removing his old-time mitt from a pocket*). Look, kid, a minute ago I was shaggin' fly balls at Forbes Field—and the next thing I knew I was standing here.

JOEY. That's impossible. Forbes Field is gone. They tore it down.

HONUS. That's impossible. They just built it!

JOEY (*a challenge*). If you're Honus Wagner, tell me what your batting average was in 1900.

HONUS. That was a pretty good year. I hit .381.

(*JOEY stares at HONUS. Beat. Then he quickly consults his huge baseball encyclopedia.*)

JOEY. OK. Lucky guess. How many bases did you steal in 1907?

HONUS. I think it was 61.

JOEY. *Total luck.* What about 1908? How many hits did you have?

HONUS. I had 201. (*proudly*) And I hit *10* home runs. Only one guy hit more. Tim Jordan of the Brooklyn Superbas—he cranked out *12* of 'em.

JOEY. Twelve? There's guys who can hit like *60* or *70* of them.

HONUS (*lifts a baseball from JOEY's glove or nightstand*). Playin' with balls like this? Hard as a rock?

JOEY. Yeah, I guess.

HONUS (*reaches into his pocket and brings out a baseball of his own, dirty and soft and beat-up*). Try hittin' one of these.

(*tosses this ball to JOEY*)

JOEY (*regarding the ball*). It's all squishy.

HONUS. It's dead is what it is. You gotta smack the stuffing out of it just to get it outta the infield. One time, though, at an exhibition game, I sent a ball like that over an outfield fence — *403 feet away*. They called it a world's record.

JOEY. For the longest ball ever hit?

HONUS. I didn't hit it, kid. I *threw* it.

(*JOEY is staring at HONUS as his MOM's voice is heard from offstage.*)

MOM. Joey?

JOEY. Yeah, Mom?

MOM. Who are you talking to?

JOEY (*finally lets it sink in and, looking at HONUS, he speaks, simply*). Honus Wagner.

HONUS. And who might you be?

JOEY. Me? I'm Joey. I'm, uh, Joey Stoshack.

HONUS. What do your friends call you?

JOEY (*beat*). Uh, they call me . . . Joey—Joey Stoshack.

HONUS. I'll call you *Stosh*. How's that?

JOEY. Stosh. (*beat*) That's cool.

HONUS. My friends call me Hans. Now, can you tell me which streetcar I catch to get back to the park?

JOEY. *Streetcar?* What year do you think it is?

HONUS. It's 1909, of course. (*JOEY hands a calendar to HONUS.*) What's the joke, Stosh? That says two-oh-oh-six!

JOEY. Yep.

HONUS. Jumpin' jehoshaphat! *What did you do*—cast a magic spell or something?!

JOEY. I don't know what I did!

HONUS (*hands the card back to JOEY, growing worried*). Well, whatever you was—you better *undo it,* 'cause I got a game tomorrow!

JOEY (*frustrated*). I don't know how to *undo it!*

HONUS. What was it you did before?

JOEY. All I did was hold onto that card. *See, there's this thing that happens—*

HONUS. *Just try it again, will ya?* I need your help.

JOEY (*beat*). Sure. OK. (*Stares at the card, holding it tightly. Beat.*) But, can I ask you something?

HONUS. Sure.

JOEY. Didn't they offer you a lot of money to print these cards?

HONUS. Sure they did. But sometimes there's the easy thing to do, and the *right* thing. And nobody can tell you which is which. It's up to you. (*extends his hand*) Good to meet you, Stosh.

(*They shake hands.*)

JOEY (*to audience*). His hand was the size of a baseball mitt—just like I'd read. And bigger than his hand, were his *stories.*

(*music under*)

HONUS. One time at Forbes Field I was playin' the outfield, and a fella hit a ball over the fence and right into the smokestack of a train! I hollered to the engineer to "pull the lever" and he did. Out came a big burst of steam—*and the baseball,* which I caught for the final out. And then . . .

JOEY. He just kept telling stories and I kept holding onto to that card, hoping I could get him back to 1909.

HONUS. There's the time I hit a ball that went *under* the pitcher's arm and *still cleared the outfield fence.*

JOEY (*lies back in his bed*). I closed my eyes. I tried to imagine Honus Wagner back at Forbes Field, shagging flies in the outfield. (*The CRACK OF A BAT and HONUS's eyes go up, his mitt ready, as though he is tracking a long, arcing fly ball.*) And that ball is well hit and Honus is after it on the dead run, further and further. He keeps going back— (*The light on HONUS begins, slowly, to fade.*) But he's not going to get it, not this time—because that ball is going . . . (*Lights fade more.*) going . . . (*Lights continue to fade.*) gone.

(*Lights to black.*)

END OF ACT I

ACT II

(*The little league baseball field. The BLUEBIRDS TEAM is on the field. A light isolates JOEY.*)

JOEY (*speaks to the audience*). The next day, I still had the card . . . but there was no sign of Honus Wagner. Maybe I had sent him back to Forbes Field. Or maybe he'd never been here at all. Either way, everything now was back to normal. (*beat*) *And we were playing the Ravens.* (*The RAVENS TEAM enters carrying a miniature coffin.*) The Ravens are the best-coached team in the league. They call "I got it" on fly balls, they remember how many outs there are, and they always throw to the right base. They even do something my dad calls "the lost art of hitting the cutoff man." (*The members of the RAVENS TEAM open the coffin. The RAVENS PITCHER removes a few black baseball bats.*) The only thing worse than how they dress, is the way they *act*.

RAVENS PITCHER (*in a fierce whisper*). Death to the Bluebirds.

(*The RAVENS CATCHER removes a faux tombstone from the coffin and sets it near JOEY. The tombstone reads "BLUEBIRDS, R.I.P."*)

JOEY. And the only thing worse than how they act is the way they play—

RAVENS CATCHER (*in a whisper*). Say your prayers, Dumbo.

JOEY. Because they're *really good.*

(*The RAVENS TEAM take their places for the game.*)

VOICE OF UMPIRE. Play ball!

JOEY. The good news for me is I'm gonna sit right here till it's over. (*moves to the bench. SOUNDS OF THE GAME are heard under the following.*) I kind of like the bench. It's better than making the last out. Supposedly there is this every-kid-must-play rule, but luckily our coach pays no attention to it.

(*JOEY's COACH enters. No cell phone.*)

COACH (*clapping his hands*). C'mon now, guys and gals. We're only down three runs and their pitcher's startin' to tire. I feel a BIG INNING COMIN' ON. (*The BLUEBIRDS TEAM, including JOEY, cheer.*) We just need *oneheckuvalot* of base runners. OK. Laman's up, Parks on deck, Bradley in the hole. Atkins, Meyer, and Noland—you be ready, 'cause we're gonna bat around and PUT UP SOME MIGHTY CROOKED NUMBERS!

(*more cheers as DAD approaches COACH*)

DAD. What about Stoshack?

COACH. Who's that?

DAD. Joe Stoshack. He's your backup shortstop.

COACH. And who might you be—his *agent?*

DAD. I'm his dad.

COACH. Uh-huh.

DAD. And it's the last inning.

COACH. Uh-huh.

DAD. And I happen to know there's an every-kid-must-play rule.

JOEY. Dad, no!

DAD. So, I'd appreciate it if you could please—

COACH. You want my whistle, is that it?

DAD. No, I don't want your whistle. I want my son to play.

JOEY. Dad, please!

COACH. Well, unless you're wearing this whistle, you're not gonna tell me how
    to run my team. *Capisce?*

DAD. Look, I don't want to argue with you in front of my son, but—

JOEY. Dad, really—I'm fine. I don't need to play!

DAD. But Joey, I *know* you want to—

JOEY. No, I don't.

COACH. There you go, Pops. You heard the kid. Now could you please put butt
    to cushion, and let me orchestrate an amazing comeback here? Thank you
    just *oneheckuvalot. (calling toward the field)* OK, two outs—Bradley, make
    him pitch to you!

JOEY. And Coach was right. With two outs, the Ravens pitcher did start to tire.
    He walked Bradley and Atkins—

COACH. Good eye! Take your base!

JOEY. And then Billy Meyer knocked them both in with a triple!

COACH. Atta boy, Billy!

JOEY. We were only down by one run with a man on third and our best hitter,
    Andy Noland, coming up!

COACH *(calling off)*. C'mon, Noland—you're up!

JOEY. And then a terrible thing happened.

COACH *(to the unseen player)*. You WHAT?

JOEY. Andy Noland set down his bat—

COACH. You've got to be KIDDING.

JOEY. And he took his mom's hand—

COACH. NOLAND, where are you GOING? A BASE HIT WILL TIE THE GAME.

JOEY. And then he and his mom walked away, got in their car, and drove off.

COACH. NOLAND—DON'T YOU DO THIS TO ME!

JOEY. But it was hopeless. Andy Noland had left the game. *He had a dentist appointment.* (beat) And, of course, that meant—

COACH. STOSHACK!

(*a groan from the BLUEBIRDS TEAM*)

JOEY. Oh, no.

COACH. GET UP THERE!

JOEY. Do I have to?

COACH (*resigned*). You're all I got, son.

DAD (*thrilled*). C'mon, Joe—knock that run in!

(*DAD hands JOEY his bat and batting helmet.*)

JOEY. WHY CAN'T *I* HAVE A DENTIST APPOINTMENT?!

VOICE OF UMPIRE. Batter up!

(*JOEY takes his place in the batter's box, similar to Act I. Lights now gradually isolate JOEY at bat, downstage. The RAVENS PITCHER is facing offstage left, as before. A chant is now heard repeatedly, coming from the RAVENS TEAM: "Sto-Shack, Sto-Shack, he's a No-Hack!"*)

JOEY. As I stepped in the box, I made up my mind: I was *not going to swing*— NO MATTER WHAT. Because if you don't swing, *you can't miss.*

(*The pitch comes in. JOEY takes it.*)

VOICE OF UMPIRE. Strike one!

COACH. Take the bat off your shoulder!

DAD. OK, next one.

JOEY. Oh, man! That was a *fat one*—right down the middle!

DAD. C'mon, Joe, NICE AND EASY NOW.

(*Another pitch. JOEY takes it.*)

VOICE OF UMPIRE. Strike two!

COACH (*simultaneously*). What are you waitin—

DAD (*simultaneously*). Be ready, now.

JOEY. Man, oh, man—that was a *marshmallow!* Right down the heart of Broadway! I stepped out of the box, looked at my dad.

DAD. YOU CAN DO IT, JOE!

JOEY. Looked at my coach.

COACH (*punching numbers into his cell phone*). OK, who's ready for pizza?

JOEY. Looked at the pitcher.

RAVENS PITCHER (*a whisper, as before*). I'm gonna bury you, Stoshack.

JOEY. And now I was *mad*. I got back in the box. I gave that pitcher my mean-est stare—and there it came. (*The pitch is thrown, but comes to JOEY in slow motion.*) It was a CREAM PUFF—just beggin' me to HIT IT INTO NEXT WEEK! (*Now the pitch comes at real speed. JOEY swings the bat PING!*) AND I DID IT!!! (*Lights instantly isolate JOEY, as music and cheering are heard under the following.*) I raced to first, still looking for where the ball had landed. And Billy Meyer, he raced home and stepped on the plate. And I kept running, looking for the ball—past second and on my way to third! Because I HAD HIT THAT BALL HARDER THAN ANYONE HAD HIT A BALL ALL SEASON. AND IT WENT— (*Lights expand to reveal the RAVENS CATCHER. The music and cheering suddenly stop.*) STRAIGHT UP!

(*The ball falls harmlessly from the sky and into the RAVENS CATCHER's waiting mitt.*)

VOICE OF UMPIRE. Yooouuurrreee out!

RAVENS CATCHER (*tosses the ball to JOEY, whispering*). Rest in peace.

(*The RAVENS TEAM leaves, and COACH is speechless as DAD approaches JOEY.*)

DAD. Man, you smacked that thing, Joe! That would have been a home run—

JOEY (*dejected*). If we played in an elevator shaft.

DAD. You'll get 'em next time.

JOEY. Why do you always say that? "Get 'em next time."

DAD. Well . . . that's what my dad always told *me*. And what his dad told him. Hey, did you know *my* grampa once saw Honus Wagner play at old Forbes Field? (*smiles*) Do you know what he'd do if *he* got in a slump? He'd walk up to the plate, and then—

JOEY. Then he'd switch over, and bat left-handed.

DAD (*surprised*). Yeah, that's right.

JOEY. He'd smack a line drive and next time up he'd go back to batting right-handed. His slump was over.

DAD. Did I already tell you that?

JOEY (*silent, looking away*). Hey, Dad? Did you ever think of selling any of your cards? I mean, if you had one card that was *really, really valuable* and you knew it would make Mom *really, really happy* to not have to worry about money for a *really, really long time?*

DAD (*smiles*). I never had any cards like that, Joe.

JOEY. But if you *did*.

DAD. Those cards belong to *you* now. You can do whatever you want with them.

JOEY (*hopeful*). You mean it?

DAD. As long as it's OK with your mom. (*Hearing this, JOEY's face freezes.*) Want to get a bite to eat? (*JOEY just shrugs.*) Well . . . can I give you a ride home?

JOEY. Mom said I could walk.

DAD (*beat*). OK. Well . . .

(*DAD starts to give JOEY a hug, but JOEY quickly says—*)

JOEY. Dad . . .

(*JOEY holds up his palm, where DAD now gives him a high-five.*)

DAD. Love you.

JOEY. See ya.

(*DAD goes. JOEY packs up his mitt and the ball, grabs his bat, and starts to go, walking past the bench where HONUS is now sitting. HONUS has his bat with him.*)

HONUS. See ya, Stosh.

JOEY (*not looking up*). Yeah. See ya—(*JOEY stops, does a double take. HONUS is wearing a pair of old brown suit pants with suspenders and a simple blue work shirt.*) Honus? No way! You're really here?!

HONUS. If I'm not, you better stop talkin' to yourself.

JOEY. But *how?*

HONUS. You fell asleep listenin' to my stories—

JOEY. Sorry.

HONUS. So, I went for a walk. Found these clothes that an old lady was throwin' out—pretty nice, huh? Then I came and watched you play.

JOEY. Oh, no.

HONUS. Looks like you're in a batting slump. Happens to everyone.

JOEY. I'm not in a *slump. That's the way I hit.*

HONUS. You know, Stosh, you've got a lot of natural talent, but the thing is—

JOEY. Yeah, I know, here it comes. The old pep talk. *Play hard, keep trying, don't give up.* I've heard it a million times.

HONUS. You're over-striding.

JOEY. What?

HONUS (*picks up a bat, demonstrates*). You're stepping too far with your front foot. That pulls your back shoulder down. Your elbow dips and your wrists come in under the ball. Leads to a pop-up every time. (*HONUS hands the bat to JOEY. He takes his own [wooden] bat and places it downstage from JOEY's front foot to keep him from over-striding.*) Now, try it again. Here comes a Walter Johnson fastball. (*JOEY swings, nice and strong. HONUS continues, pleased.*) How about that.

JOEY. Wow, thanks.

HONUS (*looking more closely at the aluminum bat*). So, what year did they run out of *wood?*

JOEY. Kids' bats are aluminum nowadays.

HONUS. When you hit the ball, it doesn't even go "smack." It goes "*ping.*" A baseball's not supposed to go "*ping.*"

JOEY. Lots of things have changed, Honus. Like the designated hitter. It means the pitcher doesn't have to bat.

HONUS. That crazy idea's been around forever. It'll never catch on.

JOEY. Well, it *caught on.*

HONUS. Don't tell me, in the *American League,* right?

JOEY. Right.

HONUS. Pitchers get away with everything! Rubbin' the ball in the dirt, spittin' tobacco juice and god-knows-what-all onto it. That thing comes at you like a brown slobberin' snake.

JOEY. But I bet you still *hit it.*

HONUS. It's a game of *failure,* Stosh, and the great ones are the ones who fail *just a little bit less* than the rest. You know the difference between a .250 hitter and a .300 hitter? *One more hit every week.* But it's that *one more hit* that's the hardest to come by.

JOEY. Man, I'd love to play in the big leagues—even just once.

HONUS (*stares at him for a moment*). C'mon, let's toss it around.

JOEY. *Really?*

(*HONUS nods, taking his mitt out of his back pocket. JOEY quickly grabs his mitt and a ball. They play catch during the following.*)

HONUS. Remember, there ain't much to bein' a ballplayer if you're really a *ballplayer.*

JOEY. Who taught you to play—your dad?

HONUS. We never saw much of him. He was down workin' in the mines. It was my brother Al—

JOEY. Folks called him "Butts."

HONUS. That's right. He's the one taught me to play. One day he got offered a tryout in Steubenville, but he didn't want to go. So, I hopped a freight and took his place.

JOEY. And nobody noticed?

HONUS. Nah. He and I used to switch places all the time. Next thing I knew, this fellow from Louisville —

JOEY. Ed Barrow.

HONUS. That's right. You know Ed?

JOEY. I Googled him.

HONUS. You what?

JOEY. Never mind.

HONUS. Ed Barrow saw me throwin' lumps of coal clear across the river.

JOEY. I read that it was "rocks in a train yard."

HONUS. Well, it might of been. The best story is always the true one.

JOEY. So, he signed you up on the spot?

HONUS. Nope. I told him I wasn't interested, just to see what he'd do. He said, "Isn't there somethin' I can give you — somethin' you'd really like to have?" I said, "I'd like to have a *bag of bananas*." He ran out and got one! And I signed for $35 and a bag of bananas.

JOEY. Nowadays, players make like $10 million a year!

HONUS. Stosh, I spent 12 years in the big leagues before I finally made $10 thousand a year. And I don't care what anyone says, 10 grand is the most any man should be paid to throw and hit a ball.

(*They continue to play catch.*)

JOEY. Is it true that on ground balls you'd scoop up and throw a whole bunch of dirt and rocks and they'd arrive at first base along with the ball?

HONUS. What do *you* think?

JOEY. Sounds made up.

HONUS. Well, how 'bout the time a ball got passed me at short, but one of my dogs jumped out of the stands and fetched it. I picked up the dog, with that ball in his mouth, and I touched the runner comin' into second. You know what they called that?

JOEY. (*groans*). A *dog tag*.

HONUS. How about that! And then there's the time a jackrabbit came runnin' across the field just as I was chargin' a slow roller. In my hurry, I picked up the rabbit instead of the ball—and threw him all the way to first. It was a close play, but you know what the ump said?

JOEY (*another groan*). You got him by a *hare*.

HONUS. Atta boy, Stosh!

JOEY. I know one thing you never did.

HONUS. What's that?

JOEY. Make the *last out*, like I always do.

(*Pause as HONUS stares at JOEY. Then lights begin to isolate HONUS in the batter's box. CROWD SOUNDS begin to be heard under the following.*)

HONUS. 1903. The first World Series ever played. My Pirates against the Boston Pilgrims. Ninth inning, two outs, nobody on—and I was the last chance for the Pirates.

(*The SINGING BOSTON FANS are heard under the following dialogue.*)

BOSTON FANS (*singing under*). HONUS, AT BAT YOU LOOK SO BADLY. STRIKE THREE, AND SIT YOU DOWN. BEANTOWN HAS HAD ENOUGH OF WAGGY. TAKE THE TRAIN NOW, GET OUT OF TOWN! GO FIND ANOTHER TEAM TO HIT FOR. PITTSBURGH IS JUST THE PITS. AND EVER MORE, HONUS, YOU ARE A PHONY, PHONY, PHONY!

HONUS (*overlapping the song*). Those crazy Boston fans had made up a song for me.

JOEY. But you didn't even hear it, right? That's what the players always say.

HONUS. Well, they're lying. I heard every word of it. And what's worse— those Boston fans couldn't sing to save their lives.

(*The singing fades into SOUNDS OF THE CROWD as the SPORTSWRITER appears.*)

SPORTSWRITER. And now it fell to the great Honus Wagner, premier batsman of the National League.

HONUS. As I dug in, Stosh, I already knew . . .

SPORTSWRITER. The count was oh-and-two against him. And there on the mound, in the gathering gloom, Big Bill Dineen peered in for the sign.

HONUS. I knew exactly what he was going to throw.

SPORTSWRITER. The Mighty Dutchman readied his bat.

HONUS. And I knew exactly what I was going to *do with it*.

SPORTSWRITER. And now the windup. And the pitch, fast as an arrow, shooting toward the plate—

HONUS. And here it came.

SPORTSWRITER. The Great Wagner's mighty shoulders began to heave. And those in the crowd will swear that his very frame began to creak and shiver, as he swung his bat with a force unmatched in the game.

(*HONUS swings in slow motion.*)

HONUS. And I got ready to hear the best sound a ballplayer can ever hear — and I don't mean the sound of a "*ping.*" I mean that wonderful "*smack.*"

JOEY. And you heard it, right?!

SPORTSWRITER. And everyone heard it, all at once, that unmistakable sound—

JOEY. Honus?

SPORTSWRITER. Of the ball crashing into the catcher's waiting mitt. (*HUGE, AMPLIFIED SOUND of the ball landing in a mitt*) The Great Wagner, the Mighty Dutchman had made the final out. The Series was over. The failed, fallen champion left the field alone, in defeat.

(*HONUS stands there silently. The SPORTSWRITER is gone.*)

HONUS. I love this game more than anything else on earth. But sometimes, Stosh, baseball is nothin' but *organized humiliation.*

(*pause*)

JOEY. My Dad would say, "Get 'em next time."

HONUS. That's the plan, Stosh, but first you gotta get me back home.

JOEY. I tried, Honus.

HONUS. Well we gotta try again. I got a big game tomorrow!

JOEY. Meet me at my house tonight. My mom will be asleep by 10.

HONUS (*strong*). *I'm countin' on you, Stosh.*

(*HONUS goes as lights shift to JOEY's front yard. His MOM is talking to BIRDIE. He carries a sturdy black briefcase, which is handcuffed to his wrist.*)

MOM. Yes, Mr. Birdwell, I'm glad you stopped by.

BIRDIE (*overly polite*). It was my pleasure.

MOM. It's all a misunderstanding, I'm sure.

(*JOEY arrives.*)

JOEY. What is he doing here?

MOM. Joey, this is Mr. Birdwell from the baseball card shop.

BIRDIE. Hello, young fellow. How are you this fine day?

JOEY. Oh, gimme a break, Birdie.

MOM. We've been talking about something you may have mistakenly acquired from him.

JOEY. *Something I WHAT?*

MOM. I'm sure it's nothing you did on purpose.

JOEY. I didn't do anything! He's the one who tried to trick me and—

BIRDIE (*overlapping as JOEY says "anything"*). Now, now, now, Joey, let's not get ahead of ourselves here.

MOM. Mr. Birdwell, I'd like to speak to my son.

BIRDIE. I understand. (*to JOEY with a hint of menace*) See ya 'round, slugger.

(*JOEY glares at BIRDIE, who exits.*)

MOM. *Well?*

JOEY. Nothing he told you is true!

MOM. You don't have a baseball card that's worth a lot of money?

(*Pause. She stares at him.*)

JOEY. OK. So *that* part's true.

MOM. He says he sold it to you by mistake.

JOEY. And *that's* a LIE. I took it to his shop to see if it was the real thing, and when I wouldn't sell it to him—

MOM. Joey, where'd you get this card?

JOEY (*beat*). I found it . . .

MOM. Mm-hmm.

JOEY. At Miss Young's house . . . in a box of stuff she told me to throw away.

MOM. Mr. Birdwell says it's worth over a thousand dollars.

JOEY. Mom, the last one of these that sold went for $1.2 million.

MOM (*stares at him in silence*). Can I see it?

(*JOEY hands MOM the card. She looks at it. He puts his arm around her.*)

JOEY. Mom, I don't know how to break this to you, but all our worries are OVER. You can quit your job and buy a new car and I can go to college and get a degree in statistical analysis, so I can start my own baseball consulting firm when my Major League career is over. (*MOM looks JOEY straight in the eyes. JOEY is immediately defensive.*) Don't ask me if I told her because, RE-MEMBER, she told me I could keep *anything I found up there.*

MOM. Joey—

JOEY (*overlapping*). And don't ask me to give it back to her because *she doesn't want it!*

MOM. *Listen to me*—

JOEY (*overlapping*). MOM, all our problems are SOLVED.

MOM (*sharp*). Not if we're taking things that don't belong to us. Not if we can't tell the truth to each other.

JOEY (*grabs the card back*). I knew I shouldn't have told you.

MOM. You give that card back to Miss Young.

JOEY. I knew you'd screw this up for us!

MOM. It's the right thing to do and you know it.

JOEY. You *want* us to be unhappy—just to punish *Dad*.

(*rushes off*)

MOM. Joey!

(*Lights isolate JOEY.*)

JOEY. Why did I go and tell her the *truth*?! I should have told her I found it *lying on the street*. See what happens when you tell people the truth?!

(*A separate area. DAD is speaking with MOM.*)

DAD. Do you know how excited he must have been to find that card?

MOM. It doesn't belong to him, Tom, and I would like you to *please back me up on this.*

DAD. When I gave him my collection, he asked me, "What's the hardest card to find in the whole world?" And I told him it was the Honus Wagner T-206. And he *remembered that*, whereas most people would have just thrown it away in the trash.

MOM. Where it belongs.

DAD. How can you say that?! It's a piece of *history*. It could change our lives.

MOM. You sound just like Joey.

DAD. The money from this card—

MOM. Would not change a thing *between you and me.*

(*JOEY steps into their midst.*)

JOEY. Then what about me? It's *my* card. Doesn't anybody care what *I* think?

MOM (*simultaneously*). Go back upstairs, please. Right now.

DAD (*simultaneously*). Hi, Joe, your mom and I are just—

JOEY. What happened to "You can do this, Joey; you're old enough to make decisions on your own"?

MOM. Not this time, Joey.

JOEY. But, Mom—

MOM (*with a glance at DAD*). We've decided that the card belongs to Miss Young, and you'll give it back to her tomorrow.

JOEY. No, I won't.

MOM. Suit yourself.

JOEY. Dad, say something!

MOM. I'll take it to her myself.

JOEY. NO!

DAD. Joey—

JOEY. You won't find it! You'll never find it!

(*JOEY races off as lights shift to JOEY's room at night. HONUS is there, paging through some of JOEY's baseball card binders. He is wearing his baseball uniform.*)

HONUS. You said 10 o'clock, right, Stosh?

JOEY. *What?* Oh, yeah.

HONUS. And you've got that card?

JOEY (*regarding his parents downstairs*). I'm not giving that card to *anyone*.

HONUS (*regarding the cards*). Can't get used to these Pirates uniforms—and this letter "h." There's no "h" in Pittsburgh. And what's with these *numbers* on the *player's backs*?

JOEY. Those are their . . . numbers.

HONUS. Like this number nine. (*trying to pronounce it*) Maz-err-ohh—

JOEY. Bill Mazeroski. Hit the most famous home run in Pirates history.

HONUS (*another card*). Roberto . . .

JOEY. *Clemente.* Best right fielder of all time. Had an arm like a rocket.

HONUS (*another card*). And this number 24—

JOEY. That's Barry Bonds when he was still a Pirate. Now he's the greatest home run hitter in baseball.

HONUS. This *skinny little guy?*

JOEY. He's kind of . . . *filled out.* He might pass Babe Ruth on the all-time home run list.

HONUS. Take it from me, Stosh, nobody will EVER pass Roger Connor. As of last year, he's got *138 home runs.* Let's see someone top that!

JOEY (*smiles*). Just you wait, Honus.

HONUS (*with passion*). I'll tell you whose card you should have: John Henry Lloyd. They call him "Pop" Lloyd. Plays in the Negro Leagues. Best short-stop I've ever seen.

JOEY. Wish I could see him play.

HONUS (*beat*). Come with me.

JOEY. What do you mean?

HONUS. Let's try it, Stosh, maybe that card works *both ways.*

JOEY. But, Honus—

HONUS. I've seen your time. Let me show you how we play ball in *mine.*

(*The PHONE RINGS in the room. It's a chirpy little ring. HONUS, of course, does not know what the sound is.*)

JOEY (*regarding the phone*). Get that!

HONUS. Get what?

JOEY. The phone—quick! Before it wakes up my mom!

(*The PHONE KEEPS RINGING.*)

HONUS (*regarding the noise*). You got a bad cricket problem in here, Stosh.

(*JOEY jumps past HONUS and answers it.*)

JOEY (*into phone*). Hello!

(*A light on BIRDIE. In one hand, his cell phone. In the other, his briefcase.*)

BIRDIE (*into phone*). Hi, there, *slugger.*

JOEY. Who's this?

BIRDIE. This is the guy standing *right outside your window.* I heard you talkin' to yourself in there, Joey.

JOEY. Leave me alone, Birdie—

BIRDIE. Oh, believe me, I will. As soon as I have that card, I will leave you *very, very alone.*

HONUS. Everything OK?

BIRDIE. Now, why don't you just open your window and drop that card into my hand. OK?

(*pause as JOEY stares toward the window*)

JOEY. OK.

(*JOEY hangs up the phone and the light on BIRDIE goes out.*)

HONUS (*concerned*). Stosh?

(*JOEY takes out the Honus Wagner T-206 card and holds it in his hand, looking in the direction of the window.*)

JOEY (*with conviction*). I wish I was bigger. I wish I could make my own decisions. I wish I was *all grown up.*

HONUS (*regarding the card*). Feelin' anything?

(*music begins*)

JOEY (*closing his eyes*). Hey, Honus. In 1909, is everything in black and white? Like all those old pictures?

HONUS. No, friend, *the past is in color. In bright . . . beautiful . . . color.*

(*The SPORTSWRITER appears. Music from the era plays, as before.*)

SPORTSWRITER. And as morning dawns on the city of Detroit, the Tigers faithfully begin the great march to Bennett Park—that hallowed place where their beloved Tigers will attempt to bring the first world championship to this great city by the lake. But take heed, Tiger Rooters, though you have the incomparable Ty Cobb on your side, your rivals also have a man, a man among men: Johannes Peter Wagner, the Flying Dutchman. Here they are, folks, the two greatest players in baseball—brought together right here in Detroit. Let the games begin!

(*In a hotel room. Lights rise on JOEY. He is under the covers, asleep. An OLD-TIME CAR HORN sounds very loud and JOEY sits up with a start.*)

JOEY. HUH?! (*beat*) Honus? Honus, are you here? (*Next to the bed is a brass wind-up alarm clock. JOEY lifts it.*) Twelve-thirty! I slept till 12:30?! Wait a minute—Mom never lets me sleep that late, even on Saturday. (*stares at clock*) Wait—this isn't my clock. This clock has hands. (*looking around*) And this isn't my room.

(*HONUS enters, wearing his uniform. He is in the midst of shaving, a towel tossed over his shoulder.*)

HONUS. Thought you'd never wake up, Stosh.

JOEY. Where are we?

HONUS. The Pontchartrain Hotel. Detroit, Michigan.

JOEY. But Honus, *when* are we?

(*HONUS hands JOEY a calendar.*)

HONUS. Have a look.

JOEY. October . . . *1909*!

HONUS. Yep.

JOEY. But I'm not even born yet.

HONUS. Then how come you're all grown up?

JOEY. What?

HONUS. Have a look in that mirror.

(*JOEY goes to the [unseen] mirror in the room. The previously oversized baseball jersey he slept in now fits him snugly.*)

JOEY. Hey—my shirt shrunk.

HONUS. Think again, big fella.

(*HONUS steps out of the room.*)

JOEY (*to audience*). It was true! I was *hairy* in places that I used to be smooth. My breath tasted *really bad* in my mouth. My whole body kind of *smelled*. And I needed a *shave*! I was . . . *disgusting*. I was . . . A MAN!

(*JOEY is making muscles in front of the mirror as HONUS returns, finished shaving and holding a small duffel bag.*)

HONUS. Hey, Muscles—we gotta go. (*HONUS tosses JOEY a coat and hat.*) Put these on. And maybe on the way we'll get you some new shoes.

JOEY. *I like these sh—*

HONUS. C'mon, now—I don't want to miss batting practice.

JOEY. Why do you get dressed here? Aren't there locker rooms at the stadium?

HONUS. Welcome to the good old days, Stosh.

JOEY. But Detroit's in the American League. You'd never play the Tigers, un-less— (*dawns on him*) It's . . . the *World Series*.

HONUS. Told you I had a big game today.

(*HONUS goes and JOEY follows as lights isolate JOE and HONUS. The SOUND OF A BUSTLING CROWD.*)

FRIENDLY FAN. Good luck today, Honus!

HONUS. Thanks a lot.

HECKLER. Cobb's gonna roll all over you, Dutchman!

HONUS (*smiles*). We'll see about that.

(*Two LADY FANS approach wearing fancy hats. They each carry scorecards and hold a fountain pen.*)

FIRST LADY FAN. Mr. Wagner, could you please sign this for my son? His name's Hiram.

HONUS (*signing it*). For Hiram . . .

SECOND LADY FAN. And could you sign this for my son, as well?

HONUS. Happy to do it.

SECOND LADY FAN. And could you maybe write it, "with love?"

HONUS. OK. Sure. And the name?

SECOND LADY FAN. Um, his name is . . .

(*The LADY FANS are about to bust up with giggles.*)

FIRST LADY FAN. Lydia.

HONUS (*winks at JOEY, signs*). "To . . . *Lydia*, with love."

FIRST LADY FAN (*whispers to SECOND LADY FAN*). He's doing it!

SECOND LADY FAN. Oh, thank you, Mr. Wagner. (*HONUS hands her the score-card.*) And you know something? You're just as ugly *in person.*

(*HONUS just smiles as the FIRST LADY FAN turns to JOEY.*)

FIRST LADY FAN. And who's this? Are you a ballplayer?

HONUS (*before Joey can respond*). He's my brother.

(*The FRIENDLY FAN enters, patting JOEY, shaking his hand, etc.*)

FRIENDLY FAN. Hey, Butts! Butts Wagner! How ya doin'?

HONUS. He's great!

FRIENDLY FAN. Where you playing now, Butts? Haven't seen you since Brooklyn in '98.

(*The LADY FANS hold their scorecards in front of JOEY and he signs them quickly during the following.*)

HONUS (*regarding JOEY*). Well, his knee was a little banged up.

FRIENDLY FAN (*as he goes*). Hope we see you next year, Butts!

JOEY. OK. Thanks.

(*The LADY FANS take their signed scorecards and hurry off.*)

SECOND LADY FAN (*as they go*). Butts Wagner—never heard of him.

FIRST LADY FAN. He's as ugly as his brother!

(*The HECKLER approaches. Around his neck and shoulders are various pots and pans, whistles, etc., as well as a small megaphone.*)

HECKLER. Hey, Butts—your brother's gonna get creamed today!

JOEY (*not backing down*). Oh, yeah? Who says?!

HONUS. Don't let 'em get to you, Stosh.

HECKLER. Bet he makes the *last out* like he did in '03!

(*The HECKLER goes as HONUS hands JOEY a ticket and a quarter.*)

HONUS. Here's your ticket. And two bits for some food.

JOEY. Thanks, Honus.

HONUS. And one more thing. I want you to watch me every inning when I come off the field. If I look up at you and do this— (*pats his left shoulder twice with his right hand*) I want you to come down to the tunnel behind our bench. Is that clear?

JOEY. Sure, but—

HONUS. Remember the sign.

JOEY (*imitates the sign*). I got it.

(*HONUS turns to go.*)

JOEY (*cont'd*). Honus, this is like a dream come true.

HONUS. Not yet, it ain't.

(*Bennett Park in Detroit. Red, white, and blue bunting unfurls around the stage. JOEY finds his seat directly behind the two LADY FANS and between the FRIENDLY FAN and the HECKLER. Several of the fans wave Tigers pennants. The HECKLER uses his noisemakers throughout. The SOUND OF THE CROWD [live and recorded] is heard, rising and falling, as needed. The ANNOUNCER'S VOICE can be heard [recorded or amplified].*)

ANNOUNCER'S VOICE. Welcome one and all, to Game 7 of the 1909 World Series, between your American League champion Detroit Tigers.

(*LOUD CHEERS as TY COBB appears and tips his cap.*)

JOEY. Is that Ty Cobb?!

HECKLER. What're you—some kind of joker?! Of course that's the Great Ty Cobb!

ANNOUNCER'S VOICE. And their opponent today—the National League champions, the Pittsburg Pirates.

(*HONUS joins TY COBB at home plate as JOEY stands and CHEERS [seemingly the only Pirates fan in the park].*)

JOEY (*a hip-hop chant*). OH, YEAH—GO PIRATES! GO PIRATES!

(*The other fans glare at him.*)

HECKLER. Go back to the coal mines, Smokestack.

JOEY (*to the HECKLER*). It's Stoshack!

FIRST LADY FAN. I thought it was Butts.

JOEY (*Beat. Offers food.*) Cracker Jack?

(*The LADY FANS turn away in a huff as lights now feature HONUS and TY COBB at home plate, each holding a bat.*)

HONUS. Young Mr. Cobb.

TY COBB. Mr. Wagner.

HONUS. Game 7.

TY COBB. Yep.

HONUS. Someone's gonna go home the world champion today.

TY COBB. And someone's gonna lose and go back to Pittsburgh. (*HONUS smiles. Beat.*) You're lookin' at my hands.

HONUS. I'm wonderin' if you stole my grip. Hands a little bit apart, slide 'em up and down a bit, dependin' on the pitch.

TY COBB. I don't steal nothin' from nobody.

HONUS. I'll remember that.

(*Pause. They wave, tip their caps, etc., to the cheering crowd.*)

TY COBB. So, what do you fellas hunt up there in Pennsylvania?

HONUS. Oh, we go out for squirrel and rabbit and all sorts of small game.

TY COBB. Down in Georgia, we go after *birds*.

HONUS. Do you now?

TY COBB. You should come down South when the season's over. You and me could do a little bit of shootin'.

HONUS. Sounds good. (*Pause. TY COBB is staring at HONUS.*) Somethin' else on your mind?

TY COBB. They say you're the most *popular* man in baseball.

HONUS. Whoever "they" are.

TY COBB. Oh, believe me, I know exactly who *they* are.

HONUS. And they say you're the most *feared*. Say you'd climb a mountain just to punch an echo.

TY COBB. Baseball is a red-blooded sport for red-blooded men—and all the little mollycoddles had better stay out of it.

HONUS. It's a *game*, young man.

TY COBB. No, sir. It's something like a *war*.

VOICE OF UMPIRE. Play ball!

(*The crowd CHEERS. HONUS and TY COBB part as the game begins.*)

JOEY (*to audience*). With the Tigers down four to nothing in the fifth, the Great Ty Cobb came to bat.

(*TY COBB steps into the batter's box.*)

HECKLER. C'mon Cobb, show these Pittsburgh rubes how it's done!

(*TY COBB swings—SMACK!*)

JOEY. Cobb slapped the ball to right field for a hit. I'd never seen anyone run so fast in my life. And now he was on first base, like a wild horse caught in a pen. He took a huge lead, taunting the pitcher, and then he pointed down at Wagner.

TY COBB. You better look out, Krauthead! On the next pitch, I'm *comin' down*!

HONUS. I'll be ready!

(*A LOW, HAUNTING DRONE is heard as lights isolate JOEY.*)

JOEY. And sure enough, on the next pitch, Cobb broke for second! Honus caught the ball, straddling the bag. (*Now a shaft of light illuminates the base, revealing the very end of TY COBB's slide in slow motion.*) And Cobb's spikes went *right into Wagner's arm!* And Wagner tagged Cobb *right across the face!*

(*The AMPLIFIED SOUND of HONUS smacking TY COBB across the face with his mitt*)

VOICE OF UMPIRE. Yoouu'rree oouutt!

HONUS (*standing over him*). Remember: You don't steal nothin' from nobody.

(*The DRONE continues as TY COBB slowly rises, face-to-face with HONUS.*)

JOEY. Cobb stood up, his face covered with blood, and I *waited for a fight to break out.* (*After a hard stare, HONUS and TY COBB part, respectfully.*) But Cobb ran back to the dugout, Honus went back to short, and the game went on.

(*APPLAUSE from the crowd*)

HECKLER. You got his number, Ty, you'll get him next time!

JOEY. The inning ended and Honus came toward the dugout— (*HONUS does the signal.*) The signal! I got out of my seat and raced down behind the Pirates bench.

(*JOEY approaches HONUS, who is taking off his uniform shirt [or producing a second one from his duffel bag].*)

HONUS. Quick, Stosh. Get out of those clothes and put this on.

JOEY. Why?

HONUS. Cobb got me pretty good on that slide. My arm's cut up and I can't hold a bat.

JOEY. But what do you want me to do?

HONUS. I want you to be my designated hitter.

(*HONUS is putting the baseball jersey on JOEY.*)

JOEY. What?!

HONUS. Said you wanted to play in the majors, right?

JOEY. Well, yeah, *someday.*

(*HONUS slides JOEY's pants up to his knees and tucks them into his dark socks.*)

HONUS. I'm the fourth man up this inning. So, if anyone gets on, you're going to come up to bat.

JOEY. You've got to be crazy—

HONUS. Didn't you say it was your dream come true?

JOEY. Yeah, but I was thinking maybe spring training or something—this is the World Series!

(*HONUS puts his cap on JOEY's head.*)

HONUS. So, what could be better than that?!

JOEY. BUT, HONUS—

(*HONUS shoves him toward the field just as a light isolates JOEY.*)

ANNOUNCER'S VOICE. Now batting for Pittsburgh—the shortstop, HONUS WAGNER!

(*HUGE TAUNTS and JEERS from the crowd as JOEY stands frozen for a moment, then approaches the batter's box, bat in hand. He digs in. The TIGERS PITCHER is on the mound.*)

JOEY. I pulled his cap way down over my eyes. I stepped into the rear of the batter's box like Honus always did. I gripped the bat the way he did.

HECKLER. THROW HIMALITTLE CHIN MUSIC, GEORGE!

JOEY. I stared out at the mound and tried to look ready.

(*The pitch comes in. JOEY takes it. The sound of a ball hitting the mitt loudly.*)

VOICE OF UMPIRE. Strike one!

JOEY. But I wasn't ready. I wasn't ready at all!

HECKLER. ATTA BOY, WABASH!

JOEY. I'd never seen a ball come at me that fast. Before I knew what hit me—

(*The next pitch comes in. JOEY takes it. The sound of a ball hitting the mitt, as before.*)

VOICE OF UMPIRE. Strike two!

HECKLER. YOU'RE WASHED UP, WAGNER, GO BACK TO THE COAL MINES!

JOEY. And now I was really in a hole. I smacked the bat down on home plate.

TY COBB (*from right field*). Hit it here, Wagner, so I can drill you in the head with it!

JOEY. I dug my cleats in and I spit on the ground, just because, well, I had to do *something*!

HECKLER (*as he leaves the stands*). Hey, Wagner—could your ears be any bigger?! YOU LOOK LIKE AN ELEPHANT!

(*The LADY FANS laugh and the crowd begins to chant "STRIKE HIM OUT! STRIKE HIM OUT! STRIKE HIM OUT!"*)

JOEY. And then, just before Wabash George Mullin started his windup, I glanced into the dugout to see if Honus was watching. (*beat*) But I didn't see him anywhere. What I did see was an amazing thing— (*Music begins under the following.*) My teammates weren't packing up the gear like they usually did—my coach wasn't ordering pizza. NO! They were leaning toward me.

They were nodding their heads like they just knew, they just knew I could do it! And that was the greatest feeling of all. (*beat, smiles*) Well, maybe the second greatest feeling.

ANNOUNCER'S VOICE. And here's the oh-two pitch to Wagner— (*The pitch comes in. JOEY takes a great, clean swing at it, and SMACK!*) And there's a drive down the third base line! It's gonna clear the bases! Leach will score! Here's Clarke coming around to score and Wagner's not stopping at second, he's going for third. And here comes the throw from Jones—and it's off-line. It gets away from Schmidt and now Wagner's on his feet. He's heading home—and they're not gonna get him! Wagner scores! Pirates seven, Tigers nothing!

(*HUGE CHEERS and music playing as the lights shift. The SPORTSWRITER arrives, notebook in hand.*)

SPORTSWRITER. How'd you do it, Hans? What's the secret?

JOEY (*a la HONUS*). Well, there ain't much to bein' a ballplayer—if you're really a ballplayer.

SPORTSWRITER (*jotting this down*). Is that so?

JOEY. I remember once in Louisville, all our bats were broken. So the batboy handed me an ax to hit with. Well, I swung at the first pitch and split that ball clean in half—*hit a single to right and a double to left!*

(*TY COBB approaches JOEY. Seeing TY COBB, the SPORTSWRITER rushes off.*)

TY COBB. Mr. Wagner.

JOEY (*tentatively*). Yes?

TY COBB. You're as good as advertised. (*JOEY is speechless.*) I'll see you down South.

JOEY. OK.

TY COBB. Bring your guns. (*TY COBB leaves as HONUS appears, opposite, carrying his duffel bag. During this scene, JOEY takes off the uniform top, cap, etc., until he's back in his contemporary clothes.*)

HONUS. I knew you could do it, Stosh!

JOEY. But what if Cobb hadn't spiked your hand?

HONUS. Oh, I'd-a thought of something. Once I saw you all grown up, I knew I had to get you into the game. And, hey, I've got somethin' else for you. (*rummaging through his duffel bag*) A whole bunch of those baseball cards with my face on 'em—they gave 'em to me down at the factory. You might as well have 'em.

JOEY. How many do you have?

HONUS. Oh, probably about 20 of 'em. Now, what in the devil happened to those?

JOEY (*to audience*). And as I was doing the math in my head—20 cards times $1.2 million each . . .

(*A PIRATES TEAMMATE enters with a champagne bottle.*)

PIRATES TEAMMATE. A toast to the man who outhit and outran the Mighty Cobb!

HONUS. Hey, Smitty, you seen those cards I had?

PIRATES TEAMMATE (*reaches into his pocket*). HIP, HIP, HOORAY! (*tosses a large handful of confetti into the air above HONUS's head, with a laugh*) I told you they were good for something!

HONUS (*regarding the confetti*). Well, Stosh, there's your cards. Sorry about that.

PIRATES TEAMMATE (*shaking JOEY's hand*). Stosh, I'm Phenomenal Smith. Good to meet you. Why don't you come out with us? Me, Ducky Hemp, Peakaboo Veach—we'll meet you at the hotel. WA-HOO!

(*The PIRATES TEAMMATE dances out of the room, joyous. But now JOEY is looking at something else in HONUS's bag.*)

HONUS. What is it, Stosh? You're white as a ghost.

JOEY. That picture—who is that?

HONUS (*removes half of a torn photograph from the bag*). Oh . . . that's Amanda. She and I were gonna get married. When I went away to spring training, we tore this picture in half—said we'd put it back together when I got home.

JOEY. But why didn't you get in touch with her?

HONUS. Time went by. I heard someone else was courtin' her—figured she probably didn't want to hear from me. Tell you what, though . . . I never forgot about her. (*JOEY reaches into his pocket and removes the other half of the photograph. He shows it to HONUS.*) Now, where'd you get that?

JOEY. Amanda Young lives down the street from me.

HONUS. She's still alive—in your time?

JOEY. She's *really* old. But she never married. (*beat, excited*) Hey, why don't you come back with me!

HONUS. No . . . I had my chance with Amanda. That's over and done.

JOEY. But, Honus—

HONUS. Sorry, Stosh, but I belong here. (*HONUS gives the two halves of the photograph back to JOEY.*) Hey, since you know the future, maybe you can tell me how long I stayed in the game?

JOEY. Till 1917.

HONUS. I'll be 43.

JOEY. You hit .265 that year.

HONUS. Ouch. No wonder I called it quits.

JOEY. But then the Pirates asked you back, to be a coach. And you did that until—

(*stops*)

HONUS. Till when? Till I died? (*off JOEY's look*) It's OK. You can tell me. What year was that?

JOEY. 1955. You were 81.

HONUS (*silent, looking away*). Somethin' I gotta ask you, Stosh. (*beat*) Did I ever play in another World Series? (*JOEY is staring at him.*) No, don't tell me. Everybody needs somethin' to hope for.

JOEY. Well, I guess I should be getting back. I mean forward.

(*JOEY extends his hand and they shake.*)

HONUS. Come visit me sometime, OK?

JOEY (*holds up the baseball card*). Already got my ticket. (*HONUS picks up his duffel bag and leaves as JOEY turns to the audience.*) And as he walked away, I realized— (*stops, worried*) I had *no idea how to get home!* I knew how to get to the past, but how was I gonna get to the *future*? I tried everything. I tried imagining the cards in my room at home, but nothing worked. (*stops*) WAIT. (*reaches into his sneaker and pulls out a piece of cardboard*) LARVELL BLANKS. MY HERO. MY FAVORITE PLAYER OF ALL TIME. (*stands, holding the card*) And, yep. Sure enough, right away my hands started to *tingle*. (*music begins*) And I wished I was a *kid* again. Just plain old Joey Stoshack, living with my mom in my house in Pittsburgh, Pennsylvania, at good ol' two-oh-oh-six . . .

(*A downstage area. MOM is holding JOEY's backpack and a paper sack.*)

MOM. Joey, you're gonna be late for school.

JOEY. *Mom?*

MOM. I packed up your breakfast. You can take it with you on the bus.

JOEY. Mom, *what year is it?*

MOM. I think you mean what *time* is it? And it's time you got movin', buddy!

JOEY. But have I been, like, *gone* for a couple days or anything?

MOM. I think I'd know if you were. And listen, I want you to make your own decision about that baseball card. OK?

(*JOEY nods as MOM goes. A light isolates JOEY.*)

JOEY. That night I walked down to Miss Young's. It was getting dark. And just like always, the wind was blowing the trees against her house.

(*MISS YOUNG's yard. BIRDIE and CHUCK jump out of the shadows and grab JOEY. CHUCK gets JOEY in a full nelson as BIRDIE holds the baseball bat. BIRDIE takes JOEY's backpack from him during the following.*)

BIRDIE. Well, well, well.

CHUCK. We got him now, dude.

BIRDIE. I gave you a chance to give me that card, Stoshack —

JOEY. Let me go!

BIRDIE. But now I'm gonna have to *take it*.

JOEY. I don't have it!

BIRDIE. I think that's a *fib*. Do you think that's a fib, Chuck?

CHUCK. *Fib* with a capital "P-H."

JOEY. You lied to me, Birdie — you told me that card was worth 20 bucks!

BIRDIE. The value of a card comes down to two things, Stoshack: supply and demand. (*CHUCK tightens his grip as BIRDIE lifts the bat.*) I demand it. You supply it.

JOEY. Birdie — NO!

(*MISS YOUNG's voice is heard from offstage.*)

MISS YOUNG. DROP IT!

(*BIRDIE freezes and CHUCK turns to see MISS YOUNG holding a very old rifle.*)

CHUCK (*races off*). Duuuuuuude —

MISS YOUNG. I said drop it!

BIRDIE. *What's this?*

MISS YOUNG. What's it look like? I'm an old lady with a gun.

BIRDIE. It's not loaded.

MISS YOUNG. Want me to *show* you? (*She lifts the rifle with intent and aims it at BIRDIE.*) I got nothin' to lose. What're they gonna do — put me away for *life?* (*BIRDIE is frozen.*) Now, I suggest you drop that bat. (*BIRDIE drops the bat.*) Joseph, what's all this about?

JOEY. I brought you something.

(*JOEY reaches into his pocket and removes the Honus Wagner T-206 card.*)

BIRDIE. I knew it!

MISS YOUNG. Quiet, batboy. (*JOEY hands the card to MISS YOUNG. She looks at it briefly.*) Where did you get this?

JOEY. I found it in your attic.

MISS YOUNG (*sharply*). I told you to throw all that stuff away.

JOEY. Yes, I know, but— (*MISS YOUNG puts the rifle in JOEY's hands and begins to tear the card into a handful of pieces.*)

MISS YOUNG (*adamant*). What's past is past and what's gone is gone and there's no point in going back.

BIRDIE (*dying at the sight*). No! No, don't! Oh, no, please—nooooooooooooo!!!

MISS YOUNG (*drops the pieces of the card into the trash can*). When I tell you to throw something in the trash, I expect you to do it. (*to BIRDIE*) And you. You should be ashamed of yourself—picking on a little kid like that. Don't let me catch you 'round here again.

BIRDIE. That's more than a million bucks!

MISS YOUNG. And get a rag. Your head is sweating. (*BIRDIE grabs his bat and looks up at JOEY.*)

JOEY. Bye, bye, Birdie.

(*BIRDIE storms off. When he's out of sight, MISS YOUNG gestures to the rifle.*)

MISS YOUNG. You can throw that away, too. Hasn't worked in 50 years. (*JOEY puts the rifle in the trash.*) What's this half-a-million bucks stuff?

JOEY. That's what that card was worth.

(*Beat. She looks in the direction of the trash, then back to JOEY.*)

MISS YOUNG. And you brought it back to me?

JOEY. Sometimes there's the easy thing and the *right thing*.

(*JOEY reaches into his pocket and pulls out the torn photograph.*)

MISS YOUNG. That's the picture I showed you.

JOEY. Yes.

MISS YOUNG. I told you to throw that away, too.

JOEY. Sorry.

MISS YOUNG. Did you throw *anything* away? (*JOEY now produces the other half of the photograph from HONUS. He hands it to MISS YOUNG. Slowly, she puts the two halves of the photo together, completing the picture.*) My, oh, my . . . there we are.

JOEY. He never forgot about you. (*off her look*) He told me.

MISS YOUNG. That's impossible.

(*JOEY puts his hands on the photograph, as well, so that they are both holding it.*)

JOEY. Hold onto this photo—really tight.

MISS YOUNG. Joey, what are you doing?

JOEY. And close your eyes.

MISS YOUNG (*doing so*). But why?

JOEY. Do you feel it? In your hands?

(*Music: the lovely solo trumpet version of "Take Me Out to the Ball Game," as before.*)

MISS YOUNG (*feeling it now*). Well, I don't know—

JOEY. In your fingers?

MISS YOUNG. It's like . . . *electricity.*

JOEY. Do you want to go there?

MISS YOUNG. Joey—

JOEY. Do you want to go *back*?

MISS YOUNG (*pause*). Yes. Yes, I do.

(*music plays as JOEY speaks to the audience*)

JOEY. And then Miss Young began to *smile*. A smile I'd never seen her smile. And it made her look young. (*MISS YOUNG begins to slowly walk upstage toward the huge replica of the Honus Wagner T-206 card and into the distance, into the light.*) And the wrinkles on her face slowly faded away, and her hair turned from grey to blonde, and she was beautiful and young. And she was going . . . going . . . (*MISS YOUNG turns back, waves, and is . . .*) gone.

(*Music fades out as COACH immediately enters, buoyant. MOM and DAD enter from opposite sides. A Little League baseball field.*)

COACH. Just *oneheckuva* game, *Stosh*. From here on out, you're my starting shortstop!

JOEY. Thanks, Coach.

COACH. And brush your teeth—these dentist appointments are killing me.

(*COACH goes.*)

DAD (*to JOEY*). Two singles and a triple. I told you you'd get 'em next time.

JOEY. You saw the whole game?

MOM. Yes, he did. Including the double play.

JOEY. We got him by a hare. (*Beat. Regarding himself and DAD.*) Hey Mom, can we go get some pizza?

(*Beat. MOM looks at DAD.*)

MOM. Just be home by nine, OK?

(*DAD nods. JOEY and DAD exchange a high-five. JOEY turns to give the same to MOM, but she just opens her arms, demanding a hug, which he gives her.*)

DAD. I'm proud of you, Joe, for giving that card back.

MOM. You never told me what Miss Young said.

JOEY (*simply*). She just smiled.

(*MOM goes as JOEY reaches into his backpack and discovers the vintage Pirates cap he wore in the World Series.*)

DAD. You're a Pirates fan now?

JOEY (*smiles, puts the cap on*). Hey, Dad, can we toss it around?

DAD. I thought you were hungry.

JOEY. Just for a minute.

DAD. Sure.

(*Music plays as JOEY gives DAD his mitt and picks up another that's been left near the bench. They begin to play catch.*)

JOEY (*to audience*). I never told them about going back in time. But I wish my mom could have seen me, all grown up into a man. And I wish my dad could have seen that old ballpark, the way the game used to be played. (*beat*) Which I guess is not so different from today. In right field, Ty Cobb charged the ball—and in one motion, he *scooped it from the ground and fired it on a rope to nail the runner at third.* Just like Clemente. And just like Ichiro. And just like some kid somewhere in Single-A, who no one's ever heard of. (*beat*) At least not *yet.*

(*The game of catch continues as the SPORTSWRITER appears in the distance.*)

SPORTSWRITER. Great is baseball. The national tonic.

DAD. It's getting dark, Joe.

SPORTSWRITER. The reviver of hope.

JOEY. Just a couple more, Dad.

SPORTSWRITER. The restorer of confidence.

JOEY. Just a couple more . . .

(*Lights fade.*)

END OF PLAY

Jackie & Me

Steven Dietz

Premiere production, Chicago Children's Theatre, 2011

Production credits from the premiere of *Jackie & Me* and details concerning performance rights are included in the acting edition of the play as published by Dramatic Publishing.

Cast of Characters

(6m., 2w., doubling as indicated)

JOEY STOSHACK: a 10-year-old boy (played by adult actor).

JACKIE ROBINSON: a 28-year-old ballplayer.

MOM / WOMAN (at fountain) / MRS. HERSKOWITZ

DAD / MAN (at fountain) / DIXIE WALKER / DELIVERY MAN / BROOKLYN KID 1 / PHILLIES CATCHER

MS. LEVITT / RACHEL ROBINSON / JAYHAWKS CATCHER

COACH / BRANCH RICKEY / EDDIE STANCKY / BABE RUTH

FLIP VALENTINI / BROOKLYN KID 3 (Young Flip) / LEO DUROCHER / PEE WEE REESE / REPORTER / POLICEMAN

BOBBY FULLER / ANT / BROOKLYN KID 2 / BEN CHAPMAN

Others:

GROUNDSKEEPER

UMPIRE'S VOICE

JAYHAWKS PLAYERS

YELLOW JACKETS PLAYERS

STUDENTS

ANNOUNCER

DODGERS PLAYERS

PHILLIES FANS

PHILLIES PLAYERS / SCHOOLBOY ROWE

PHILLIES CATCHER

YELLOW JACKETS CATCHER

KID IN A CAP

OTHER MEN (with BABE RUTH)

Time and Place

The Present. And 1947. Pittsburgh. New York City. Brooklyn. Philadelphia.

Setting

An open playing space that will depict a variety of locales.

LITTLE LEAGUE BASEBALL FIELDS

JOEY'S HOME

A CLASSROOM

FLIP'S FAN CLUB: a glass case displays baseball memorabilia

BRANCH RICKEY'S OFFICE: chairs and a desk with an old-fashioned black phone

A DRINKING FOUNTAIN: a fountain with a sign hanging nearby that reads "WHITES ONLY"

THE HOTEL MCALPIN: a hotel room with a small mirror hanging

THE DODGERS CLUBHOUSE a locker room with baseball equipment, lockers, and towels

EBBETS FIELD: the Dodgers baseball field

A BROOKLYN STREET

HERSKOWITZ GROCERY: a corner grocery in Brooklyn

SHIBE PARK: the Phillies baseball field

THE VISITOR'S CLUBHOUSE (SHIBE PARK): a locker room

A DARK ALLEY: in the Bronx

THE VISITOR'S CLUBHOUSE (YANKEE STADIUM): a locker room

YANKEE STADIUM

JOEY'S BEDROOM

Note on Casting

It may be desirable, but is not required, to use three or four additional non-speaking cast members (or "supernumeraries") to fill out the teams, classroom, crowds, etc.

Note on Updating

The present year, and thus the names of any current ballplayers mentioned, may be updated as needed.

ACT I

(In the darkness, a lone trumpet plays "The Star-Spangled Banner," quietly and mournful at first, as a shaft of light slowly rises on a GROUNDSKEEPER. The GROUNDSKEEPER is slowly "chalking" the first [or third] base line as a light rises on JOEY STOSHACK, alone.)

JOEY *(to audience)*. There's something you should know about me. I've got a *special power*. When most kids hold an old baseball card in their hand, it's just a piece of cardboard. But for me ... well ... *(And now, with the white chalk line nearly complete, the song grows louder, more joyful, and is joined by voices: "Oh, say does that star-spangled baaaanner yet waaaaaaaaaave...")* when I hold a baseball card, *my hand starts to tingle*... *("O'er the laa-aand of the freeee...")* and that baseball card... *("... and the hooooome of the...")* it becomes a *time machine!* *("... braaaaaaaaaaaave")*

UMPIRE'S VOICE. Play ball!

(A LITTLE LEAGUE BASEBALL FIELD. All that is required onstage is the pitcher, BOBBY FULLER, and perhaps a few JAYHAWKS PLAYERS [the opposing team] and some YELLOW JACKET PLAYERS [JOEY's team] in the distance. JOEY's COACH stands to one side. JOEY, in his uniform, puts on his batting helmet and lifts his bat, ready to hit.)

BOBBY FULLER & JAYHAWKS PLAYERS. NO BATTER, NO BATTER, NO BATTER, NO BATTER!

COACH. Come on, Joey, give 'er a good rip.

JOEY *(to audience)*. It's the first game of the year, the score is tied—and my team, the Yellow Jackets, really needs a hit.

BOBBY FULLER. You can't hit, Stoshack!

JAYHAWKS PLAYERS *(chanting)*. Sto-shack, Sto-shack, He's a No-Hack!

JOEY. And they need that hit from me.

BOBBY FULLER. You couldn't hit water if you fell out of a boat!

(JAYHAWKS PLAYERS laugh, etc.)

COACH. Little bingo now, buddy!

JOEY. Two outs, two men on—and the pitcher for the Jayhawks is a kid I cannot stand.

BOBBY FULLER *(winds up, saying)*. Hey No-Hack—you're so ugly, when you look in the mirror it turns the other way! *(pitches)*

(JOEY swings and misses.)

UMPIRE'S VOICE. Strike one!

(*JAYHAWKS PLAYERS laugh, cheer, etc.*)

JOEY. His name is Bobby Fuller, and I know it's not right to say this—

BOBBY FULLER. Hey Slow-Sack—

JOEY. But *I hate that kid.*

BOBBY FULLER (*winds up again*). You're so dumb, you took a ruler to bed to see how long you slept! (*pitches*)

(*JOEY swings and misses.*)

UMPIRE'S VOICE. Strike two!

(*JAYHAWKS PLAYERS laugh, cheer, etc.*)

JOEY. Time out! (*Steps out of the batter's box. Speaks to audience.*) I could feel the blood rushing to my face! I knew I was about to blow up.

BOBBY FULLER (*to JAYHAWKS PLAYERS*). Hey, I think little Jo-Jo-Girl is scared of me!

JOEY. But right then I thought of what my mom always says when I'm about to lose my temper—

(*a quick light on MOM*)

MOM. You can't let it get to you, Joey. You've got to *turn the other cheek.*

JOEY. *But I am running out of cheeks to turn!*

(*MOM is gone.*)

UMPIRE'S VOICE. Batter up!

JOEY (*digs in at home plate*). The coaches are always talking about "being a good sport" and "treating the other team with respect."

BOBBY FULLER. Hey, Low-Crack—

JOEY. The Little League has *very strict rules about this stuff*—

BOBBY FULLER. You know the only thing dumber than a box of hammers?

JOEY. But I guess this kid never got the message!

BOBBY FULLER (*starts his wind-up*). A big, dumb, ugly *Po-lack!*

(*BOBBY pitches. JOEY swings extra hard and misses.*)

UMPIRE'S VOICE. Strike three—you're out!

BOBBY FULLER & JAYHAWKS PLAYERS (*arms in air, celebrating*). YESSSSSSSSS!!!

(*All action freezes as JOEY stands, holding his bat, literally shaking with anger.*)

JOEY. OK. You can call me ugly and dumb. You can make fun of how I play. But nobody—*nobody*—makes fun of my heritage. I'm proud to be Polish, proud to be a Stoshack. (*lifts the bat as he speaks the following*) And that's when I felt my arm lifting that bat into the air.

COACH (*steps in*). Take it easy, Joey. He struck you out fair and square.

JOEY. But Coach—

COACH. We're not gonna lose our temper here, are we? If you get thrown out, we'll be out of players and we'll have to forfeit the game. You wouldn't do that to your teammates, would you?

BOBBY FULLER. Hey, Stoshack, just so you know, I like Polish people. They throw fun parties. And you know when a Polish party is over? When someone flushes the punch bowl!

(*Quick beat. Then JOEY attempts to hurl the bat at BOBBY FULLER just as COACH grabs the other end of the bat, leaving JOEY's arm to continue forward without the bat as he yells.*)

JOEY. Take it back!

(*Now JOEY jumps atop BOBBY FULLER, punching him as they fall to the ground, immediately surrounded by all of the JAYHAWKS PLAYERS, the YELLOW JACKET PLAYERS, and the UMPIRE until JOEY disappears into the middle of the fight. COACH rushes to the fight and tries to pull the JAYHAWKS PLAYERS and the YELLOW JACKET PLAYERS away.*)

JAYHAWKS PLAYERS (*as needed*). GET HIM, BOBBY! STUPID POLACK! FIGHT! FIGHT! FIGHT! KICK HIS BUTT!

COACH (*as needed, with JAYHAWKS PLAYERS*). JOEY—NO! STOP IT! GET OFF OF HIM! RIGHT NOW!

(*JOEY appears downstage, talking to the audience. His uniform is torn up and his helmet is gone. NOTE: The fight continues upstage as though JOEY is still in their midst.*)

JOEY. Man oh man—it was brutal under that pile of bodies! Everyone was punching at me and I was punching at them and there was blood and spit and everything smelled really bad and I said a whole lotta words that I'm never supposed to say—and the next thing I knew, the umpire had thrown me out and we had to forfeit the game and Coach had a hold of Bobby Fuller by the neck—

(*COACH is holding BOBBY FULLER with one hand and JOEY's baseball cap in the other.*)

COACH. Run along now, Bobby.

BOBBY FULLER (*breaks into a grin and runs off, saying*). Good game, Polack!

JOEY (*to COACH*). Did you hear that?!

COACH. You could have killed him with that bat!

JOEY. But what about the things he said?!

COACH. Joey, you already cost your teammates the game — don't make it worse.

JOEY. OK, I know. I'm sorry.

COACH. You've got a problem, young man. And you're not gonna play again in this league till you solve it.

(*JOEY puts out his hand, asking for his cap. COACH stares at JOEY but does not give him back his cap. COACH goes, leaving JOEY alone. At JOEY'S HOME. DAD and MOM approach from opposite directions. DAD has his coat on and he holds his Yankees baseball cap. MOM is dressed in her nurse's uniform. She has JOEY's backpack.*)

DAD. He did what?

MOM. He got in a fight.

DAD. Who started it?

MOM. What does it matter who —

DAD. I've always told him that it's wrong to fight, but if another kid starts it, sometimes you have to —

MOM. He started it. Joey started it.

DAD. You're sure?

MOM. The Little League commissioner called me, said he thinks Joey has a problem — that he needs help.

DAD (*a slight smile*). Anger management classes or something?

MOM. Is this funny to you?

DAD (*serious*). No, I'm just —

MOM. Because if it is —

DAD (*overlapping*). He's a kid, Beth. He got in a fight and that was wrong, but I'm sure he's already learned his lesson. (*JOEY appears. He sits and plays with his Nintendo DS [or Game Boy].*) Right, Joe?

JOEY (*quiet*). Hi, Dad.

DAD. You do know it was wrong — what you did?

JOEY. Yeah.

(*awkward pause*)

DAD. School OK?

JOEY. Yeah. It's good.

(*beat*)

DAD. OK…Well, you should be thinking of what you'd like to do this weekend.

JOEY (*eagerly*). Maybe Wild Mountain! They've got this gigantic new roller coaster that goes—

MOM. I don't think your dad meant something quite that…

JOEY. Fun?

MOM. *Expensive*. Money's a little tight right now—for all of us.

DAD. OK, whatever it is, you let me know and we'll figure something out, all right? See you Friday, buddy. (*DAD opens his arms to give JOEY a hug, but JOEY lifts his hand to give DAD a fist bump.*) Love you.

(*DAD gives the fist bump and goes. MOM is staring at JOEY.*)

JOEY. What's to eat?

MOM. We've talked about this, you know.

JOEY. Yes, I know, but—

MOM. If you can't control your temper, you're not going to play baseball.

JOEY. Mom, what if Ty Cobb's mom had told him to control his temper?! He wouldn't have been Ty Cobb!

MOM. I'm not raising Ty Cobb here! I'm talking about *you*, Joey. You are done with baseball until you can change your ways.

JOEY. Is that what the commissioner said?

MOM. He suspended you for two games.

JOEY. Two games?! I can't believe—

MOM. But *I'm* suspending you for the whole season. (*JOEY stares at her in disbelief.*) Something, or someone, has to get your attention.

JOEY. The whole season?! You can't do that!

MOM. I think it's what you need.

JOEY. We'll you're wrong!

MOM. Joey—

JOEY. And just because you had a crappy day and money's tight and you're mad at Dad doesn't mean you have to take it out on—

MOM. Joey. There it is again.

JOEY. What?!

MOM. *Your temper.* (*beat*) I'm not saying it's easy. We all get mad, we all get frustrated sometimes and wish we could just break something.

JOEY. Is Dad out of work again?

MOM (*this stings, a beat*). OK. See, right now—what I'm feeling right now—is an example of what I'm talking about.

JOEY (*hands her some small object*). You wanna break this?

MOM. No.

(*pause*)

JOEY. Did you get in a fight over what I did?

MOM. Joey, why do you—

JOEY. Because it seems like things are worse now—and that maybe it's because of me.

MOM (*firm, kind*). It's not you. It's just . . . the way things are right now. I want you to focus on your temper, on not letting it—

JOEY. Yeah, I know, I will—

MOM. *You need to promise me, Joey.*

JOEY. And then you'll let me play?

MOM. We'll see. (*She musses his hair and goes, saying the following.*) Dinner in five.

JOEY (*turns to the audience*). "We'll see." Every kid knows what that means. "We'll see" is what parents say when they want to say "no" to you . . . *as slowly as possible.*

(*The CLASSROOM. The teacher, MS. LEVITT, addresses the STUDENTS.*)

MS. LEVITT. And this year, for our black history unit, we're going to do something a little different. Instead of doing written reports on an influential African American, this year you'll be doing *oral reports*, which you'll present to the entire class— (*The STUDENTS and JOEY grumble.*) And the report judged as the most well researched and presented will win—

STUDENT. Probably like a *sticker* or a new *eraser*!

(*The STUDENTS laugh, groan, etc.*)

MS. LEVITT. That student will win three all-day passes to Wild Mountain.

JOEY (*stunned, thrilled*). No . . . way.

MS. LEVITT. Now—

JOEY (*his hand immediately shoots up*). Ms. Levitt? Ms. Levitt? Ms. Levitt?

MS. LEVITT. No, Joey, not this time.

JOEY. Oh, come on!

MS. LEVITT. You cannot write about a ballplayer again. You always do that—

JOEY. How about a retired player?

MS. LEVITT. Joey, this is a history class—

JOEY. OK, how about a *really old retired player who is almost dead?!*

MS. LEVITT (*beat*). Joey, listen to me —

JOEY. I HAVE GOT TO WIN THOSE PASSES TO WILD MOUNTAIN!

MS. LEVITT. It's time to broaden your horizons. There is more to life than baseball.

JOEY (*beat, to audience*). *Did she really just SAY THAT?!*

MS. LEVITT (*handing out papers*). Here is a list of notable black Americans from which you will select one person to profile.

JOEY (*reading from list*). Frederick Douglass. Harriet Tubman.

MS. LEVITT (*looking at JOEY*). Keep in mind that you are to use *only the names on this list.*

JOEY. Sojourner Truth. Langston Hughes.

MS. LEVITT. And the goal of your research is to discover, as best as you can —

JOEY. Paul Robeson. Rosa Parks.

MS. LEVITT. What it might have felt like to *be them.*

JOEY. George Washington Carver.

MS. LEVITT. To *live like they lived, in their day.*

JOEY. Booker T. WAIT A MINUTE — (*stops suddenly, having seen another name*) There it was! The perfect name!

MS. LEVITT. Did you find someone, Joey?

JOEY. Yes, ma'am. And I know just how to do my research! (*a light on JOEY*) I rode my bike to the new baseball card shop in my neighborhood. It's called Flip's Fan Club. It's run by this old guy named Flip Valentini who is probably, like, *70 years old.* He tells stories about things like typewriters and rotary phones and TVs that had ears made out of rabbits. I never really knew any of my grandparents, but I guess Flip is what a grandparent would be like if they were way cooler than your mom and dad.

(*AT FLIP'S FAN CLUB. FLIP VALENTINI enters wearing an old cardigan sweater, rearranging the merchandise in his display case.*)

FLIP. Jackie Robinson!

JOEY. Yep.

FLIP. You came here lookin' for a Jackie Robinson card!

JOEY. I'm doing a report on him for school.

FLIP. So, you like Dem Bums, huh? That's what everyone called 'em, you know. The *real Dodgers* — not those thievin' Hollywood hotshots out in Los Angeles. I'm talkin' 'bout the real Trolley Dodgers, that played in Brooklyn, New York—

JOEY. At Ebbets Field—

FLIP. Oh, kid, you're takin' me back! I grew up there, ya know. On Flatbush Avenue—right under the "L." I can still hear that thing rumble by while me and my buddies are havin' an egg creme or playin' 'round the johnny pump or just sittin' on the stoop *fozzying* away the hours.

JOEY (*to audience*). Sometimes Flip would speak in another language.

FLIP (*off of JOEY's look*). Oh, you don't know about Fozzying? Well, lemme hook you up. See, Fozzying was this game we played where you'd flip cards against a wall or the stoop, and whoever got their card the closest got to keep the other guy's cards.

JOEY. You did this with baseball cards?!

FLIP. I was real good at it. That's how I got the name "Flip."

JOEY. What happened to those cards?

FLIP. Oh, they got pretty beat up. And I had some nice ones, too. I had the whole team from '55: Jackie, Pee Wee, Eddie, Campy, and the Preacher.

JOEY. You should display them.

FLIP. I wish I could. When I grew up and left home, my mom found this old box of cards, all ragged and beat-up, and she *threw 'em out.*

JOEY. No way.

FLIP (*wistfully*). Broke my heart, Joey. Think a parent can't break a kid's heart? *Think again.* I wonder about those cards all the time. (*indicates to a place in his shop*) If I still had 'em, I know right where I'd put 'em.

JOEY. They'd be worth a lot of money.

FLIP. Oh, but I'd never sell 'em. You don't sell your memories when your memories are all you got. (*dramatically produces a baseball card*)

JOEY. Wow—that's a beauty.

FLIP. 1951. Jackie hit .338. Stole 25 bases, including home.

JOEY. I was looking for a 1947. His rookie year.

FLIP. The year he made history.

JOEY. That's right!

FLIP. Wish I could help you, Joey.

JOEY. You don't have one?

FLIP. Nobody does. They didn't make 'em.

JOEY. What?!

FLIP. After the war, paper and ink were scarce. So there's no Jackie Robinson rookie card at all.

JOEY. *But how am I going to get back to 1947?!*

FLIP. Come again?

JOEY (*to audience*). My plan had completely fallen apart!

(*FLIP reaches into an unseen cabinet [or goes into the "back" of the store] for a moment.*)

FLIP. Tell you what, Joey: I do have one thing that might help you out. (*produces a framed set of 13 cards*) In '47, the Bond Bread Company signed Jackie Robinson to endorse their bread. There are 13 Bond Bread cards—with a different photo of Jackie on each of 'em.

JOEY. *Wow.*

FLIP. Nice, huh?

JOEY. Is there any way I could *touch* one of them. Just for a second?

FLIP. Well, they're pretty special, Joey, but you bein' a Brooklyn fan and all . . .

(*FLIP takes one of the cards out and hands it to JOEY. [possible projection of the card]*)

JOEY (*to audience*). On the back of the card was a picture of a loaf of bread— and the words "Folks, why not eat the bread that Jackie eats?" And better yet, there it was—the tingling in my hands. Just like with a real baseball card!

FLIP. Whatcha think?

JOEY. It's perfect, Flip. How much is it?

FLIP (*laughs*). Oh, I can't part with these.

JOEY. Well, how about just one of 'em?

FLIP. Can't break up the set, Joey. But if you want, you could take a picture of 'em—include it in your report.

JOEY. If you ever *did* break up the set . . . how much would one card be?

FLIP. About 700.

JOEY. *Dollars?*

FLIP. Yep. (*beat*) Unless . . .

JOEY. Yes?

FLIP. What?

JOEY. You said "unless."

FLIP (*playing him*). Did I?

JOEY. Yes, you said—

FLIP. Unless . . . it was more of a *loan*. When's your report due?

JOEY. Two weeks.

FLIP. And how much money you got?

JOEY. Twenty dollars.

FLIP. Well, if I *loaned it to you* for 10 bucks a week, that would come to—

JOEY. Twenty dollars!

FLIP. But then I'd have to have it back—

JOEY. Sure.

FLIP. In *mint condition*, just like it is now.

JOEY. It's a deal! (*FLIP gives JOEY the card in exchange for the $20 bill.*) Why are you doin' this, Flip?

FLIP. Because I'm a lousy businessman! Because I love the game *more than the money the game can make*. A good businessman don't have that problem— he can up and move his team out of Brooklyn because it'll make him some money. But a true fan . . . (*lifts his vintage Brooklyn Dodgers cap and puts it on*) A true fan could never let his team go . . . not for all the money in the world.

JOEY (*to audience, holding up the Bond Bread card*). I had my ticket back! Now I just had to tell you-know-who.

(*At JOEY's home. His MOM enters, wearing a nurse uniform, just off of work. JOEY approaches her.*)

MOM. Can you not—just this once—*go to the library* to research your report?!

JOEY. Mom, no one goes to the *library* anymore.

MOM. But do you really have to fly back to 1947?

JOEY. I don't actually fly, Mom.

MOM. Well what do you do? How do you get there?

JOEY. I told you. I hold an old baseball card in my hands, close my eyes, and I wish I was back in that player's time. My hand starts to tingle, and when I open my eyes, I'm there.

MOM. But how can—

JOEY. And then I use a baseball card from the *present* to get me home. It works every time!

MOM. *Once*, Joey! You've done it *once before*. With (*pronounced Hoe-ness*) Honus—

JOEY (*correcting, Hawn-ess*). *Honus* Wagner.

MOM. And what if that was just a fluke? An accident?

JOEY. It wasn't, Mom.

MOM. And what if you get in a fight and hurt yourself? In 1947, there are no antibiotics, no CAT scans, no—

JOEY. I'll be careful.

MOM. What if you can't *get back home?*

JOEY. Mom, this is *educational.* This is for *school.* (*turns to audience*) OK, that's my best shot. Usually if I say it's educational, Mom will fall for it. If that doesn't work, I'm sunk.

(*JOEY turns back to MOM, expectant.*)

MOM (*firm, conditional*). You can't miss any school.

JOEY. I won't. This is Friday. I have three nights to do what I need. That's plenty of time.

MOM. I expect to see you in your bed *first thing Monday morning*—

JOEY (*starts to go*). OK.

MOM. And Joey— (*He stops. She looks him in the eye.*) *Watch your temper.*

JOEY. I promise. (*MOM goes. JOEY continues talking to audience as he packs.*) I put some jeans and T-shirts in my backpack. A notebook for my report. I wrapped my DS (*or Game Boy.*) in an old towel. Then I picked a current card out of my collection—Ken Griffey Jr.—to get me back home. Once I threw in my mitt and a toothbrush, I was all set.

(*Doorbell rings.*)

MOM (*offstage*). JOEY, WILL YOU GET THAT?

JOEY. Whenever Mom won't answer the door, that means my dad's come over. She must have told him what I was going to do.

(*DAD enters. He is carrying a large, old leather satchel.*)

DAD. 1947, huh? You think it'll work again?

JOEY. It's got to. (*regarding the satchel*) Were you planning to go with me?

DAD (*smiles*). Wish I could. No—I brought you something, Joe.

(*brings out a baseball card in a protective plastic sleeve*)

JOEY. For real? Babe Ruth—1932!

DAD. I want you to have all the Yankee greats in your collection someday, and there's none greater than the Babe.

JOEY (*admiring the card*). This can be my birthday *and* my Christmas present, OK?

DAD. No—it's just something I wanted to do. (*referring to JOEY holding the card, hopeful*) *Hand tingling?*

JOEY. Yeah, a little.

DAD. Hey, did I ever tell you about the Babe's famous "called shot"?

JOEY (*to audience*). Only a million times.

DAD. The 1932 World Series against the Cubs—the Babe comes up to bat at Wrigley Field. And you know what he does?

JOEY (*nodding his head yes*). No, what?

DAD. He *points to the centerfield fence*! Like he's saying, "I'm going to hit the ball *right there!*"

JOEY. "And what happens?"

DAD. *He does! On the very next pitch!*

JOEY. It might just be a story. One of those myths—made up by baseball fans.

DAD. You're absolutely right.

JOEY. I guess we'll never know.

DAD. *Or maybe we will.* (*off of JOEY's look*) You could find out, Joe! You could use that card and go back to 1932—and you could see for yourself.

JOEY. But Dad, I'm—

DAD. It's the biggest mystery in all of baseball, and you could solve it!

JOEY. I'm going back to '47—to meet Jackie Robinson.

DAD. Yes, I know but—

JOEY. I'm not going to meet Babe Ruth. (*starts to hand the card back*) Maybe some other time.

(*But DAD does not take it.*)

DAD. No. That's yours. You keep that. (*beat*) I bought you your first set of cards, remember. Just like my dad did for me. (*regarding the satchel*) This was Grampa's satchel, you know. His initials, which are the same as yours, are right on there. I thought it should belong to you.

JOEY. Thanks.

DAD. Might be good for your trip—looks like the old days, won't attract attention. Plus, it's got a secret pocket here on the inside— (*gesturing, "See there, isn't that cool?"*) and it's also got a lot of extra room inside.

JOEY. OK, great.

(*pause*)

DAD. You know, Joe . . . I never thought I'd have to say this . . . and I hope you won't have to say this to your son . . .

JOEY. Dad, it's OK, just say it.

DAD. I need your help. I'm tryin' so hard, but I'm fallin' behind. And it's making things real hard for your mom, and for you.

JOEY. No, we're OK, we'll be—

DAD. A little bit of money would, I don't know, go a long way toward making things better.

JOEY. And it would get you two back together. Mom said that!

DAD (*beat*). No, Joe, I don't think she did.

JOEY. OK, no, not in so many words, but if things were just—

DAD. I made a promise to her. And to you. And I want to keep that promise.

JOEY. But where will we get the money? (*JOEY is staring at DAD. Then JOEY [not DAD] looks down at the leather satchel. JOEY gets an idea.*) Cards. (*to DAD*) I could fill Grampa's satchel with cards from the olden days—then bring 'em home and sell them! Is that what you were thinking?!

DAD. The idea had crossed my mind, yes—

JOEY. It's a great idea! I can't believe we didn't think of this before!

DAD. But when you told me there weren't any new cards in '47, I started thinking that maybe—

JOEY. But Dad, there'll be cards from '46 and '45 and '44 and '43—people'll probably just give 'em to me for free!

DAD. And if they don't . . . (*pulls out a bill*) . . . here's $20. Buy up as many cards as you can.

JOEY. You got it.

DAD. Thanks, Joe. (*JOEY puts his backpack inside the leather satchel as MOM appears, carrying some food for JOEY's trip. DAD continues to MOM.*) I think he's all set. (*to JOEY*) Come home safe. Don't worry your mother.

JOEY. OK. Bye, Dad. (*DAD goes. JOEY turns to MOM.*) You could say something to him, you know.

MOM. I've said plenty. (*regarding the food*) OK, I packed some tuna sandwiches, carrot sticks, and a couple of your favorite cookies—

JOEY. Mom, they have food in 1947.

MOM. Remember to wear your coat, keep an eye on your things, and—

JOEY. Right.

MOM & JOEY. Mind your manners.

(*MOM gives JOEY a kiss on his forehead, then looks at him for a good long moment.*)

MOM. Bye, Joe.

(*MOM goes.*)

JOEY (*to audience*). It was weird. My mom had never called me "Joe" before. It made me feel sort of grown up. (*Music/sound as lights isolate JOEY, alone.*) I got my stuff together. I took out my Jackie Robinson Bond Bread card and I thought of 1947 . . . what it must have felt like to live back then—to live like Jackie Robinson—and sure enough, my hands started tingling . . . and I drifted away . . . thinking of Ebbets Field . . . Brooklyn, New York, and Jackie Robinson stealing home . . . (*Music/sound builds as an office [a desk and chairs] is assembled around JOEY, who remains asleep on the floor, until an OLD-TIME PHONE RINGS LOUDLY and lights bump up, and we are now in BRANCH RICKEY'S OFFICE, New York City, 1947. JOEY is awakened by the phone. He sits up and looks around, disoriented. He goes to the [old, heavy, black] phone and stares at it. He lifts the receiver and tries to find something to push to answer it, but instead he hears a voice on the other end.*) Oh! What? Hello?! Rickey? No, this is Joey. Joey Sto—what? Oh, *Mister* Rickey? *Branch* Rickey? I—I'm pretty sure he's dead. Yeah. He used to run the Brooklyn Dodgers back in— (*sees a calendar in the room*) *1947!* (*to audience*) It worked! I'm here! (*into the phone*) What—the *funeral*? Oh, I'm not sure when that is. Just check the website, I guess. I'm sure they'll—

(*The caller's voice can still be heard mumbling out of the phone. JOEY is trying to find a button to push to end the call as BRANCH RICKEY appears behind JOEY.*)

BRANCH RICKEY. Just set it down. (*JOEY turns, startled.*) Drop it in the cradle. He'll shut up. (*JOEY puts the receiver down in the cradle and the voice stops.*) God, how people love to talk, huh? I grew up with a kid who would never stop yammerin'. To this day, reporters call his office the "Cave of the Winds"— and you know what I say to that? (*JOEY shakes his head no.*) I say: *Get used to it, fellas,* 'cause that kid was me! How'd you get up here, son, are you lost?

JOEY. Umm, I was just doing some research for school. A history project.

BRANCH RICKEY. Oh, I love history. Tell me who's in that picture right there.

JOEY. Abraham Lincoln. The 16th president.

BRANCH RICKEY. Easy one, I know. How about that picture?

JOEY. Leo Durocher. Manager of the Dodgers. And, later, the Giants.

BRANCH RICKEY (*with a laugh*). Oh that's a good one—me lettin' Leo go manage the Giants. That'll happen the same year pigs can fly.

JOEY. Then pigs might fly in 1948.

BRANCH RICKEY (*amused*). Next year, huh?

JOEY. I looked it up.

BRANCH RICKEY. You looked it up?

JOEY (*realizing*). I mean . . . that's just what I *heard*.

BRANCH RICKEY. What's your name, son?

JOEY. Joey. Joey Stoshack.

BRANCH RICKEY. What do your friends call you?

JOEY. They call me Joey. Joey Stoshack.

BRANCH RICKEY. I see.

JOEY (*proudly*). Except for Honus Wagner. He called me—Stosh (*rhymes with "wash"*).

BRANCH RICKEY (*a smile, playing along*). You knew ol' Hans, did you? The two of you pal-ed around together?

JOEY. Well, actually—

BRANCH RICKEY. I have dreams like that, too, Joey. I dream I'm there at Lincoln's side during the Civil War. See myself there with the Wright Brothers at Kitty Hawk. Imagine if history was somethin' we could go *visit*—whenever we wanted? Wouldn't that be *grand*?

JOEY (*a smile*). *Totally* grand.

BRANCH RICKEY. And wouldn't it be grander still if we could *make a little history of our own.* (*gestures to a window in the room*) Look at that boy, Joey. There in the window. See that reflection? That's a boy who loves baseball. (*JOEY is looking at the reflection in the window.*) And tell me this: Why on earth can't that boy play ball alongside white boys?

JOEY (*pointing to window*). Who is that, sir?

BRANCH RICKEY. Pardon me?

JOEY. That boy outside the window?

BRANCH RICKEY. You pullin' my leg, Joey?

JOEY. No, sir, I just—

BRANCH RICKEY. That's you! That's your reflection in the window! I'm talkin' about you!

JOEY (*to audience*). Something had happened. I still felt like me—but my skin, my hair . . . something had changed.

BRANCH RICKEY. It'll be a cryin' shame if we don't do right by *kids like you.*

(*BRANCH RICKEY arranges some papers and a pen on his desk, preparing for a meeting, while JOEY is still looking at his reflection. IMPORTANT NOTE: there must be no change in JOEY's physical appearance. He remains a kid with white skin. From this moment on, until noted otherwise, all of the other character's will view him, and treat him, as an African-American kid, circa 1947.*)

JOEY (*to audience*). Something very weird was happening. The kid in the window — *the African-American kid in the window* — kept looking at me. I raised my hand, he raised his.

BRANCH RICKEY. A colored man can go off and fight against Hitler now, can't he?

JOEY (*to audience*). I turned my head, he turned his.

BRANCH RICKEY. Well, I say if he can die for his country, why can't he *play* for his country?!

JOEY (*to audience*). The last time — with Honus Wagner — I had wished I could be all grown up, and when I went back in time, I *was.*

BRANCH RICKEY. And better, yet, why can't he play for the Dodgers?!

JOEY (*to audience*). Now, I'd wondered what it was like to be Jackie Robinson . . . and when I got back to 1947, I was a kid with black skin!

BRANCH RICKEY. Baseball won't be America's game until *all Americans can play it.*

JOEY (*to audience*). I always thought if I was another color, that I'd *feel* — I don't know . . . *different.* But I still just felt like *me.*

BRANCH RICKEY. You a ballplayer, Joey?

JOEY. Yeah, sure.

BRANCH RICKEY. Well, maybe one day you'll get to play in the Negro Leagues —

JOEY. *Me?*

BRANCH RICKEY. Unless, of course, you'd rather play for the Dodgers.

JOEY. But aren't there rules?

BRANCH RICKEY. Not a ONE of 'em. NOWHERE is it written that a black man can't play in the Major Leagues —

JOEY. Then what's stopping —

BRANCH RICKEY. But the owners of the teams have an *unwritten rule* between them. And remember, Joey, it's the *unwritten rules* that are *written most deeply.* (*The PHONE RINGS and BRANCH RICKEY answers it immediately, speaks into phone.*) Rickey. (*beat*) Send him in. *And hold my calls.* (*hangs up the phone*) I've got a meeting now, son. You gotta scadaddle. (*regarding JOEY's things*) Don't forget your stuff.

JOEY. But, Mr. Rickey, I came here because I'm trying to meet —

(*And now a man is standing behind JOEY, seen only by BRANCH RICKEY. He wears a crisp suit and carries a hat. This is JACKIE ROBINSON.*)

BRANCH RICKEY. Jackie Robinson.

JOEY (*to BRANCH RICKEY*). Yes, how did you know?

JACKIE (*formal, polite*). Mr. Rickey. (*Hearing the voice behind him, JOEY turns and sees JACKIE.*) Oh my gosh— (*to audience, amazed*) Standing there was— (*to JACKIE*) I mean, wow . . . *you are*—

BRANCH RICKEY. The man knows his own name, kid. Now, if you'll excuse us—

JACKIE (*extends his hand to JOEY*). I'm Jackie Robinson. Folks call me Jack.

JOEY. I'm Joey Stoshack. Folks call me . . . *Stosh.*

BRANCH RICKEY. I bet your mom's waitin' for you . . . *Stosh.* I'll have my secretary walk you down to the lobby—

JOEY (*not wanting to go*). But . . .

BRANCH RICKEY (*overlapping*). Mr. Robinson and I have some things to discuss.

JACKIE. The boy can stay. It's fine with me.

(*JOEY looks to BRANCH RICKEY, hopeful. BRANCH RICKEY leads JOEY away from JACKIE.*)

BRANCH RICKEY (*whisper*). OK, just for a minute . . . but you *cannot talk.* Not a word. Got me?

(*JOEY nods. BRANCH RICKEY and JACKIE now begin to stare at each other in silence.*)

JOEY (*to audience*). And I waited as they stared at each other. Waited for history to be made.

(*BRANCH RICKEY turns away and moves to the chair behind his desk, sits.*)

BRANCH RICKEY (*finally*). You know why you're here?

JACKIE. Yes, sir. A fellow told me to meet with you. Said you were gonna start up a Negro League team here in Brooklyn. The Brown Dodgers.

BRANCH RICKEY. Yes, that was my plan. Till I had a new thought. A bigger thought. (*BRANCH RICKEY and JACKIE continue to stare at each other across the room.*) I've been talking to lot of people, Jack. People out West, in California, who knew you in school. They say at UCLA you lettered in four sports in one year.

JACKIE. That's true.

BRANCH RICKEY. And no one had ever done that. Only you.

JACKIE. Yes, sir.

BRANCH RICKEY. And baseball was your best sport?

JACKIE. No, sir. It was my worst.

BRANCH RICKEY. You were even better at football and basketball and track?

JACKIE. Yes, sir.

(*beat*)

BRANCH RICKEY (*quickly*). I could beat you at tennis.

JACKIE (*just as quick*). No sir, you could not.

BRANCH RICKEY. Bowling.

JACKIE. No.

BRANCH RICKEY. Horseshoes, Checkers, Ping-Pong.

JACKIE. No, no, and no.

BRANCH RICKEY. You don't lose, is that it?

JACKIE. *Not happily, no.*

BRANCH RICKEY. *Neither do I, Jack.* (*beat*) But I'm talking about doing something that's never been done.

JACKIE. You're not starting up a team here in Brooklyn, are you, Mr. Rickey?

BRANCH RICKEY. No, Jack, I've already got a team. They're called the Dodgers. And I want you to play for 'em.

JOEY (*to audience*). Finally! Now all that had to happen was for Jackie Robinson to say yes! (*JOEY turns expectantly to JACKIE. JACKIE is silent.*) But he didn't say anything! (*The PHONE RINGS and JOEY immediately answers it.*) I SAID HOLD MY CALLS—we're tryin' to make some history here!

(*JOEY hangs up the phone, hard, as BRANCH RICKEY shoots him a look. JOEY returns to where he was watching.*)

BRANCH RICKEY (*to JACKIE*). You're a polite young man. Credit to your mother. She taught you good manners.

JACKIE. Yes, sir, she did.

BRANCH RICKEY. So, where'd you get that temper? Word is you're a hothead, Robinson. You were a hothead in the military and you're the same way on the field. You've got a mean streak in you, an angry streak—is that true?

JACKIE. I suppose you could—

BRANCH RICKEY (*sharply*). *I suppose you could ANSWER THE QUESTION.*

(*A hard, sharp look from JACKIE to BRANCH RICKEY.*)

JACKIE (*icily*). I have a temper, yes.

BRANCH RICKEY. Good. You're gonna need it. And you're gonna need to know *how to use it.* See, I know you can hit and run and throw, but that's not gonna be enough. (*BRANCH RICKEY stands and approaches JACKIE, build-ing in intensity.*) What'll you do, Jack? When all your teammates go to a restaurant and you're not allowed to eat there? When you have to stay in a separate hotel, ride on a separate bus, walk in the back door rather than the front?!

JACKIE. I'll do what it takes, Mr. Rickey.

BRANCH RICKEY. Well I hope you know what it "takes" when those voices start sayin', "Hey Nappy Head, get your butt to the back of the line."

JACKIE (*trying to stay cool*). Mr. Rickey—

BRANCH RICKEY. "Where'd you steal that suit—off the back of a white man?"

JACKIE. Please, sir—

BRANCH RICKEY. "Why don't you go back to the cotton fields where you belong? Baseball's a white man's game—"

JACKIE. Listen now—

BRANCH RICKEY (*overlapping*). "And uppity coons like you are fit for nothin' but shining our shoes, ain't that right?!" (*JACKIE's fists are now clenched at his side, rage in his eyes, as BRANCH RICKEY makes a fist, like he's about to punch JACKIE.*) I said, "AIN'T THAT RIGHT, BOY??!!" (*A frozen moment: BRANCH RICKEY's fist is ready to strike. JACKIE is staring fiercely into BRANCH RICKEY's eyes. BRANCH RICKEY continues speaking in a hard whisper.*) What will you do, Jack, when you hear all that?

JACKIE. You want a man who's *afraid to fight back?*

BRANCH RICKEY. No. *I want a man with enough courage NOT TO.* (*beat*) A man who knows how to *use* his temper. I want him to put his temper into *the game.* If you lash out at ANYONE—even ONCE—it's over. You'd have to promise me. You'd have to learn to turn to the other cheek. (*beat*) Can you do that, Jack?

(*silence*)

JOEY (*whispers to audience*). And after a very long silence, Jackie Robinson said . . .

JACKIE. Yes, sir.

(*BRANCH RICKEY extends his hand and JACKIE, after staring at it for a moment, shakes his hand.*)

JOEY (*quietly*). *Yes!*

BRANCH RICKEY. I've got some papers for you to sign.

(*JACKIE sits at BRANCH RICKEY's desk and signs the papers.*)

JOEY (*to audience*). Jackie Robinson was 28 years old. He signed for the Major League minimum of $5,000. Baseball now had 399 white players . . . and one black. I looked at the picture of Leo Durocher in Mr. Rickey's office. When some of his players complained about playing with Robinson, Leo Durocher told 'em—

(*a quick light on LEO DUROCHER*)

LEO DUROCHER (*crusty as all get out*). I DON'T CARE IF THE GUY IS YELLOW OR BLACK, OR HAS STRIPES ON HIM LIKE A— (*mouths the word*)

JOEY (*quickly, covering*). BEEEEP!

LEO DUROCHER. —*ING ZEBRA*! I'M THE MANAGER OF THIS TEAM AND I SAY HE PLAYS.

JOEY (*to audience*). That was close.

(*LEO DUROCHER is gone.*)

BRANCH RICKEY (*to JACKIE, regarding the papers*). Starting now, it's just you and me. We've got no army. There's almost nobody on our side. We can only win if we convince the world that you're a great ballplayer and a fine gentleman. Oh, Jack, there's one more thing—

JACKIE. Yes, Mr. Rickey?

BRANCH RICKEY. Once you're done turnin' the other cheek, I want you to steal home.

JACKIE (*finally, a smile*). Yes, sir. (*turns to JOEY*) See you later, Stosh.

JOEY (*awed*). Bye.

(*JOEY watches JACKIE as he goes.*)

BRANCH RICKEY. Well . . . you think he can do it?

JOEY. Yes, I do.

BRANCH RICKEY. Let's hope you're right. And about some of that language I used—

JOEY. It's OK, I've heard kids talk like that at school.

BRANCH RICKEY. I'm sorry to hear that.

JOEY. This time it was different, though . . .

BRANCH RICKEY. Why's that, Stosh?

(*JOEY is once again looking at his reflection in the window. He touches his face with his fingers.*)

JOEY. This time it was about me.

(*BRANCH RICKEY puts an arm around JOEY. They start offstage.*)

BRANCH RICKEY. C'mon, I'll have my secretary get you a Coke.

JOEY (*looks back to phone*). Oh, Mr. Rickey, I think I told someone you were dead.

BRANCH RICKEY. You probably made their day.

(*A light on JOEY as BRANCH RICKEY exits.*)

JOEY (*to the audience*). I wanted to see Ebbets Field before it got dark. I tried to ask directions, but no one would look at me. Then a policeman raised his nightstick and said —

POLICEMAN'S VOICE. Move along now, boy.

JOEY. I'd left the food from my mom in Branch Rickey's office. I was hungry and thirsty, and I was really hot *in the coat my mom had made me wear.*

(*A DRINKING FOUNTAIN. A WOMAN is getting a drink from the fountain. A MAN is in line behind her. He holds a newspaper. He stands in such a way that he blocks a sign near the fountain. JOEY approaches the fountain and gets in line behind the WOMAN. Seeing JOEY, the MAN steps out of line.*)

JOEY (*to the MAN, politely*). Oh, thank you. (*The MAN begins to walk in a slow circle around JOEY, giving him a hard stare. We can now see the sign fully. It reads "WHITES ONLY." The WOMAN, having finished her drink, turns, sees JOEY, and gasps.*) What is it, ma'am? (*The WOMAN holds her purse tightly to her chest as the MAN taps JOEY on the shoulder with his now rolled-up newspaper. JOEY turns to the MAN and the MAN points to the sign.*) What? Oh — I didn't see that . . . (*dawns on him*) Do you mean they really can't — (*stops, corrects himself.*) That . . . I really can't . . . (*The WOMAN spits at JOEY's feet as she rushes past him.*) Hey!

(*The MAN gets right in JOEY's face.*)

MAN. You got something to say, black boy?

JOEY (*to audience*). And then I saw it — there in the eyes of that man *who didn't know me at all.*

MAN. Well?

JOEY. All he knew was that my skin was black. And what I saw in his eyes . . . was hate.

(*The MAN now turns and drinks from the fountain, gives JOEY a final look, and then leaves. A black woman has appeared behind JOEY. She has seen the previous incident. She carries an infant in one arm and a small bag in the other. This is RACHEL ROBINSON.*)

RACHEL. Thirsty? (*JOEY turns. He nods. RACHEL sets the bag down.*) There's water in the bag. You're welcome to some. (*regarding the small thermos*) Not much left. Jackie Jr. was hot, so I let him suck on the ice cubes. Go ahead and finish it. (*JOEY drinks as RACHEL coos to the baby and also gives JOEY a good looking over. RACHEL continues, indicating the water fountain.*) You didn't see that "WHITES ONLY" sign?

JOEY. I saw it. But I . . . (*voice trails off*)

RACHEL. But you stayed in line, anyway? (*JOEY nods. RACHEL continues kindly, warmly.*) Be smart about the fights you pick. Stay brave—but be smart about it.

JOEY. Yes, ma'am.

(*JACKIE enters.*)

JACKIE. Sorry about that, Rae, Mr. Rickey wanted me to pose for some photos with— (*stops, seeing JOEY*). Hey—it's Joey, right? I mean, *Stosh.*

JOEY. Either one is fine!

JACKIE. This is my wife, Rachel, and my little son, Jack Jr.

RACHEL (*sees JOEY's satchel*). Are you here visiting, Joey?

JOEY. Yeah, I'm doing a report for school.

RACHEL. And where's your mom?

JOEY. She's back home in the future—*I mean Pittsburgh.*

JACKIE. You came to New York all alone?

JOEY. Sort of, yeah.

RACHEL. And where are you staying?

JOEY. Well, I thought I'd go down around Ebbets Field, maybe find a place to—

RACHEL. This is no place for a Negro boy to be alone. You'll come back to our apartment tonight. And tomorrow, first thing, we'll get ahold of your mother.

(*RACHEL exits. JACKIE lifts JOEY's satchel and heads off after RACHEL. A light on JOEY.*)

JOEY (*to audience*). So that night I stayed with the Robinsons. They were renting a room at the Hotel McAlpin, not far from the Empire State Building. They made me a bed on the couch, but I couldn't sleep.

(*THE HOTEL MCALPIN, New York City. JOEY is looking in a small mirror. He begins to rub his face and his skin with his fingers as JACKIE appears behind him, holding a baseball.*)

JACKIE (*with a smile*). It don't rub off, Stosh.

JOEY (*stops, turns*). Oh, yeah, I wasn't—

JACKIE. My brothers and me used to do the same thing. Sit on our beds and look at all the white kids out the window. Waiting to throw rocks at us because of our skin. There was only one thing to do.

JOEY. What's that?

JACKIE. Throw our rocks harder than they did. (*laughs*) My brother Mack — he could throw harder than anyone. And run? Mack won a silver medal at the Berlin Olympics. Came in second to Jesse Owens in the 200-yard dash.

JOEY. I didn't know that.

JACKIE. Spent my life tryin' to be as good as my big brother. You got someone like that, Stosh? Someone you hope you'll be like?

(*JOEY is looking right at JACKIE.*)

JOEY. Yep.

JACKIE. You got a mitt in that bag?

JOEY. Uh . . . yeah. Of course.

JACKIE. I can't sleep. Opening-day jitters. How 'bout we go outside and have a catch?

(*JACKIE goes as . . .*)

JOEY (*to audience*). And we did! Right in the middle of New York City! There was an alleyway behind the hotel — (*A MIDTOWN ALLEY AT NIGHT. STREET SOUNDS are heard.*) And under the light of an old street lamp, I was playing catch with Jackie Robinson!

(*They play catch.*)

JACKIE. I keep thinking about all the Negro families who'll be there tomorrow — all comin' to watch me play.

JOEY. It's history.

JACKIE. No, Stosh, it's baseball. History is all the people who *won't* be there tomorrow. All the black ballplayers who never got the chance — Rube Foster, Buck O'Neill —

JOEY. Moses Fleetwood Walker —

JACKIE. You know about him?

JOEY. Another school report. I got an A.

JACKIE. The thing is, tomorrow I'm *playin' for them — for all those men that never got the chance.* And if I fail . . .

JOEY. You won't fail.

JACKIE. How do you know? (*JOEY says nothing. JACKIE takes off his mitt and stares at the palms of his own hands.*) Want to know how to travel back in time, Stosh?

JOEY. Um . . . sure.

JACKIE. Just look at your hands. (*JOEY does.*) A man has his father's hands. My father was a sharecropper. His father was a slave. Eighty years ago these hands were picking cotton. (*beat*) What's your dad do for work?

JOEY. He's . . . sort of between jobs right now.

JACKIE. Well . . . *you help him out.* Any way you can. That's what a son is supposed to do.

(*JACKIE exits. A light on JOEY. SOUNDS of the BASEBALL FIELD are heard under.*)

JOEY (*to audience*). The next morning—there it was! Ebbets Field! It was like a *shrine.* The seats were so close to the field that the upper deck actually *hung over* the outfield grass. An announcer called out—

ANNOUNCER. FANS IN THE OUTFIELD, PLEASE REMOVE YOUR CLOTHING!

JOEY. Which meant the fans should take their coats off the top of the outfield wall, where they'd hung them!

ANNOUNCER. THANK YOU!

JOEY. And on this day, Ebbets Field was filled with black families. All dressed up—the men in hats, the women in dresses and gloves. They wore buttons that said "I'm for Robinson." (*JACKIE appears.*) We got to the clubhouse door. *No black player had ever stepped through that door.*

(*Possible projection of a famous photo of JACKIE ROBINSON on the clubhouse door.*)

JACKIE. C'mon, Stosh, it's time.

JOEY (*to audience*). And with that he opened the door . . . and we were IN.

(*THE DODGERS CLUBHOUSE. A brash kid in a Dodgers uniform walks up to JACKIE. This is ANT.*)

ANT. You Mr. Robinson?

JACKIE. Yes, I am.

ANT. Here. (*ANT hands JACKIE his jersey.*) Rest of the uniform's in your locker. Over there in the corner.

JACKIE. In Montreal I wore number 20, but if you don't have that, I wore number 5 for the Monarchs, and—

ANT. The *Monarchs?*

JACKIE. Kansas City.

ANT. You mean—in the *Negro Leagues?*

JACKIE. Yes.

ANT. Well, round here rookies get the number that's left. (*regarding JACKIE's jersey*) And that's it.

(*JACKIE unfurls the jersey, displaying his number: 42.*)

JACKIE. Forty-two? That's a football number. Who wears somethin' like that?

ANT. Nobody wanted it. So it's yours. (*Three DODGERS PLAYERS enter: DIXIE WALKER, EDDIE STANKY, and PEE WEE REESE. They say nothing to JACKIE as he walks silently through their midst with his jersey and then he is gone. ANT turns to JOEY.*) What're you lookin' at? Never seen a clubhouse?

JOEY. No—I mean, yeah, lots of 'em.

(*The DODGERS PLAYERS finish dressing, tying their shoes, readying their mitts, etc. DIXIE WALKER holds a letter-sized piece of paper.*)

ANT. Well, if you're the new clubhouse kid, get to work.

(*ANT tosses JOEY some towels.*)

JOEY. Oh, OK. Who are we playing today?

ANT. The Braves.

JOEY. Atlanta?

ANT. *Atlanta what?*

JOEY (*to audience*). Wait—the Braves moved to Atlanta much later. (*to ANT*) I mean Milwaukee. The Milwaukee Braves.

ANT. *Milwaukee?*

JOEY (*to audience*). And that was wrong, too—

ANT. *Geez—do you know anything about baseball?*

JOEY. Because before they went to Milwaukee, they were—

ANT. *Boston.* The Boston Braves.

DIXIE WALKER. Hey, Ant, you got a pen?

ANT. Sure, Mr. Walker. (*ANT gives DIXIE WALKER a pen and he signs the paper.*) That's Dixie Walker—great hitter and our best outfielder. (*DIXIE WALKER hands the paper to EDDIE STANKY, who also signs it.*) And that's Eddie Stanky—second baseman. They call him The Brat. (*DIXIE WALKER and EDDIE STANKY bring the paper over to PEE WEE REESE.*) And over there . . .

JOEY (*in awe*). Pee Wee Reese. The real guy. He's Flip's favorite player.

ANT. Who's Flip?

JOEY. Just . . . a guy I know.

(*PEE WEE REESE looks at the piece of paper as DIXIE WALKER and EDDIE STANKY move away and finish their preparations.*)

ANT. Well, *boy*, I gotta lot of work for you to do.

JOEY (*to audience*). And I felt my neck get tight.

ANT. My daddy says you colored people are real good workers.

JOEY (*to audience*). And my breath get short.

ANT (*starts to leave*). Just remember who's boss.

JOEY (*to audience*). And my hand made a fist!

(*JOEY starts after ANT but is intercepted by JACKIE, now in uniform.*)

JACKIE. Don't do it, Stosh—

JOEY. Did you hear how he talked to me?!

JACKIE. Heard it for years. But we made a promise, remember?

JOEY. *You* made a promise to Mr. Rickey, but not me. I didn't make any—

(*Quick light on MOM.*)

MOM. *You need to promise me, Joey.* (*JOEY looks at the image of his MOM.*)

JOEY. OK. Maybe I did. (*whispers to MOM*) This is a locker room, Mom . . .

MOM. Oh, sorry.

(*Lights snap out on MOM as JACKIE steps in front of the other DODGERS PLAYERS and addresses them.*)

JACKIE. Gentlemen, I hope you'll let me say this one thing before the game starts. (*Beat. The DODGERS PLAYERS stop and stare at JACKIE, motionless.*) Some of you may not like me because I'm a Negro. You have a right to feel that way. Thing is, I'm not here to be liked. I'm here to play baseball. *I only ask for your respect.* Thank you.

(*silence*)

JOEY (*to audience*). And nobody said *anything.* Jackie just walked away, out the clubhouse, up the tunnel to the field.

(*JACKIE is gone. DIXIE WALKER refers to the paper in PEE WEE REESE's hand.*)

DIXIE WALKER. Well? Anybody else need to sign it?

EDDIE STANKY. Reese, after you sign it, bring it with you.

JOEY (*to ANT*). Sign what?

(*PEE WEE REESE stands, still holding the paper, as DIXIE WALKER and EDDIE STANKY grab their mitts and leave, followed by ANT, who calls to JOEY.*)

ANT. Grab those bats, will ya?

(*ANT is gone. JOEY watches as PEE WEE REESE, having read it, slowly sets the paper down, not signing it. Then he grabs his mitt and heads out as music plays and lights reveal . . . EBBETS FIELD. The GROUNDSKEEPER has finished chalking the* white chalk line and JACKIE stands on the field. He is facing the line. The voice of the ANNOUNCER is heard.)

ANNOUNCER. Welcome Dodger faithful to the opening game of the 1947 campaign! Today's game will feature the visiting Boston Braves— (*Back in the clubhouse, JOEY lifts the paper that PEE WEE REESE set down and looks at it.*) Taking on the home club, your own Brooklyn Dodgers.

(*The DODGERS PLAYERS jog onto the field and take their places, but JACKIE does not move. Separate lights reveal BRANCH RICKEY and RACHEL, looking on.*)

BRANCH RICKEY. Let the record show that history was made here, Tuesday afternoon, in Brooklyn's Ebbets Field, when number 42 . . .

RACHEL. Jack Roosevelt Robinson, grandson of a slave . . .

(*JACKIE walks out and over the white chalk line onto the field.*)

BRANCH RICKEY. . . . trotted out onto the green-swept diamond with the rest of his Dodgers teammates.

JOEY (*reading the paper*). "We, the undersigned players of the Brooklyn Dodgers, hereby state that we wish to be traded or released—rather than be forced to take the field with a colored man."

ANNOUNCER. PLAY BALL!

(*Lights rush out.*)

END OF ACT I

ACT II

(*THE DODGERS CLUBHOUSE. Music plays and the DODGERS PLAYERS [DIXIE WALKER, EDDIE STANKY, and PEE WEE REESE] file in, happy, victorious, holding cans of beer, laughing and talking, as JOEY holds up a scorecard.*)

JOEY (*to audience*). The scorecard for April 15, 1947, shows that the Dodgers beat the Braves 5 to 3. Jackie Robinson reached base on a sacrifice bunt, scored a run, and handled several chances at first base without error. What it doesn't show . . . (*JACKIE enters and the DODGERS PLAYERS immediately go silent. Music out, abruptly.*) is that it *had happened.* A black man had taken the field and played ball in the Major Leagues. And . . . *the world did not stop.* The game of baseball went on.

(*EDDIE STANKY tosses JACKIE a can of beer.*)

EDDIE STANKY. Here you go, rookie. Nice bunt.

JACKIE. Thanks.

(*JACKIE stares at the can of beer.*)

EDDIE STANKY. Something wrong?

JACKIE. No, it's just . . . I don't drink.

(*JACKIE tosses the beer back to EDDIE STANKY.*)

DIXIE WALKER (*unlit cigar in mouth*). Or smoke either, I bet.

JACKIE. No, I don't.

EDDIE STANKY. So what do you do for fun?

(*JACKIE just stares at them.*)

DIXIE WALKER. Well?

PEE WEE REESE (*breaks through the tension*). Probably somethin' a lot smarter than you guys do. (*to DIXIE WALKER and EDDIE STANKY*) C'mon, let's get some supper.

DIXIE WALKER (*regarding EDDIE STANKY*). You comin' along, Colonel?

EDDIE STANKY. It's your turn to pay, Dixie.

(*The DODGERS PLAYERS gather up their things.*)

JOEY. History had been made . . . but *nothing stopped*. Even though Jackie's bat and glove and uniform were all going to the Baseball Hall of Fame one day. (*The DODGERS PLAYERS walk past JACKIE, ignoring him.*) Inside that clubhouse, it felt like just another game. *No one even shook his hand.* (*JACKIE is alone at his locker.*) Good game today.

JACKIE. Not bad. But not good enough.

JOEY. At least it's over, though, right? That first game. It must be good to know —

JACKIE. Stosh, *it's not over.*

(*JACKIE starts off toward ANT, who is entering. ANT does not get out of JACKIE's way. ANT is holding two large canvas bags.*)

ANT. Lotsa folks lookin' for you, Mr. Robinson —

JACKIE. All right, thanks.

ANT. So you're gonna want to use the back door.

(*ANT points to an [unseen] door in the opposite direction.*)

JACKIE. *Say again.*

ANT. Back door. That's where they're havin' everybody wait for you. Don't want to make a scene out front.

(*JACKIE is staring at ANT, who holds his ground, chewing his bubblegum.*)

JACKIE (*to JOEY*). See, it's just *getting started.*

(*JACKIE leaves in the direction ANT suggested as ANT tosses one of the canvas bags to JOEY, saying the following.*)

ANT. The uniforms get washed down the hall. (*ANT empties the contents of the other bag at JOEY's feet: baseball cleats, lots of them. He tosses JOEY a can of shoe polish and a brush or rag.*) I wanna be able to see my shiny white teeth in the toes of those cleats.

JOEY. Hey, look, Ant—

ANT. And you're lucky—that black shoe polish won't even show up on your skin.

(*ANT now sits nearby, opens his* Amazing Stories *magazine and blows bubbles as he reads. JOEY works on the cleats.*)

JOEY. Good game, huh?

ANT (*not looking up*). Robinson got lucky. He's not gonna last. My dad said you colored guys aren't tough enough to play real baseball.

JOEY. Wanna bet he's named Rookie of the Year?

ANT. There's no such thing as the Rookie of the Year.

JOEY. There will be.

ANT (*with a laugh*). Oh, because you know the future, do you?!

JOEY (*playing along*). Yeah, because I'm an alien that landed in a spaceship and I know the future!

ANT (*beat*). *What did you say?*

JOEY. Forget it.

ANT (*suddenly more serious*). *Where'd you get those shoes?*

JOEY. What? They're my old Nikes. They're just— (*to audience*) I *should not* have worn these shoes.

ANT. They look . . .

JOEY. Weird, I know.

ANT (*intensely*). *Futuristic.* Of or pertaining to the future.

JOEY. I know what it means.

ANT. So maybe you'd like to tell me this: *Have you ever been to Roswell, New Mexico?* (*before JOEY can answer*) It says right here in *Amazing Stories* that a spaceship, a spaceship from *outer space*, landed there in the desert.

JOEY (*trying to laugh it away*). Well it wasn't me!

ANT (*very serious now*). Hey, don't laugh, this is real. *Aliens are WITH US. They are IN OUR MIDST.* (*ANT, suspicious now, gives JOEY a very wide berth as he leaves.*) See you tomorrow, Shine Boy from Mars.

JOEY (*to audience*). But I wouldn't see him tomorrow. I just needed to buy a few baseball cards for my dad, say goodbye to Jackie and Rachel, and then use my Ken Griffey Jr. card to get me home.

(*On A BROOKLYN STREET. Music and sounds fill the stage.*)

JOEY (*to audience*). The streets of Brooklyn were like a carnival without rides. Radios blared out of the windows, sirens wailed, every stoop and every window was filled with people talking in languages I didn't understand—including a language they called "Brooklyn-ese."

(*A KID IN A CAP runs across the stage, pointing into the distance.*)

KID IN A CAP. G'Jooma! G'Jooma! G'Jooma! G'Jooma!

JOEY. And that turned out to be a *Good Humor* ice cream truck! Vendors were selling corn and fish and pots and pans and hats and scarves—

BROOKLYN KID 2 (*from offstage*). So throw it already!

(*JOEY now stands near a group of three BROOKLYN KIDS [with YOUNG FLIP as BROOKLYN KID 3]. They all wear Dodgers caps. Their backs are to us and we don't see their faces till noted. The BROOKLYN KIDS are flipping cards [Fozzying] against a stoop.*)

JOEY. But nowhere I looked was anyplace selling baseball cards.

BROOKLYN KID 1. Nah—not even close!

BROOKLYN KID 2. Your turn—hurry up!

BROOKLYN KID 3 (YOUNG FLIP). Don' rush me!

JOEY. Excuse me, is there a baseball card store around here?

(*The BROOKLYN KIDS don't stop playing.*)

BROOKLYN KID 1. Beat it, jungle bunny.

BROOKLYN KID 2. Go back to Harlem.

BROOKLYN KID 1 (*to BROOKLYN KID 3 [YOUNG FLIP]*). C'mon, throw da cards!

JOEY (*trying to stay cool*). Look, I don't want any trouble—

BROOKLYN KID 1. You hard-a-hearin', darkie? We said scram.

JOEY. I'm just trying to find a place that sells baseball cards.

BROOKLYN KID 3 (YOUNG FLIP). You mean *bubblegum cards?*

JOEY. Yeah, that's right.

BROOKLYN KID 2. Stop yappin', Flip, it's your turn.

BROOKLYN KID 3 (YOUNG FLIP). Try the grocer on the corner of Flatbush. They might have some there.

BROOKLYN KID 1. Geez, Flip, are you gonna fozzy the cards or what?!

BROOKLYN KID 3 (YOUNG FLIP). I'm fozzyin' all right and I am takin' you down!

(*BROOKLYN KID 3 [YOUNG FLIP] is about to throw a card.*)

JOEY. WAIT!

(*BROOKLYN KID 3 [YOUNG FLIP] stops. BROOKLYN KIDS 1 and 2 stand and surround JOEY, like they plan to beat him up.*)

BROOKLYN KID 1 (*simultaneously*). Wwwhazzatt?!

BROOKLYN KID 2 (*simultaneously*). Wwwhhooooaa!

BROOKLYN KID 1. YOU LOOKIN' FOR A FIGHT, BOY?!

BROOKLYN KID 2. 'CAUSE WE GOT ONE FOR YOU!

JOEY (*to BROOKLYN KID 3 [YOUNG FLIP]*). Is your last name Valentini?

YOUNG FLIP. Yeah, what's it to ya?

JOEY (*to audience, excited*). *I know the guy this kid is gonna be!* (*to YOUNG FLIP, regarding the cards*) What are you throwin' there?

YOUNG FLIP. My Dodger cards, of course. I got the whole team. *Now why don't you mind your own—*

JOEY. Can I give you a piece of advice?

(*BROOKLYN KIDS 1 and 2 grab JOEY.*)

BROOKLYN KID 1 (*simultaneously*). Who is this Weisenheimer?!

BROOKLYN KID 2 (*simultaneously*). Only if you wanna piece of his fist!

JOEY (*to YOUNG FLIP*). Don't throw those cards. Keep 'em nice and new. And when you get older and move out of the house, take those cards with you, *so your mom won't throw 'em away!*

(*BROOKLYN KID 1 suddenly points to something in the distance.*)

BROOKLYN KID 1. G'JOOMA! G'JOOMA! G'JOOMA!

BROOKLYN KID 2. FLIP, COME ON!

(*BROOKLYN KIDS 1 and 2 rush off.*)

YOUNG FLIP (*turns to JOEY*). See ya later.

JOEY (*a knowing smile*). You will.

(*YOUNG FLIP rushes off. A light on JOEY.*)

JOEY (*to audience*). I found the grocer on Flatbush Avenue. Some stores had signs that said "Negro Entrance At Back," but not this one.

(*A corner grocery, HERSKOWITZ GROCERY. MRS. HERSKOWITZ is sweeping up.*)

JOEY. Excuse me? Do you . . . serve colored people in here?

MRS. HERSKOWITZ. There's only one kind of people I don't serve.

JOEY. Who's that?

MRS. HERSKOWITZ. Yankee fans. You're not one of them are ya?

JOEY. No, ma'am. Dodgers all the way. I love Dem Bums.

MRS. HERSKOWITZ. Good boy. What can I do you for?

JOEY. I want to . . . um . . . buy some bubblegum cards. I have $20.

MRS. HERSKOWITZ. Are you *meshuga*?

JOEY (*to audience*). I didn't know what that meant. So I said nothing.

MRS. HERSKOWITZ. You gotta be crazy to ask something like that. Of course
    I don't sell bubblegum cards.

JOEY. But the kids outside said—

MRS. HERSKOWITZ (*reaches into a box or behind a counter*). *I give 'em away.*

(*She sets a box of cards in front of JOEY.*)

JOEY. You *what*?

MRS. HERSKOWITZ. What a racket. All these companies bring cards in
    here—want me to hand 'em out when I sell their goods. It's a promotion
    they say. I say it's a racket. Take as many as you want.

JOEY. Really?

(*A DELIVERY MAN enters wearing a uniform that prominently features the words
"BOND BREAD." He is pushing a handcart.*)

DELIVERY MAN. Heya, Mrs. Herskowitz, howyadoin'?

MRS. HERSKOWITZ (*looking at JOEY*). I'm nuttin' but chicky. Right, young
    man?

JOEY. Ummmmm . . .

DELIVERY MAN. I'll put the bread in back. Oh, and I'm spozed to give you
    these— (*He hands her a package.*) They want 'em cleared outta the warehouse.

MRS. HERSKOWITZ. What is it?

DELIVERY MAN. Some kind of promotion.

(*The DELIVERY MAN heads off as MRS. HERSKOWITZ tosses the package to JOEY
and leaves, saying the following.*)

MRS. HERSKOWITZ. See what I mean! Have at it, kid. And keep rootin' for
    Dem Bums. This is gonna be our year!

JOEY (*to audience, regarding the package*). There they were!

A full set of the Bond Bread cards with Jackie Robinson on every one of 'em.
    And they were *mint*. (*The DELIVERY MAN is leaving, wheeling his cart past*

JOEY.) Pardon me, sir? (*holds up the cards*) You said there were more of these somewhere?

DELIVERY MAN. At the warehouse. Hundreds of 'em.

(*The DELIVERY MAN checks an invoice while JOEY turns to the audience.*)

JOEY (*to audience*). And right then I realized: *This is why we study math in school!* If nowadays one pack was worth 5,000 bucks, that meant 10 packs would be 50,000! A hundred packs would be a half a million dollars! (*to DELIVERY MAN*) Could I go with you to the warehouse and get more of these cards?

DELIVERY MAN. How's that gonna work, kid? What am I gonna say to my boss when he asks why I'm givin' rides to Negro boys in my truck?

JOEY. But, I just—

DELIVERY MAN. You want those cards, be here tomorrow mornin'—8 o'clock *sharp*. I'll bring you everything I got.

JOEY. *Tomorrow?* But I need to get *home*—

DELIVERY MAN. Upta you, kid.

(*The DELIVERY MAN exits. THE HOTEL MCALPIN. RACHEL holds a large bin of mail—some opened, some not—which she sets down. JACKIE is nearby.*)

JACKIE. Most of the letters are real nice, Rae.

RACHEL. Yes, I know. But how come the ones *I* open always say something like this . . . (*RACHEL shows a letter to JACKIE.*) We need to show it to Mr. Rickey, show it to the police.

JACKIE. There's nothing they can do. You know that.

(*JOEY enters.*)

RACHEL. Joey, there you are! Did you get lost?

JOEY. I was looking for a gift for my dad.

RACHEL. And I've been trying to find your mom. I called the operator. There's no Stoshack on Grant Street in Pittsburgh.

JOEY. Well, no, not *yet*.

JACKIE. Not *yet?*

JOEY. But there will be! My parents get married in about 50 years and then—

RACHEL. Joey, you're not making any sense. I need you to tell me your real name and where you really live. Your mom must be so worried about you—

JOEY. Look, I can explain—

RACHEL (*to JACKIE*). We may need to take him to a doctor.

(*RACHEL has put her palm against JOEY's forehead.*)

JACKIE. Not feelin' well, Stosh?

JOEY. Really, it's no big—

RACHEL. I think you're having delusions.

JOEY. No, I'm not having delusions—

RACHEL (*simultaneously*). Well, it sure—

JACKIE (*simultaneously*). Easy now—

JOEY (*suddenly exclaims*). *I'M FROM THE FUTURE!*

JACKIE. You're *what?*

JOEY (*a deep breath, then the truth rushes out*). I got a Bond Bread card from a guy named Flip Valentini, who's a kid right now in Brooklyn, but in the future's gonna be an old guy in Pittsburgh and I traveled back in time to meet you so I can do a report and win free tickets to Wild Mountain but I can't leave until I meet the delivery guy at Herskowitz Grocery—tomorrow morning—8 a.m. sharp! (*RACHEL and JACKIE stare at him.*) Oh, and in the future I'm a *white kid.*

RACHEL (*beat*). I'll get the number for the doctor.

(*RACHEL exits but JACKIE is still staring at JOEY.*)

JACKIE. The future, huh?

JOEY. Yes.

JACKIE. How is it?

JOEY. Umm . . . it's cool. We have . . . you know . . . Hybrids and laptops and Nanos and Wiis. Which are . . . just . . . *things we have.*

JACKIE. Don't you wish you could, Stosh? Really see that far into time . . .

JOEY. Wait, I can prove it to you.

(*JOEY quickly takes out his Ken Griffey Jr. baseball card and hands it to JACKIE.*)

JACKIE (*reads*). "Ken Griffey Jr."?

JOEY. Look at the dates.

JACKIE. Wait a minute—

JOEY. See?

JACKIE. It says "Seattle" on his jersey. They wouldn't put a team way out on the West Coast.

JOEY. The Dodgers will be out there, too, someday. Along with the Giants.

JACKIE. OK, now you're talkin' crazy. Next thing you'll tell me is that Satchel Paige is still pitching. He told me he planned to pitch forever!

JOEY. He sort of did. But he's gone now. Like the Negro Leagues.

JACKIE. What do you mean — *gone?*

JOEY. Other players followed you to the majors — and the Negro Leagues just kind of . . . died out.

JACKIE. What players?

JOEY. Roy Campanella, Don Newcombe, Larry Doby —

JACKIE. Well, if they follow me, I hope they do better than I have. I'm not hitting. I'm pressing. Not making good contact.

JOEY. It's just a little slump —

JACKIE. I hear what they're sayin', Stosh — sayin' Mr. Rickey made a mistake, picked the wrong fella, say they're thinkin' of sending me back down to the minors —

JOEY. They're not gonna do that.

JACKIE (*not believing*). You know that, do you? I had big hopes, Stosh. For my mother, my family. For Rachel and my little boy. I wanted to make 'em proud of me.

JOEY. They are. They will be.

JACKIE. *You know that, too, huh?*

JOEY. Yes.

JACKIE. Players make it to the big leagues and they want to wear number 3 like the Babe, or number 5 like DiMaggio. I hoped, someday, some player comin' up would want to wear this old football number — 42. Well, since you know the future, Stosh, you tell me: Is anybody gonna be wearing that number?

JOEY (*beat*). No. Never again.

(*JACKIE stares at him.*)

JACKIE. You said you're writin' a report. What's it about?

(*JOEY makes a gesture that includes JACKIE, the room, everything.*)

JOEY. . . . *This.*

JACKIE. And does your teacher want you to know *everything?*

JOEY. Yes, she does.

JACKIE. *Good.* You're lucky. (*JACKIE retrieves the letter that he and RACHEL were reading earlier.*) 'Cause if you want to know everything . . . you gotta remember that everything you learn is not gonna be nice. These letters — I try to get to 'em and throw 'em away before Rachel sees 'em. Some of them talk about harming her or kidnapping the baby. (*regarding the letter*) Here's a man who took the time to write me a personal letter. In his own hand. And what does it say?

(*JACKIE hands the letter to JOEY.*)

JOEY (*reads*). "We are going to kill you . . ." (*stops before saying the next word*)

JACKIE (*quietly, firmly*). And the next word is what? The one that starts with an "n." (*JOEY just stares at him.*) It's OK, Stosh. That next word is somethin' you better *know*—somethin' you better keep *out in the open*—'cause I'm afraid they're gonna call you that word someday, and when they do, you're gonna have to stand up to it in your own way. Now, what is it?

(*Beat. Then, finally . . .*)

JOEY (*reading, this is hard for him*). "We are going to kill you . . . nigger." (*JACKIE nods, supportive. JOEY continues.*) "We have done it before. And you are next."

JACKIE (*quiet praise*). There you go.

(*JACKIE now takes the letter from JOEY and throws it in the trash.*)

JOEY. I'd want to *find that guy. Find him* and *hit him*—hit him so hard! *Don't you want to do that?!*

JACKIE. You have *no idea.*

JOEY. I mean, I know it's wrong to fight, but—

JACKIE (*firmly, eye-to-eye*). It's not wrong to fight, Stosh. The question is *how. How are we going to fight?* With our fists—or with *something more?*

(*JACKIE turns and moves away.*)

JOEY (*to audience*). It got real quiet in that room, for a long time. (*pause*) I told Jackie he was going to win Rookie of the Year, told him soon he'd be the league MVP and one day he'd be in the Hall of Fame—told him he'd be part of huge changes in America and that one day in the future the president of the United States would throw out the first pitch on opening day . . . and that president would be a black man.

(*JACKIE looks up at JOEY.*)

JACKIE (*a smile*). Rae's right. You need a doctor.

(*JACKIE exits. A light on JOEY.*)

JOEY (*to audience*). The Dodgers were going to Philadelphia for their first road game of the season and Jackie invited me to go with them. But before I left, I needed to get those Bond Bread cards.

(*A package of Bond Bread cards slides onstage and lands at JOEY's feet.*)

DELIVERY MAN (*from offstage*). HERE YOU GO, KID.

JOEY. Everything was working perfectly! (*puts the cards in his satchel*) The next day we arrived in Philadelphia, the City of Brotherly Love.

(*Outside of the ballpark. BRANCH RICKEY is talking up a storm to a REPORTER, who is trailing him.*)

BRANCH RICKEY. And you know what he said to me? "You can't bring that *black fella* here, Branch. We're not ready to have *one of his kind* on the field in Philadelphia!"

REPORTER (*taking notes*). Herb Pennock said that?

BRANCH RICKEY. Yes, Herb Pennock—the man who runs the Phillies. He says that if we came here with Jackie Robinson on our team, his Phillies would refuse to take the field! I was shocked. I was astounded.

REPORTER. What did you say?

BRANCH RICKEY. I said that's GREAT NEWS, Herb, we'll chalk up three victories by FORFEIT and I'll save a bundle of money on travel!

REPORTER. Perfect! Thanks, Mr. Rickey—

(*JACKIE and RACHEL enter. He holds a suitcase, she holds the baby.*)

BRANCH RICKEY. Here he is now. You can talk to him yourself. (*to JACKIE*) Something wrong, Jack?

JACKIE. They wouldn't take us.

BRANCH RICKEY. Who?

JACKIE. The hotel. Against their policy. No colored folks allowed.

BRANCH RICKEY (*livid, to the REPORTER*). You hear this?! I want you to write it down and put it in ink: The Dodgers will never again stay at the Benjamin Franklin Hotel. Not so long as I'm in charge. (*The REPORTER exits, writing, as BRANCH RICKEY grabs the suitcase, saying the following to RACHEL.*) I'm gonna find you the best hotel in Philly. (*to JACKIE*) You and Stosh better go, Jack, it's nearly game time. (*to RACHEL, with concern*) And, Mrs. Robinson, if you'd rather not go to the game, I can—

RACHEL (*firm, certain*). Oh, I am going. Thank you, Mr. Rickey, but *I am going to that game.* (*RACHEL steps toward JACKIE.*) You ready?

JACKIE. Are you? (*RACHEL nods, and JACKIE continues with a wry smile.*) Oh, and if you can't find me out there . . . I'll be the guy wearin' number 42.

(*RACHEL manages a smile as JACKIE leaves with JOEY. THE VISITOR'S CLUBHOUSE [SHIBE PARK]. ANT enters, carrying some equipment.*)

ANT. We don't need any help today.

JOEY. I'm here with Jackie. He said I can put my stuff in his locker.

ANT. Why don't you let me do it? Don't you *trust me?*

(*ANT smiles and leaves as JOEY puts his satchel away and DIXIE WALKER enters, getting ready for the game. JOEY stops and stands still, staring at DIXIE WALKER.*)

DIXIE WALKER. You need somethin', kid?

JOEY. Dixie Walker, right? My dad has your baseball card.

DIXIE WALKER. Hope he gave you the gum.

JOEY. The gum was pretty old by the time he got the card.

DIXIE WALKER. Yeah, they gotta do somethin' about that.

JOEY. Can I ask you something?

DIXIE WALKER. You a reporter?

JOEY. Sort of. (*DIXIE WALKER nods, "Go ahead." [Possible projection of a team photo].*) In the team photo for this year . . . everyone on the Dodgers is looking at the camera. *Except you.* You turned your head. Looked away. (*beat*) Why would you do that?

(*music under, slow and quiet, "The Star-Spangled Banner" [instrumental]*)

DIXIE WALKER. Son . . . I got nothin' against Robinson or any of the rest of you Negroes. But you gotta understand—most the fellas on this team are Southern boys. And where we come from, you keep everything *separate* and everybody's happy. Ain't nothin' personal. That's just the way it's always been.

(*Now the music builds and continues, as lights reveal: Shibe Park, Philadelphia. JACKIE runs onto the field and stands between PEE WEE REESE and EDDIE STANKY, their hats placed over their hearts for the national anthem.*)

JOEY (*to audience*). There had been more death threats—and it wasn't just Jackie and Rachel who knew about 'em. The players knew about 'em, too.

(*PEE WEE REESE and EDDIE STANKY each very slowly begin to inch away from JACKIE, leaving him standing alone.*)

PEE WEE REESE. Not so close there, Jack.

JACKIE. What're you fellas doin'?

EDDIE STANKY. Just taking precautions. In case he's not a good shot.

JACKIE. Who?

EDDIE STANKY. One of these Philly nut cases with a rifle.

PEE WEE REESE. Don't worry, Stanky, you're safe.

EDDIE STANKY. How do you figure that?

PEE WEE REESE. The way you been hittin'—the Phillies *want you* to bat today.

(*"The Star-Spangled Banner" concludes.*)

UMPIRE'S VOICE. Play ball!

(*JOEY watches from the stands, sitting next to RACHEL.*)

JOEY (*to audience*). It was Jackie's first game away from home—and it was nasty. One of the Phillies intentionally spiked Jackie at first base. The Phillies pitcher threw bean-balls at Jackie's head. And the Phillies manager, Ben Chapman, turned out to be the worst of them all.

(*BEN CHAPMAN paces in the Phillies dugout. We also see several PHILLIES PLAYERS.*)

BEN CHAPMAN (*hands cupped, yelling*). Hey, Robinson, my last pitcher missed your head, but this new one's gonna nail you.

(*The PHILLIES PLAYERS laugh.*)

JOEY. Jackie was playing first base, right by the Phillies dugout.

BEN CHAPMAN. We're gonna send you back to the cotton fields where you belong!

JOEY. He looked like he was about to boil over. And the fans were just as bad.

(*JEERS/TAUNTS from the PHILLIES FANS are heard. The chant is similar to the "Sto-shack" chant from the top of play.*)

PHILLIES FANS (*a loud chant*). JACK-IE, JACK-IE, NO-GOOD BLACK-IE!

(*Repeat, etc.*)

JOEY (*concerned*). Finally, Rachel stood up—right in the middle of all of them.

RACHEL. Sometimes I think I can block it all out with my back. If I stand between these people and Jack, I believe I can stop him from hearing all these words.

PHILLIES FANS (*a burst of cheers*). GO PHILLIES! GET HIM NOW! HERE WE GO!

BEN CHAPMAN. How's it feel to know some hunter's got your head in his sights. LINE HIM UP, BOYS. (*The PHILLIES PLAYERS lift their baseball bats and pretend to use them as rifles, shooting at JACKIE.*) Blam! Splat! Pop your head open like a watermelon!

PHILLIES PLAYERS. Pow! Pow! Got him!

JOEY (*to audience*). And then, as they were doing this, an amazing thing happened—

BEN CHAPMAN. We might not get you today—

JOEY. From his position at shortstop, Pee Wee Reese, a Southern boy from Louisville, Kentucky, walked over toward Jackie . . .

BEN CHAPMAN. But it's gonna happen, darkie, and you're gonna be sorry.

JOEY. And when he got there . . . the great Pee Wee Reese didn't say anything. (*PEE WEE REESE has walked over to JACKIE. Facing BEN CHAPMAN, PEE WEE REESE casually rests his elbow on JACKIE's shoulder, friendly, like a buddy.*) He didn't have to.

(*The crowd has gone SILENT. The PHILLIES PLAYERS slowly lower their bats and sit down.*)

BEN CHAPMAN. What do you think your doin', Reese?! You in love with this colored fella—is that it?! (*PEE WEE REESE and JACKIE just stare at him.*) *I asked you somethin'!*

PEE WEE REESE (*cool, firm*). Know what I wish, Chapman. I wish Jackie hadn't promised not to fight. 'Cause he could throw you over that outfield fence if he wanted to.

BEN CHAPMAN. Oh you think so, huh?

PEE WEE REESE. Why don't you pick on somebody who can *fight back*?!

(*Still staring at BEN CHAPMAN, PEE WEE REESE pounds his mitt, hard. And JACKIE pounds his mitt, hard. BEN CHAPMAN is silent as the DODGERS PLAYERS now hustle back to their positions, exiting.*)

JOEY (*to audience*). The inning ended. I ran down near the field—as Jackie came in and got ready to bat.

JACKIE. Sorry you had to hear all that, Stosh.

JOEY. But didn't you want to take his head off?!

JACKIE. *Oh, you bet I did,* but remember—we gotta put our fight into *the game.*

ANNOUNCER. Now batting for Brooklyn—

JOEY. *But how?*

ANNOUNCER. Number 42, Jackie Robinson.

(*BOOS/JEERS from the PHILLIES FANS. SCHOOLBOY ROWE is [perhaps] seen on the mound as JACKIE digs in, ready to hit.*)

JOEY (*to audience*). The first pitch from Schoolboy Rowe went right at Jackie's head.

(*JACKIE flings himself to the ground to avoid the pitch.*)

BEN CHAPMAN (*still pacing and ranting*). Atta boy, Rowe, put the darkie in the dirt!

JOEY (*to audience*). On the next pitch, Jackie slapped a single to right. He took his lead at first, bouncing back and forth, driving the pitcher nuts, then he stole second! And one pitch later, he stole third! Schoolboy Rowe was nervous now. And even Chapman was running out of things to yell.

BEN CHAPMAN (*at a loss*). JUST—C'MON, GET 'IM—GET THAT ROBINSON GUY!

JOEY (*to audience*). Rowe had pitched a shutout. If he could keep Jackie from scoring, he'd win the game.

RACHEL. They just need one run to tie.

JOEY. Yeah, but Stanky's up and he's in a terrible slump.

RACHEL. Doesn't matter, Joey. Jack's gonna take care of it. He just needs the
right pitch . . .

(*JACKIE is now dancing off third base.*)

JOEY (*to audience*). And then it happened.

RACHEL. . . . *a good jump* . . .

JOEY. Schoolboy Rowe went into his windup —

RACHEL. . . . *and a little luck.*

JOEY. And Jackie broke from third — racing the ball to home plate! BUT OK,
WAIT A MINUTE! *This is why we study SCIENCE!* (*JOEY once again "stops
time," stepping between the ball coming to the plate and JACKIE. All action freezes.
JOEY continues to audience.*) The runner is 90 feet from home plate. The ball is
60 feet from home plate. A fast runner might reach a speed of 20 miles per
hour, but the ball is going at least 80 miles an hour and it is *30 feet closer to
home plate!* This tells us that SCIENTIFICALLY it has to be *IMPOSSIBLE*
to steal home — AND YET . . . (*The action begins again. JOEY continues speaking, to audience.*) Jackie beat the ball to the plate!

(*JACKIE slides in as the PHILLIES CATCHER applies the tag.*)

UMPIRE'S VOICE. Safe!

JOEY. He stole home! Tie game! And the Dodgers come back to WIN!

(*Music: "Did You See Jackie Robinson Hit That Ball?" performed by the Count Basie
Orchestra. JACKIE stands and stares directly at BEN CHAPMAN. BEN CHAPMAN
spits on the ground and exits. JACKIE turns and there is PEE WEE REESE. The men,
black and white, shake hands. The DODGERS CLUBHOUSE. Music continues under.
It is a party atmosphere. JACKIE is being congratulated by PEE WEE REESE and
[possibly] others.*)

JACKIE. Glad you came to Philly, Stosh?

JOEY. I'll never forget it.

JACKIE. Well, make sure you say goodbye before you leave.

(*Music fades out as JACKIE and the DODGERS PLAYERS exit. ANT enters, putting
some equipment away. JOEY sees his leather satchel.*)

JOEY (*regarding the satchel*). Hey, I put this in Jackie's locker. Why's it out here?

ANT. Amazing game, huh? (*Pulls another* Amazing Stories *magazine from his
pocket.*)

JOEY. *Did you go through my stuff?*

ANT. Almost as amazing as this story I was readin'.

JOEY. I had a box of cards from Bond Bread. *What did you do with 'em?*

ANT. There's a story in here says in the future we're gonna be able to push a button and travel back to any moment in history. You believe that?

JOEY. I asked you something—

ANT. 'Course you'd need to have a little time machine. (*ANT quickly reaches into JOEY's satchel and pulls out the Nintendo DS.*) Somethin' maybe like this!

JOEY. Give me that!

ANT. I'm wise to you, Future Boy. That's where you came from, right?!

JOEY. You leave my stuff alone!

ANT. I'm gonna write it all down and send it to *Amazing Stories*—the funny sneakers, the little time machine and this— (*ANT holds out the Ken Griffey Jr. baseball card.*) Who the heck is this? *Ken Griffey Jr.?* Never heard a him or the so-called Seattle— ("*Ma-reeners*") Mariners!

JOEY (*to audience*). I had to have that card! Without that card, I'd never get home.

ANT. Come and get it, black boy!

JOE (*grabs but misses*). Gimme that card or I'm gonna—

ANT (*laughs*). You're gonna WHAT? I guess it's true what they say—you people can't control your tempers! (*JOEY takes a swing at ANT.*)

JOEY. Shut up, Ant! (*And misses him.*)

ANT. How 'bout I just divide this card in half?!

JOEY. NO!

ANT. Then tell me something: Who's gonna win the World Series this year?

JOEY. I don't know.

ANT. The heck you don't—

JOEY (*to audience*). *I really didn't know!*

ANT. You're from the future, you gotta know. You tell me who's gonna win and I'll have my old man bet all the money he's got on it—

JOEY. Look—

ANT. He's always after me about how he doesn't have enough money.

JOEY. If your dad needs money, tell him to hold onto those Bond Bread cards you stole from me. They'll make him rich.

ANT. What good are a bunch of dumb cards? I already threw 'em in the incinerator.

JOEY. You burned those cards?!

ANT. And I'll do the same with this card if you don't—

JOEY. WAIT. I KNOW THE PRESIDENTS.

ANT. Everyone knows the president! It's Harry Truman— (*starts to tear the card again*)

JOEY. NO. IN THE FUTURE. I can tell you all the future presidents and your dad can get rich every four years for the rest of his life!

ANT (*considers*). You better know 'em. (*quickly gets paper and a pencil*)

JOEY (*to audience*). And this is why we study history!

(*ANT puts the card on a bench and covers it with his baseball cap.*)

ANT. I'm puttin' your card right here till I get all the names.

JOEY. OK. The president after Truman is . . . Eisenhower.

ANT. The general from the war?

JOEY. Yep. Then Kennedy. Johnson. Nixon. Ford.

ANT. Wait—Henry Ford is dead.

JOEY. Not Henry—*Gerald* Ford. And then Carter. And then Reagan. And then—

ANT. Ronald Reagan? That guy's an *actor*. And he's not even a *good* actor.

JOEY. I promise you!

ANT. There's no way he's gonna be president of the United States! You're lyin' to me!

(*ANT reaches to grab a bat, just as JOEY quickly grabs the card from under the cap, shoves it in his pocket, and leaving his leather satchel behind, runs.*)

JOEY. See ya later!

ANT. STOP THAT KID!

(*a light on JOEY*)

JOEY. I ran out of the clubhouse with Ant right behind me. I heard him yell to a group of men—

ANT. THAT BLACK KID STOLE MY MONEY!

JOEY. And now the POLICE were after me! And I just kept running, my hand in my pocket, squeezing that card as hard as I could. I could feel the tingling in my hands. I thought about how I never got to say goodbye to Jackie, never saw him play in the World Series—so many things I still wanted to do, but there wasn't time. I had to get HOME!

(*A HUGE CACOPHONY OF SOUND: SHOUTS, HORSES, SIRENS BUILDING TO A CRESCENDO. And then FADING as lights reveal: A DARK ALLEY. JOEY is lying in a heap on the ground. His eyes are closed. A POLICEMAN nudges JOEY's body with his nightstick.)*

POLICEMAN. Whadda we got here?

JOEY. Mom, is that you . . . ? *(opens his eyes)* You're not my mom.

POLICEMAN. You got that right. Where d'ya belong, huh? Where's home?

JOEY. Pittsburgh.

POLICEMAN. Oh, geez—you're a long way off.

JOEY. Where am I? What year is it?

POLICEMAN. What *year*? It's '47, of course. And you're in the finest part of New York City. We call it the Bronx.

JOEY. That's impossible. I was supposed to go home.

POLICEMAN. Well, kid—

JOE. I held the card like I always do—

POLICEMAN *(trying to understand)*. The *card*?

JOEY. And I felt my hands tingle—

POLICEMAN *(ditto)*. Oh, *did you now*?

JOEY. But it didn't work! It didn't take me anywhere!

POLICEMAN. What is this *card* you're talkin' about?

(JOEY holds up the card, which he thinks is his Ken Griffey Jr. card.)

JOEY. My Ken Griffey Jun— *(stops, realizes)*. Wait—this isn't my Griffey card. He tricked me! Ant switched my Griffey card for one of the Bond Bread cards!

POLICEMAN. Be that as it may, kid, I gotta ask you to—

JOEY *(desperate)*. I gotta find Jackie Robinson, have him help me!

POLICEMAN *(with a laugh)*. Well, kid, I think Robinson might be busy today. He's playin' a ballgame just a couple blocks from here. Game 1 of the World Series, and my Yankees are gonna clobber Dem Bums. You stay out of trouble now!

(The POLICEMAN is gone.)

JOEY *(to audience)*. It had worked after all! I had wished to see Jackie in the World Series—and now here I was! *But I still didn't have a way to get home.*

(The ANNOUNCER's voice is heard.)

ANNOUNCER. The Fall Classic is once again in New York City, and Game 1 is at Yankee Stadium today, featuring the American League champion New York Yankees— *(CHEERS/NOISE)* Against their crosstown rivals—the Brooklyn Dodgers!

(BOOS/CHEERS/NOISE. THE VISITOR'S CLUBHOUSE [YANKEE STADIUM], 1947. JACKIE is there, in uniform.)

JACKIE. Stosh! Where you been? It's been five months!

JOEY. Yeah, I know—I'm sorry.

JACKIE. Rae and I couldn't find you. We wondered if you ever made it home.

JOEY. That's why I'm here. I need that Ken Griffey card I showed you. It's my ticket home.

JACKIE. Say again?

(PEE WEE REESE's voice is heard.)

PEE WEE REESE *(from offstage)*. Jackie, let's go. We got a game to win.

JACKIE. Hey, I held onto your bag. It had your initials on it, right?

JOEY. Right!

JACKIE. It's over there by my locker. And make sure you go up and see Rae. She's been asking about you.

JOEY. OK, but—

JACKIE *(exiting)*. I gotta go, Stosh.

(ANT appears.)

ANT. Well look what dropped back in from outer space! The Polack kid!

JOEY. *What did you say?*

ANT *(regarding JOEY's satchel)*. I saw your name in your little notebook: Sto-Shack.

JOEY. You tricked me, Ant. You switched those cards.

ANT. You're the trickster here—but now I've got it all figured out!

JOEY. *Ant, I need that CARD—*

ANT. You're not an alien! *(stands on a bench, announces)* You are a Polack kid, disguised as a black kid, sent here from the future by the Commies, to infiltrate us and learn our Atomic Secrets!

JOEY. I'm . . . *what?!*

ANT *(overlapping)*. And that thing you have in there is not a time machine! It's a top-secret recording gizmo. Probably has a *laser* in it, too!

(JOEY removes the Nintendo DS from his satchel.)

JOEY. It's for playing *games*, Ant.

ANT. You expect me to believe that?

(JOEY tosses the Nintendo DS to ANT.)

JOEY. Here—you can keep it. *Just give me my card.* You know the one.

(*ANT looks once again at the Nintendo DS.*)

ANT. It has a *real laser* in it, right?

JOEY. And an X-ray camera. All of us Alien Commie Spies from the future use them.

ANT. I knew it! (*ANT hands JOEY the Ken Griffey Jr. card.*) Here's your lousy card. Waste of money, my dad says.

JOEY (*regarding the Nintendo DS*). Oh, one thing: Be careful of the toxic spy vapors.

ANT (*holds the Nintendo DS out and away from him, scared*). The *what*?!

JOEY (*with a smile*). See ya! (*A light on JOEY. He continues, to audience.*) I left the clubhouse and made my way up to the grandstand. I could already hear the roar of the crowd. I climbed some stairs, turned a corner . . . and there it was . . . (*Organ music plays. SOUNDS of the crowd are heard.*) Yankee Stadium! "The House that Ruth Built." Man, I wish my dad could have seen it. There was red, white, and blue bunting hanging everywhere. There were Joe DiMaggio and Yogi Berra. And there were the Dodgers—all gathered at the dugout step, all gathered around number 42.

(*YANKEE STADIUM at the grandstand. JOEY joins RACHEL. She holds a Dodgers pennant.*)

RACHEL. Joey, did you make it home all right?

JOEY. I'm on my way, but first I just had to see all of this . . .

RACHEL. Well, you're just in time.

ANNOUNCER. Now batting for Brooklyn, number 42, Jackie Robinson.

RACHEL. C'MON, JACK!

JOEY (*to audience*). As Jackie came up to bat, there was some commotion a few rows away. An old man was trying to get to his seat. A bunch of people were around him, trying to help him.

(*An old man in a long coat, scarf, and hat, using a cane, appears. A few OTHER MEN are assisting him.*)

RACHEL (*whispers*). You know who that is, don't you?

JOEY. Some old man, late to the game.

RACHEL. Joey . . . that's The Babe.

JOEY. You mean . . . (*RACHEL nods. JOES continues, whispering to audience.*) *It was! It was Babe Ruth!* (*BABE RUTH is now seated. JOEY continues, to audience.*) I found the card from my dad, it was still in the hidden pocket, and I made my way through the crowd. (*JOEY has approached BABE RUTH.*) Mr. Ruth— (*holding out the card*). I wonder if you'd please—

OTHER MAN 1. The Babe is tired, kid. Some other time.

JOEY. *Please Mr. Ruth, I just—*

OTHER MAN 1. Maybe you didn't hear me —

(*BABE RUTH lifts his trembling hand and the OTHER MEN stop talking.*)

BABE RUTH. You a Yankee fan, son?

JOEY. No, sir, but my dad is. He's your biggest fan in the world.

BABE RUTH. What's his name?

JOEY. Tom. Tom Stoshack.

BABE RUTH (*signing the card*). Did he ever see me play?

JOEY. No, he wasn't born yet.

BABE RUTH. What's that?

JOEY. But now that I have your card . . . maybe someday I'll get to see you play.

BABE RUTH (*a kind smile*). Oh . . . I'm done, kid. My baseball days are long, long gone. But the thing is . . . (*BABE RUTH hands the signed card back to JOEY.*) The game of baseball is like a shiny nickel. Nobody owns it. It's passed on. From one set of hands . . . (*looking at his hands*) *to another.*

(*And now BABE RUTH lifts his hand and points toward the field.*)

JOEY. Mr. Ruth, did you really do it?

BABE RUTH. *And another . . .*

JOEY. In the '32 World Series, did you really call your shot?

BABE RUTH. *And another . . .*

JOEY (*to audience*). And I looked to where he was pointing—and it wasn't the outfield fence. He was pointing to a man in the batter's box, a black man wearing the number 42. (*Lights isolates JACKIE in the batter's box, preparing to hit. JACKIE points the end of his bat back toward BABE RUTH, a gesture of respect, the torch being passed. JOEY continues speaking, to audience.*) A man who, like so many other players, had been waiting for his chance, so much waiting. It's a "game of waiting" my dad always says, *but now the waiting was over —* (*JACKIE swings — a HUGE CRACK of a BAT, ECHOING in the air. And now a HUGE CHEER and music as lights isolate JOEY. He continues speaking, to audience.*) And the ball Jackie Robinson hit sailed into the New York sky and I was standing next to Babe Ruth—and he was *pointing at that baseball as it sailed away!* And I was holding my Ken Griffey card tight—and my hands were tingling—like a shiny nickel. The game is passed on, from Wagner to Ruth to Robinson to Mays to Aaron to Clemente to Griffey to the player that nobody's heard of yet . . . the kid they just called up today . . .

(*JOEY's BEDROOM. JOEY is lying on the floor, his leather satchel next to him. MOM nudges him with an aluminum baseball bat and he twists and turns in his sleep.*)

MOM. Joey . . . ?

JOEY (*eyes still closed*). I'm sorry, officer, I fell asleep in the alley.

MOM. You did what?

JOEY (*opening his eyes*). You're not a policeman!

MOM. Sometimes I feel like one. (*kisses him*) Now, c'mon, it's a school morning and you need some breakfast—

JOEY. But, Mom—

MOM. And then I want to hear all about your adventure.

JOEY. Mom, I've got to ask: Do I look *different* to you?

MOM. You look like you need a shower.

JOEY. No, I mean, am I sort of *another color*?

MOM. What are you talking about?

JOEY (*to audience*). And right then I saw my reflection in my window. I looked so . . . *white*. It was weird.

MOM. Well, I hope you got what you needed for your report.

JOEY. Oh, Mom, you won't believe it!

MOM. I was very worried about you. So was your dad.

(*DAD appears.*)

DAD. Welcome back, Joe.

MOM (*as she goes*). Breakfast in five.

(*JOEY and DAD look at each other.*)

JOEY (*pause, to audience*). And I didn't have to say anything. He could tell from the look on my face that I'd let him down.

DAD (*disappointed*). Oh, Joe, what happened? Was it really so hard?

JOEY. I'm sorry.

(*JOEY holds out the Babe Ruth card.*)

DAD. No, you keep that. That's yours.

JOEY. Just look. It's for you. (*DAD takes the Babe Ruth card from JOEY, looks at it. JOEY continues, to audience.*) And Dad got really quiet.

DAD. Oh my . . .

JOEY (*to audience*). It said—

DAD (*reading*). "To my good pal, Tom Stoshack. From Babe Ruth." (*DAD looks at JOEY, his face flush with joy and surprise.*) Is this . . . ?

JOEY. Yep. (*a light on JOEY. He continues speaking, to audience.*) Someone told me once that a kid can't change history. Well, all I know is that when I returned the Bond Bread card to Flip . . . (*A light on FLIP, opposite of JOEY. FLIP's back is to the audience, enabling them to see that he is holding a beautifully framed set of baseball cards. He kisses the glass, then immediately wipes the glass clean with a rag.*) He had a complete set of Brooklyn Dodgers baseball cards proudly on display. This time around, he'd kept them safe. And history was just a *little bit different.*

(*THE CLASSROOM. MS. LEVITT addresses JOEY.*)

MS. LEVITT. Mr. Stoshack, it's your turn. I suppose you've selected a ballplayer again?

JOEY. Jackie Robinson. He was on the list.

MS. LEVITT. All right. First of all, can you tell us what books, periodicals, and other research materials you employed in the creation of your biographical essay?

JOEY. I . . . used baseball cards.

MS. LEVITT. Pardon me?

(*Music under as lights isolate JOEY. He opens the notebook he carried on his adventure. He speaks to the audience as though they were the classroom: [Possible projections of JACKIE ROBINSON photos throughout the years].*)

JOEY. Jack Roosevelt Robinson was born in Cairo, Georgia, in 1919. He was the youngest of five children and he was the grandson of a slave. He was raised by his mother in a white neighborhood in Pasadena, California. He played in the Negro Leagues for the Kansas City Monarchs. Then he was signed by Branch Rickey to be a Brooklyn Dodger, and to break the color barrier in baseball, which he did on April 15, 1947. (*A light reveals JACKIE, opposite of JOEY.*) Jackie Robinson tried to live the values he believed in. Among these were courage, persistence, integrity, and commitment—*following through on the promises you make.* Later in his life, after all he'd been through, Jackie Robinson said—

JACKIE. I believe in the human race. I believe in the goodness of a free society.

JOEY. Jackie Robinson's battle was against the barriers that kept Negroes out of baseball.

JACKIE. And I believe that society can remain good only as long as we are able to *fight for it.*

JOEY. In 1955, Jackie's Brooklyn Dodgers finally won the World Series. And in 1962, he was elected to the Baseball Hall of Fame—where, once again, he broke the color barrier.

JACKIE. A life is not important except in the impact it has on other lives.

JOEY. Jackie Robinson died on October 24, 1972. He was 53 years old. His coffin was carried by his former Dodgers teammates. Thousands of fans came out and lined the streets of Brooklyn to pay their respects. Jackie was buried only a few blocks away from where a ballpark used to stand. A place now long gone. A place called Ebbets Field. (*As JOEY speaks, a giant number 42 jersey is lifted into the air [or projected], where it hovers over the stage. JACKIE watches his own number raised into the air as the light on him begins to slowly fade to black.*) On the 50th anniversary of Jackie's first game, Major League Baseball declared that the number 42 would be permanently retired throughout the major leagues. It is the first and only number in baseball to be so honored. (*JACKIE is gone.*) It is said that Babe Ruth changed baseball . . . and Jackie Robinson changed *America.* I think that's true. Because during the time I was working on this report, Jackie Robinson changed me.

(*JOEY closes his notebook and the music concludes.*)

MS. LEVITT. Joey . . . you really got all that from *baseball cards?*

JOEY (*to audience*). As Ms. Levitt handed me my *three free passes to Wild Mountain,* I just smiled.

(*A LITTLE LEAGUE BASEBALL FIELD. Day. JOEY stands on third base, wearing his batting helmet. On the mound is BOBBY FULLER. The JAYHAWKS CATCHER is behind the plate. JOEY's COACH, his MOM, and his DAD are nearby, watching.*)

COACH. C'mon, Joe, it's a tie game—we gotta get you home!

(*CHEERS/JEERS/CHANTS*)

JOEY (*to audience*). After reading my report on Jackie, Mom let me rejoin the team.

MOM (*simultaneously*). COME ON, JOE, YOU CAN DO IT!

DAD (*simultaneously*). BE READY, JOE!

JOEY (*to audience*). We're in the playoffs now, final inning. I've walked, stolen second, stolen third—and now I'm staring at *you-know-who* on the mound.

BOBBY FULLER. You're lucky you got as far as third, No-Hack. And that's as far as you're gonna get. Everybody knows a Polack *can only count to three.* (*smiles and pitches*)

UMPIRE'S VOICE. Strike one!

(*CHEERS/GROANS as needed. Music and sounds under, building as JOEY takes his lead and keeps staring hard at BOBBY FULLER.*)

BOBBY FULLER. What's wrong, Slow-Sack, *cat got your tongue?!*

COACH. DON'T LET HIM GET TO YOU, JOEY!

MOM. OTHER CHEEK, JOEY, OTHER CHEEK!

DAD. C'MON, JOE, WE NEED YOUR RUN!

BOBBY FULLER. Hey, whaddya say I strike this guy out and then come over there and KICK YOUR BUTT HOME?!

JOEY (*cool, determined*). I know how to get home, Bobby.

BOBBY FULLER (*sarcastic*). What's that supposed to mean?

JOEY (*to audience*). I started dancing back and forth at third base—just like I'd seen Jackie do.

BOBBY FULLER. You got ants in your pants, Low-Crack?! Maybe you need your mommy to come give you a hug!

JOEY. I know exactly what I need.

BOBBY FULLER. Have a good cry, Jo-Jo-Girl, 'cause this game is over!

JOEY (*to audience*). *I need the right pitch* . . . (BOBBY FULLER *winds up in slow motion.*) *a good jump* . . . (BOBBY FULLER *pitches the ball.*) *and a little bit of luck* . . .

(*JOEY, also in slow motion, breaks for home plate.*)

COAH (*simultaneously*). JOEY—NO!

MOM (*simultaneously*). THERE HE GOES.

(*All action goes to slow motion as JOEY slides in under the tag of the JAYHAWKS CATCHER.*)

UMPIRE'S VOICE. Safe!

(*CHEERS/MUSIC/CELEBRATION. High-fives all around. MOM gives JOEY a big hug.*)

MOM (*simultaneously*). What a play!

DAD (*simultaneously*). Did you see that?!

MOM. Joey, that was amazing!

JOEY. Thanks. Can we go to *Wild Mountain*?

MOM. When?

JOEY. Today—right now—I'll be in the car.

MOM (*simultaneously*). Today?

DAD (*simultaneously*). Now?

JOEY. I've got three tickets. I want us to all go *together*.

MOM (*beat, a look to DAD*). Well . . . let's talk about that over some pizza, OK?

JOEY (*simultaneously*). Great

DAD (*simultaneously*). OK.

(*DAD grabs JOEY's mitt, cap, and bat and starts off as MOM approaches JOEY.*)

MOM. I know it was hard, Joey, but you kept your cool out there.

JOEY. Thanks.

MOM. See you at the car.

(MOM goes, passing BOBBY FULLER, who approaches JOEY, sullen.)

BOBBY FULLER. My coach says I'm supposed to tell you "good game."

JOEY. Good game, Bobby.

BOBBY FULLER. And my dad says I'm supposed to shake your hand.

(JOEY puts out his hand, but BOBBY FULLER does not shake it. Instead, he turns and leaves. Music now as JOEY looks at his own outstretched hand. Then JACKIE appears [unseen at first by JOEY] and puts his hand in JOEY's. They shake hands. Separate lights reveal BRANCH RICKEY and RACHEL.)

BRANCH RICKEY. They call his name in a way no other player's name is called. They plead to shake his hand.

RACHEL. They touch his clothes as he walks by.

(JACKIE takes off his Brooklyn Dodgers cap and puts it on JOEY's head.)

BRANCH RICKEY. Jackie Robinson has never lost sight of what the game has meant to him. And what *he* has meant . . .

RACHEL. What he means *now* . . .

BRANCH RICKEY. What he will *always* mean to the people of this great land.

(JACKIE turns and walks away, vanishing into the past, as the giant 42 jersey looms beautifully above the stage. Music builds and lights fade to black.)

END OF PLAY